SECURING WINDOWS NT/2000

From Policies to Firewalls

MICHAEL A. SIMONYI

OTHER AUERBACH PUBLICATIONS

ABCs of IP Addressing
Gilbert Held
ISBN: 0-8493-1144-6

Application Servers for E-Business
Lisa M. Lindgren
ISBN: 0-8493-0827-5

Architectures for E-Business Systems
Sanjiv Purba, Editor
ISBN: 0-8493-1161-6

A Technical Guide to IPSec Virtual Private Networks
James S. Tiller
ISBN: 0-8493-0876-3

Building an Information Security Awareness Program
Mark B. Desman
ISBN: 0-8493-0116-5

Computer Telephony Integration
William Yarberry, Jr.
ISBN: 0-8493-9995-5

Cyber Crime Investigator's Field Guide
Bruce Middleton
ISBN: 0-8493-1192-6

Cyber Forensics: A Field Manual for Collecting, Examining, and Preserving Evidence of Computer Crimes
Albert J. Marcella and Robert S. Greenfield, Editors
ISBN: 0-8493-0955-7

Information Security Architecture
Jan Killmeyer Tudor
ISBN: 0-8493-9988-2

Information Security Management Handbook, 4th Edition, Volume 1
Harold F. Tipton and Micki Krause, Editors
ISBN: 0-8493-9829-0

Information Security Management Handbook, 4th Edition, Volume 2
Harold F. Tipton and Micki Krause, Editors
ISBN: 0-8493-0800-3

Information Security Management Handbook, 4th Edition, Volume 3
Harold F. Tipton and Micki Krause, Editors
ISBN: 0-8493-1127-6

Information Security Policies, Procedures, and Standards: Guidelines for Effective Information Security Management
Thomas Peltier
ISBN: 0-8493-1137-3

Information Security Risk Analysis
Thomas Peltier
ISBN: 0-8493-0880-1

Information Technology Control and Audit
Frederick Gallegos, Sandra Allen-Senft, and Daniel P. Manson
ISBN: 0-8493-9994-7

New Directions in Internet Management
Sanjiv Purba, Editor
ISBN: 0-8493-1160-8

New Directions in Project Management
Paul C. Tinnirello, Editor
ISBN: 0-8493-1190-X

A Practical Guide to Security Engineering and Information Assurance
Debra Herrmann
ISBN: 0-8493-1163-2

The Privacy Papers: Managing Technology and Consumers, Employee, and Legislative Action
Rebecca Herold
ISBN: 0-8493-1248-5

Secure Internet Practices: Best Practices for Securing Systems in the Internet and e-Business Age
Patrick McBride, Joday Patilla, Craig Robinson, Peter Thermos, and Edward P. Moser
ISBN: 0-8493-1239-6

Securing and Controlling Cisco Routers
Peter T. Davis
ISBN: 0-8493-1290-6

Securing E-Business Applications and Communications
Jonathan S. Held and John R. Bowers
ISBN: 0-8493-0963-8

Securing Windows NT/2000: From Policies to Firewalls
Michael A. Simonyi
ISBN: 0-8493-1261-2

TCP/IP Professional Reference Guide
Gilbert Held
ISBN: 0-8493-0824-0

SECURING WINDOWS NT/2000

From Policies to Firewalls

MICHAEL A. SIMONYI

A CRC Press Company
Boca Raton London New York Washington, D.C.

Library of Congress Cataloging-in-Publication Data

Simonyi, Michael A.
Securing Windows NT/2000 : from policies to firewalls / Michael A. Simonyi.
p. cm.
Includes bibliographical references and index.
ISBN 0-8493-1261-2 (alk. paper)
1. Microsoft Windows NT server. 2. Operating systems (Computers) I. Title.

QA76.76.O63 S55876 2002
005.4'4769—dc21 2002018888

Direct all inquiries to CRC Press LLC, 2000 N.W. Corporate Blvd., Boca Raton, Florida 33431.

Visit the Auerbach Web site at www.auerbach-publications.com

Auerbach is an imprint of CRC Press LLC

International Standard Book Number 0-8493-1261-2
Library of Congress Card Number 2002018888
Printed in the United States of America 1 2 3 4 5 6 7 8 9 0
Printed on acid-free paper

Contents

Preface

Approximately 5000 years ago, a group of architects and engineers descended down the corridors of Pharaoh Khufu's palace. When they approached Pharaoh Khufu, they proposed a project that would be unlike any other the known world had ever embarked upon, the construction of the Great Pyramid of Giza. Pharaoh Khufu must have been impressed or at least we know he was because he had the work commissioned. Both the architects and engineers had undoubtedly reassured Pharaoh Khufu that after his death he would be entombed and his riches would be safe from tomb robbers for all time. This author is also sure the conversation must have gone something to this effect: "Pharaoh, we have taken all precautions to guarantee that your rest will never be disturbed by mortal man. Once your body and personal effects have been sealed in the Great Pyramid, they will remain undisturbed for all eternity." Pharaoh Khufu, feeling quite confident that his architects and engineers had collectively solved the problems in dealing with his concerns of the afterlife, signed the proclamation to begin constructing one of the greatest manmade landmarks the world has ever known. Unfortunately for Pharaoh Khufu and his incredibly talented arsenal of architects, they never banked on human ingenuity and persistence. It was estimated that within 100 years of Pharaoh Khufu's entombment, the pyramid was robbed. Simple-minded but persistent thieves were able to outwit some of the greatest architects and engineers of the time. They were able to systematically circumnavigate physical barriers that if breached would surely mean an almost certain death. Although Pharaoh Khufu's architects went through almost every possible scenario to ensure the safety and security of Pharaoh Khufu and his treasures, they did not take into account that the pyramid required maintenance to ensure its impenetrable status.

At the time of his death, Attila the Hun had conquered a great deal of the known world. Far from his native home during his campaigns, it is said that his most trusted generals commissioned a troop of men to bury him and his acquired wealth where they were. After a traditional ceremony, the troop set out at night to a secret location and buried the great leader. Upon their return, they were immediately put to death in order to conceal the final resting place of Attila the Hun for all time. His generals used simple tactics and, as of today, the burial location of Attila the Hun has not been found. Although a bit extreme by today's standards, they were extremely effective. If his generals had not exercised such extreme precaution, Attila the Hun's burial site would surely have been raided, perhaps by the very men who buried him.

In any event, these examples provide a basis for what individuals will attempt to achieve some sort of security, albeit extreme and costly. It goes to show that the greater the visibility of a system, the more attractive it becomes as a target. In the case of Pharaoh Khufu, the sheer size of the pyramid would have dissuaded many in an attempt to breach it except for the truly crafty tomb robbers. To parallel, without regular maintenance and upgrading, an environment will fall into a similar vulnerability as in the case of Pharaoh Khufu's pyramid. The proper maintenance of a security environment requires constant intervention and review to apply patches and upgrades to maintain a state of integrity. If the environment lags behind the mainstream of vulnerability toolkits, unauthorized entry into the environment becomes more likely. Over time, any advanced security infrastructure will begin to show its age, and if not kept up-to-date, will be as easily penetrated as a burglar picks a padlock with a bobby pin. Alternatively, it is not possible to implement security measures the likes of Attila's generals either. Some level of visibility is always apparent on the Internet.

In today's business environment, we need to find a comfortable line of defense that keeps us from implementing security that parallels the previous examples. Small, medium, and large corporations require a good dose of security to protect themselves and their digital assets. It is no longer safe to conduct any business on the Internet without protecting it. Everything is open to attack. The better it is protected, the better off you are. But do not get complacent with technology; new vulnerabilities are being discovered all the time in systems that are seemingly secure. Implementing a well-defined security strategy will undoubtedly help in the effort to secure your business, and it does not have to be an all-out Fort Knox implementation either. We also know that not everyone has the budget or means for the ideal security solution. But the middle ground is extremely effective in thwarting the majority of these unwanted intruders, in much the same way we spray pesticides to get rid of mosquitoes. The strongest will survive or, in our case, only the truly persistent will attempt to gain access.

One of the most important questions to ask yourself regarding security is: "Of what value would it be to me to break into this site, system, or server?" If your answer is one of the following, you are in need of security:

- Financial gain
- Competitive advantage
- Disruption of an organization's ability to conduct business
- Acquire customer information
- Acquire personnel records
- Damage the reputation of the organization
- Monitor business strategy
- Acquire trade secrets
- Modify corporate information

Sometimes we tend to neglect the nature of an attack on a site, thinking their *modus operandi* is based on one of the above items. Occasionally, we deal with individuals who have nothing better to do than cause havoc. These individuals are just as dangerous to an organization and sometimes even more so because they get some sort of "intellectual high" out of the attack.

This book will specifically target perimeter security on the Microsoft Windows NT and Windows 2000 platform because this is the most commonly deployed platform for Internet computing — and as such, also the most commonly attacked platform. We will work toward the layout of a security policy and methods to implement it within an organization, as well as structure a project plan for its implementation. We will look at how to lock down a Windows NT Server for the purpose of using it as a platform for a firewall. In essence, provide the means for an organization to begin protecting itself from the Internet masses much the same way a department store uses an array of devices, cameras, and staff to thwart shoplifters.

Chapter 1

Executive Management Overview

The need for security in today's business environment is apparent. Every-day breaches in product security mechanisms surface at an alarming rate. It seems that everywhere one looks, things are getting out of hand. Every operating system is a target, every Web server is an opportunity for an attack, and every mail server is a relay point for sending spam. We have come a long way from the glass-house monolithic mainframes that were heavily guarded against unauthorized individuals and use, to an age of global public access, remote users, and a mobile workforce. We have traversed the line of secured centralized computing facilities into a mess of loosely coupled and decentralized facilities bordering on many fronts. Not only does IT have to watch out who is minding the store, but also who is knocking on the door, looking through the windows, and talking on the phone. The threats in today's business environment are real and ever-changing. Information technology (IT) cycles are moving so fast that critical areas of functionality are not being assembled correctly. Application code bases are getting so large that it is becoming unmanageable to pack every imaginable feature into an application and not expect deficiencies. In fact, we have become accustomed to these deficiencies and live with them during our daily business lives. Operating systems are becoming so large and feature-laden that most people do not even realize what is really running on a server and that these features are doorways into the heart of an organization. If not properly guarded against, they can result in great damage to the integrity of the business, loss of clients, and loss of income — three of the worst-possible effects of a security breach to an organization. Consider the breach of www.egghead.com,[1] for example, or the recent FBI investigation of alleged E-commerce site infiltration by Russian hackers. When their facilities were breached and customers' credit card information and personal information accessed, it was detrimental to the operation.

The organization loses credibility. Is this FUD (fear, uncertainty, and doubt)? No! It is reality. Script kiddies, hackers, and professional hackers are always looking for the next target — either for fun or for profit. But in any event, either case is undesirable, unwanted, and unnecessary if proper safeguards are considered and put in place. Policies and procedures, checks and balances; they need to be defined, communicated, and acted upon in a business environment.

A Need for Security

With today's rapidly collapsing timelines and the push to bring product, services, and knowledge to market, security is usually neglected. The corporate IT center can be hard-pressed when delivering computing solutions in a timely, effective, and secure manner. IT managers and directors must wrestle the four horsemen of systems development: time, money, resources, and security. Each of these is mutually exclusive and proportionate to each other. That is, one cannot have one without the other, and the effect on one has an equal impact on the others.

The role of the IT manager or director must encompass the effective dissemination of a lax or nonexistent security stance in terms that are easy to relate to. For example, a fairly common approach in delivering systems is to get version 1.0 out to market as soon as possible. Timelines are usually short, bordering on next to impossible. The budget is fairly tight and additional funding difficult to acquire. Resources are stressed and specific technology expertise may not be available or, due to budget constraints, unaffordable. In effect, these types of project cycles will typically fail to meet the desired and required outcome in more ways than one. Constantly changing requirements and specifications will have a ripple effect throughout the scope of the project, touching all areas of the IT domain from network infrastructure, server deployment, application development, testing and, last but not least, security. Typically, security can be accomplished quite easily with user ids and passwords, right? Wrong! A user id and password is not an effective defense mechanism. The rapid development of the version 1.0 product has left many deficiencies within the overall project scope. Servers have been deployed and not properly secured; and worse, they are available to the masses-at-large over the Internet. Poor applications design and testing will have left gaping holes throughout the system. Developers, in their efforts to meet timelines, have hard-coded common I/O routines to the database. The database administrator may have forgotten to encrypt passwords or applied service packs or patches to the system. The end result is the delivery of a system with more holes in it than Swiss cheese. Unfortunately, by the time the first breach has occurred, the damage is done. Whether that damage be the dissemination of customer data, access to your confidential price lists, supplier resources, or worse given the ability to your competitors to perform denial-of-service attacks against you, basically shutting down your operation. These are just a few of the many scenarios that face IT managers and directors today and undoubtedly even more issues will evolve over time. Senior management or the business stakeholders must be made aware of lax security planning. They expect a certain level of comfort and security to protect the organization, and any deficiencies in an environment must be brought to their attention before becoming an issue to the organization. By saving a dollar or two now, only to have to spend hundreds or even thousands down the road, is poor business acumen (planning). Having foresight and vision to proactively prepare an organization for a secure computing environment takes time and a great deal of skill. Knowing how to position yourself for a secure computing environment is equally important. Ask yourself these questions:

1. What are the threats to the organization?
2. Are these threats from within the organization, external to it, or both?
3. Where is the greatest threat realized?
4. What are the risks? And how do we control them?
5. Do we have the right skills to accomplish the task of developing a proper and secure computing infrastructure?
6. How do we make sure we are secure?
7. How do we maintain our level of security effectiveness over time?

These common questions can be answered at all levels of the organization. Each level of the organization will uncover areas and scenarios that other levels of the organization were not aware of or exposed to. Senior management should provide the direction for what and which people, departments, or the public should have access to information or resources. Middle management must coordinate these efforts and plan for the structure and process to accommodate senior management's mandates. The technical staff with management's direction will perform the actual assembly of these structures and processes to make them happen. During the process, varying pieces of the puzzle will fall into place; errors will be corrected and omissions added. Also, security matrices should be developed to capture the essence of the corporate security policy. Although the entire process of developing the security policy can be lengthy and time-consuming given all the facets of information security, it would be impossible to cover them all effectively in this book. The theme of this book, however, will concentrate on perimeter security and attaining a satisfactory level of security for an organization to conduct business on the Internet.

Note

1. Refer to Appendix D for a copy of the letter issued to customers of the Egghead E-commerce site.

Chapter 2

What Is Security?

Security is a very broad term and depends upon the context of its use within the computing environment. The U.S. Department of Defense (DoD) has meticulously dissected this topic into what is known as the Rainbow series of guides. For a complete listing of these guides and other information, refer to the following Web sites:

- www.fas.org/irp/nsa/rainbow.htm
- www.dynamoo.com/orange/index.html
- www.defenselink.mil/webmaster/policy/dod_web_policy_12071998_with_amendments_and_corrections.html
- www.radium.ncsc.mil
- www.itsec.gov.uk

The guides provide excellent explanations for the varying degrees of security, which are graded from levels D (the least secure), to C, B, and A (the most secure).[1] Although all of these levels have a place in their respective environments, the two that are of interest and commonplace among business communities are C (C1 and C2) and B (B1, B2, and B3). Level C is the most common occurrence and a minimum recommendation of security at the low end, followed by level B at the medium to high end of the security spectrum. Level B has been commonly referred to as a "trusted system." Most major versions of UNIX have a trusted implementation of their operating system. For example, the Sun Microsystems Operating System Solaris comes in a flavor known as Trusted Solaris, HP UX in a flavor of HP UX BLS, and Trusted IRIX from SGI. Each of these operating systems are known as level B operating systems. Microsoft does not offer a similar operating system for level B security. However, third-party options for level B security are available from Argus Sytems Group (www.argus-systems.com) and a document from http://www.trustedsystems.com/b-level.htm documents a process for attaining level

B security on Windows NT. Level C is based on "discretionary access control." Access to the physical hardware of a computer system is protected from direct access by user application programs. Subsystems of the operating system control messages sent to specific regions of the operating system that control access to the hardware of the computer system. Although all possible precautions have been put in place by the manufacturer of the operating system, it is not 100 percent secure and can be circumvented by talented individuals. Microsoft Windows NT and Windows 2000 are considered to fall into the C2 classification, although out-of-the-box, these operating systems are not completely compliant with the C2 specification. It is possible, with modifications to the operating system, to attain conformance with the C2 specification. Microsoft Windows NT 4.0 and recently Windows 2000[2] have been graded as C2 compliant. The C class security rating is typical of most deployed operating systems in the business community. (See www.radium.ncsc.mil for a listing of evaluation reports on operating systems, applications, and databases that are rated C2 compliant.) The C2 security classification requires a user id and password to gain access to the resources of a system (in this context, system refers to a target computer/server or even group of servers). One important aspect of C2 systems is that auditing is mandatory. Because the C2 classification requires the mandatory auditing of events in a computer system, the Windows NT event logger must be configured to record additional systemwide events, more than its default setting. This is just one item of many that require tuning to reach C2 compliance on the NT platform. C2 also introduces authorization levels, which provide an additional layer of security on top of file and directory access permissions. The Windows Resource Kits provide tools for helping one attain a C2 level of security on a computer system. The Windows NT 4.0 Resource Kit also provides additional tools to check for C2 compliance and Windows 2000 utilizes the Security Configuration Manager (SCM) to assist in securing a system.

The classification for level B falls into the realm of what is known as a "trusted systems environment." Level B classification encompasses all aspects of class C and the addition of mandatory access control. The B level of security also requires that change management procedures and processes be in place. It basically segregates all operating subsystems of an operating system into their own domains. For example, a computer system may have many administrators that maintain the operational integrity of a system. Each of the administrators has the ability to maintain, monitor, and control their domain; however, the domains cannot cross the boundaries of their domain or assume administrative authority over other domains.

Attaining a Level of Security

To attain a desired level of security, it will be necessary to assess the threats and risks involved with the organization. An Internet service provider (ISP) will have a vastly different assessment to its threats and risks as opposed to that of an auto parts manufacturing organization. Although there will be some overlap, each will have its own unique computing liabilities to protect and secure. Although the Department of Defense has been extremely helpful in hammering out desired security configurations for dealing with classified and top-secret installations, most business environments cannot afford the luxury of maintaining such a tight-looped security environment. This does not mean that one should not try to achieve a tight security model; it is merely how much administration overhead, procedure, and process control one can afford without incurring too much operational overhead. Again, the assessment of an organization's risks will define what level of security is required. Maintaining the integrity of corporate trade secrets in this day and age is critical and may require the implementation of a B rated system. It should be noted that the security of even the most complex environment can be circumnavigated and defeated. Individuals who deal with corporate trade secrets should sign nondisclosure statements prior to hiring that prevent them from taking corporate data and knowledge to a competitor. Making data difficult to access without proper authorization, copy, or even print is also desirable.

The Importance of Checks and Balances

The importance of checks and balances is twofold. First, a check is the process of meeting a requirement. For example, only the accounting staff is permitted access to the accounting shared directory on the corporate local area network (LAN). Procedures enforce compliance of controls by documenting appropriate actions that must be followed. Creating systemwide access profiles is an excellent method for delivering controls within an environment. The nature of the profiles — mandatory or roaming — will require management discretion; however, a hybrid deployment usually provides the best overall approach for most organizations. On the other side of the coin, balances are an audit control to make sure that the requirement or check was carried out accurately. The balances are the foundation of the environment's integrity. Reporting mechanisms assist in this process when applicable; however, there are circumstances when reporting is insufficient or not possible. Balances must be carried out either automatically or in a manual nature to verify if controls are operating correctly and within the boundaries of their requirements.

Access Controls

Access controls are the steps taken to ensure security, integrity, and proper authorization. For example, systems operations personnel have authorization to enter the computer room. They do so by way of personal access codes that identify them and permit them to enter. This prevents unauthorized access to the computer room and its facilities. In this way, the integrity of the computer room is maintained via physical access control. Access controls come in two forms: physical and logical. An example of a logical access control would be a user id and password for access to a network workstation.

Communication and Training

The heart of establishing security in a particular environment is directly related to how well an organization communicates its needs to staff at all levels. It is extremely important that all items relating to security — no matter how small and insignificant they may seem — be well-communicated to staff. Sometimes, the obvious or insignificant can lead to a catastrophic breach in security. This is similar to what David must have thought when striking down Goliath with an insignificant little stone. David banked on Goliath's ego of invincibility to disregard such a little stone as a threat. David knew what damage he could inflict with the stone but Goliath paid little attention to it, which ultimately resulted in a drastic mistake for Goliath. Although communication is critical, one must also remember to provide a means to train staff in understanding security threats as well as learning to recognize them. Appropriate staff training in security is essential. Staff members need to know their responsibilities in maintaining organizational integrity in relation to their positions.

Attaining a Level of Security

Security should be a major concern for any business organization. Determining how much security an organization requires can be a huge undertaking. Enlisting the help and guidance of a consulting body will provide the assistance required in developing a strategic security policy within a very large organization. External and perimeter security, however, should provide for less of an undertaking to assess than establishing internal security requirements. Although there is an overlap between external and internal security requirements, external security is often overlooked or neglected. When dealing with external security, all areas of contact with the outside world need to be assessed and classified for risk factors. For example, if your company CFO dials in to his computer at the office from home or on the road to check his mail, manage corporate accounts, or conduct sensitive business transactions, the organization may be at risk if there are no controls in place to allow the monitoring of what is going on. How does one know that people dialing in are who they say they are? In the past, information technology (IT) departments have been very liberal in setting up dial-in access to the corporate network using such tools as Carbon Copy or Norton PC Anywhere.[3] Although these products allow for user ids and passwords, along with dial-back options, how are they controlled? What are the guidelines for their use? Can one be sure that they are properly protected and secured from the outside world, as well as from within the organization? If the dial-in machine is breached, who is ultimately responsible, given that there were no controls defining its use, maintenance, and monitoring?

So many questions; so many things to do; so many access points. What should one do? Some opt to do little or nothing at all, either out of ignorance, time restraints, or cost. Security requires balance. One might believe that a

Fort Knox solution is necessary; but is it? Perhaps an armored car or truck would better service one's needs. Most organizations can adequately protect themselves by invoking policies and procedures and enforcing them via communication, their network operating systems, and using security devices such as firewalls on the perimeter. For those who are ignorant of security, there is no excuse for not implementing security. Not enough time? Better make some. For those who believe the costs of security outweigh their benefit, consider the following:

- The cost to rebuild and retool servers or network
- The cost of downtime while employees are sitting around waiting for production systems to come back online
- The cost of lost time, business opportunity, and reputation
- The cost of damaged or deleted data, and the time to recreate that data
- The cost of a lawsuit from clients for not adequately protecting their privacy and their business interests

The cost of implementing security is a small price to pay in light of the above possible effects of neglecting it — and a negligible amount in terms of the torrent of costs that can drown a business from not addressing security.

Almost everyone has heard the stories of network breaches from companies that have and have not implemented security measures. Does the implementation of security measures guarantee your safety? About as much as the Maginot Line helped to keep the German army out of France during World War II. No, it is not a guarantee; there are too many variables at work and it is not possible to protect an organization against *every* possible scenario. But implementing security measures will help in shutting out the vast majority of threats. Implementing security with proper reporting and analysis procedures will also help to detect and determine unauthorized activity and prepare a stand for corrective action.

Identifying Risks

Identifying risks on the perimeter of the organization should be fairly straightforward. Every access point into and out of the corporate network is a risk. Phonelines connected to modems, PBXs that interface to the corporate network for call detail reporting applications, and data lines are all vulnerable. Basically, risk identification falls into two major categories: physical security and logical security. Depending on the nature of the business, a third area of security would be employee or human resources security. Employee or Human Resources security is emerging as a fairly new topic of interest; but by any means, it has been around for a very long time. Corporate espionage comes to mind; and with the shrinking borders of the global economy come attempts to steal corporate secrets. Reverse-engineering is great, but getting the actual specifications would be better; and why not get all the R&D that went into it as well?

Physical Security

Physical security deals with securing critical computing resources or other resources that are essential for operating an organization. Securing these resources within a complex or room and allowing only authorized individuals to gain access to these resources are paramount. Physical security also covers access to computing facilities on the premises, including workstations, printers, faxes, phones, and off-site computing facilities such as laptops and workstations at employees' homes. These additional devices can be used to gain access to the corporate network and, in some cases, require little or no authorization to do so. Ensure that facilities management is aware of unlocked doors or windows that can provide access to one's place of business. In office buildings, ensure that crossover floors require keyed entry (by access card, keypunch pads, or a key). Elevators should also require keyed entry after business hours, and building security should be made aware of any special instructions regarding one's place of business. For example, a security policy may dictate that in order to remove computer equipment from the company, a signed document must be produced giving the individual authority to do so. Building security must know to challenge an individual to produce that document; otherwise, the policy is useless. Securing the physical boundaries of the organization is critical; loopholes will be taken advantage of.

Logical Security

Logical security is the act or process of defining users within the computing environment and assigning them levels of access or ability within the confines of the computing environment. Logical security covers user ids, passwords, file and directory access privileges, application access/database access privileges, as well as resource privileges (i.e., printers or faxes). The granting of use and level of use must be determined prior to granting of logical access to the environment. For example, a salesperson does not require access to computing files or resources that belong to the company's research and development activities.

Policies should be in place to handle new employees, employees changing job functions, and the termination or exit of employees from the organization. Departmental managers need to define the extent of employee permissions within the computing environment and those of the departments. The Systems department should also provide a listing of public general access areas of the environment to department heads to make them aware of potential areas in which sensitive information can inadvertently be stored.

Employee or Human Resources Security

This area of security can be a major problem, depending on the nature of the enterprise. Over the past decade, employee trust has become an alarming issue for the corporate world. Employers take for granted that the people they hire are trustworthy, loyal, and work for the good of the firm. In many cases, this is true. However, in light of poor employer–employee relationships, poor job security prospects by employers and an overall atmosphere of keeping corporate profits to only benefit shareholders, many employees leave their place of employment to join competitors. And in some cases, they take corporate knowledge with them, whether it be trade secrets or strategy. Whatever the case and whatever the reason, some prevention is necessary. Proper screening of employees who will work in sensitive areas of a company should be mandatory. Even an employee's references should be verified for legitimacy. Corporate espionage is real. Be aware and be prepared. The mail clerk may be on the payroll of the competition; yet again, so may the V.P. of Research and Development.

A very high-profile case of corporate espionage occurred during the summer of 2001. It involved one of the largest auto parts manufacturers in North America, Magna International, Inc. In this case, two executives of the firm had taken sensitive documents to a competitor and later left the organization to join the competitor.[4]

Social engineering is another area of vulnerability to an organization. Policies must be in place and well-communicated throughout the organization to discourage employees from discussing corporate activities with non-employees. Have you ever received a seemingly harmless phone call to perform a computer survey on your computing environment? How do you know it is legitimate? You may be handing out critical information regarding your computing environment to someone who will use it to mount an attack. Under no circumstances should you divulge internal corporate affairs or other information to complete strangers. You would not tell anyone that you place your valuables in the fridge to thwart thieves, would you? If you did, you might be telling them exactly where to go. Corporate confidentiality policies must be communicated throughout the organization; and, if possible, such policies should be part of an employee's hiring contract. Loose lips sink ships! Monetary loss can amount to millions in lost profit and lost opportunity when critical staff is hired away to a competitor. This is one reason why banks and financial institutions segregate job functions. They prevent the exposure of an individual having too much control and knowledge of critical business functions that if divulged would be open to analysis and possibly fraudulent activities.

Assessing Risk

Taking inventory of risk factors is fairly straightforward. For example, a department store keeps its doors locked at night to prevent theft. It also installs video surveillance systems to discourage shoplifting. The risks associated with each are fairly obvious: (1) if the store is not secured at night, the risk of theft is very likely; and (2) the video surveillance systems will deter most people from stealing. Even with these procedures in place, there is little to deter some individuals from either breaking and entering or shoplifting. In this case, the department store manager may hire security guards to patrol

Exhibit 1. Risk Assessment

Area of Concern	*Risk*	*Grade*	*Issue(s)*	*Business Impact*
Physical access to computer room	Unauthorized access to production computing facilities that can lead to intentional or accidental damage or theft of equipment; allows one to bypass logical access security by directly accessing computing facilities	3	No lock No door Room is unsecured	Financial loss of equipment and replacement of equipment; financial loss for disruption to operations, financial loss to lost business opportunity, financial loss to interruption to business processes, confidentially and damage to reputation.

the store during business hours and the perimeter after business hours. An active security presence is usually enough to deter anyone from exercising a criminal act, except of course for the truly desperate or foolish.

When assessing risk factors, they should be confined to the operating environment. Using both physical and logical security attributes to determine the level of associated risk will be necessary. The operating environment can be classified as either centralized or distributed. The risks are either internal, external, or both. Grading risk factors should be used to highlight areas of concern that should be addressed immediately or within a set period of time but no longer than one year in length.

Assessment values:

- 0: no assumed risk; no known issues or vulnerabilities
- 1: minimal risk; has potential for weakness
- 2: medium risk; has been known to have had vulnerabilities
- 3: high risk; extremely vulnerable and likely target for attack

Assessing the level of risk is the first stage in determining an organization's weakness. When performing an assessment, do not be conservative; be realistic. If there is something worth protecting, protect it; otherwise, someone will walk away with it. Draft a simple form to perform a risk assessment (see, for example, Exhibit 1.

Establishing Controls

Controls are methods by which one attains a satisfactory level of compliance to guard against risks. However, a control is not an absolute guarantee against the risk itself; it is merely a preventative measure necessary to maintain integrity. Taking the example grid from the previous risk assessment and adding additional columns to capture the control and the effects of establishing the control, the control itself requires three distinct properties to be effective:

1. Communication of a formal policy governing access to restricted facilities and the establishment of criteria for physical security access to restricted facilities
2. The placement of the control into the process
3. The ability to monitor the control in a regular fashion to determine its effectiveness, or lack thereof

In the cited example, the controls would be as follows:

1. A formal security policy is necessary to establish authorized access for the computer room. Granting authorized access for the computer room is the responsibility of the [manager/director/VP of information technology]. It is the responsibility of Human Resources to establish and maintain the physical granting of such rights on behalf of the IT department. A formal security procedure for the administration of physical security/access, including visitor authorization and chronicling of changes in physical security/access, is required.
2. Physical means to secure access to the computer room will be achieved by the installation of a door and the introduction of an electronic keypad lock. The electronic keypad lock will be interfaced with building security systems for forced-entry monitoring purposes and activity logging.
3. Maintenance of the control will be established with a monthly access list of valid key holders for the computer room. This list will be maintained by Human Resources but must be validated by the [manager/director/VP of information technology] for accuracy.

Monitoring Controls

Being aware of the risks and establishing controls to protect against these risks are the first steps in securing the environment. However, if there are inadequate measures in place to monitor these controls, their effect can be indeterminate. How does one know if they are working or not? Without a monitoring process, it is impossible to gauge the actual effect of a control. For example, take the model of the computer room risk without placing adequate reporting in the procedure to maintain a computer room access list, one can never have finite assurance of authorized access to the computer room. How does one know who has access? How can one be assured that only authorized persons have access to the computer room, and not the cleaners also? The IT manager/director/VP knows who should have access. Human Resources maintains the security log of all activity associated with authorized individuals and their keycodes from the security system. By cross-checking each other's lists, verification and integrity of computer room access is maintained. If a person and keycode are accidentally added to the security

Exhibit 2. Systems Department Responsibility Chart

Area of Concern	*Primary Contact*	*Back-up Contact*
Software support and training	Supervisor A	Supervisor B
Production systems	Supervisor B	Manager Systems
Equipment and software purchases	Supervisor A	Manager Systems
Application/database development, testing, installation, training, and maintenance	Manager Systems	Project Manager(s)
Network support	Manager Operations	Network Administrator
New project initiation	Systems Steering Committee	V.P. Systems
General systems direction and planning	V.P. Systems	Manager Systems
Help desk	Supervisor B	Supervisor A

system for the computer room, it can be identified and corrected quickly. If there is no monitoring, or the process of monitoring is lax or stretched between intervals, breaches in computer room access authorization will go undetected, leaving the organization open to vulnerability.

Responsibility and Accountability

Responsibility and accountability go hand in hand. For example, the Vice President of Information Systems (IS) is accountable for the operational integrity of the IS department. Aligning responsibility of services and equipment is critical to an organization (see Exhibit 2). Individuals must be aware of their role in the organization, their responsibilities to effectively maintain that role in accordance with operating procedures, as well as their accountability in fulfilling that role.

Information technology (IT) roles can be divided into three sections (see Exhibit 3):

1. *Management*: This section organizes, plans, and carries out directives set by business stakeholders.
2. *Development:* This section develops the strategy defined by IT management to meet the business goals of the stakeholders.
3. *Operations:* This section keeps the business operating at its highest efficiencies by continual monitoring, reporting, and correction of deviance to the systems that run the business.

Internal Systems Control Structures

For a perimeter security defense to remain relatively intact, it will be necessary to establish internal systems controls. These controls are commonly referred

Exhibit 3. Information Technology Roles

Area	Role
IT management	CIO
	Director of Systems
	Manager of Operations
	Manager of Systems Development
Development	Application architect
	Application developer
	Business analyst
	Data architect
	Project leader
	Project manager
	Quality assurance analyst
	Technical writer
Operations	Database administrator
	Network administrator
	Security administrator
	Technology architect
	Version control administrator
	Office productivity analyst
	Trainer
	Help desk analyst

to as a Change Management Control Process (see Exhibit 4). The purpose of a Change Management Control Process is to effectively manage all changes within the computing environment of an organization. A change, in any shape or form, can be defined as an activity or event that can potentially interrupt or hamper the operating service levels of an organization's computing facilities. The objective of a Change Management Control Process (or simply, Change Management Process) is to (1) prevent the introduction of ill-defined changes into a production system and (2) reduce the impact of errors or problem situations arising from the introduction of changes into the production environment. The end result of a Change Management Process is to establish an audited process for introducing changes into the production environment to protect the stability and integrity of the entire production environment.

General Process for Change Management

In general, a Change Management process must be able to handle any type of change request for the production environment. Change procedures must be able to handle simple or complex requests and even emergency implementation requests. Determining how these types of requests are dealt with

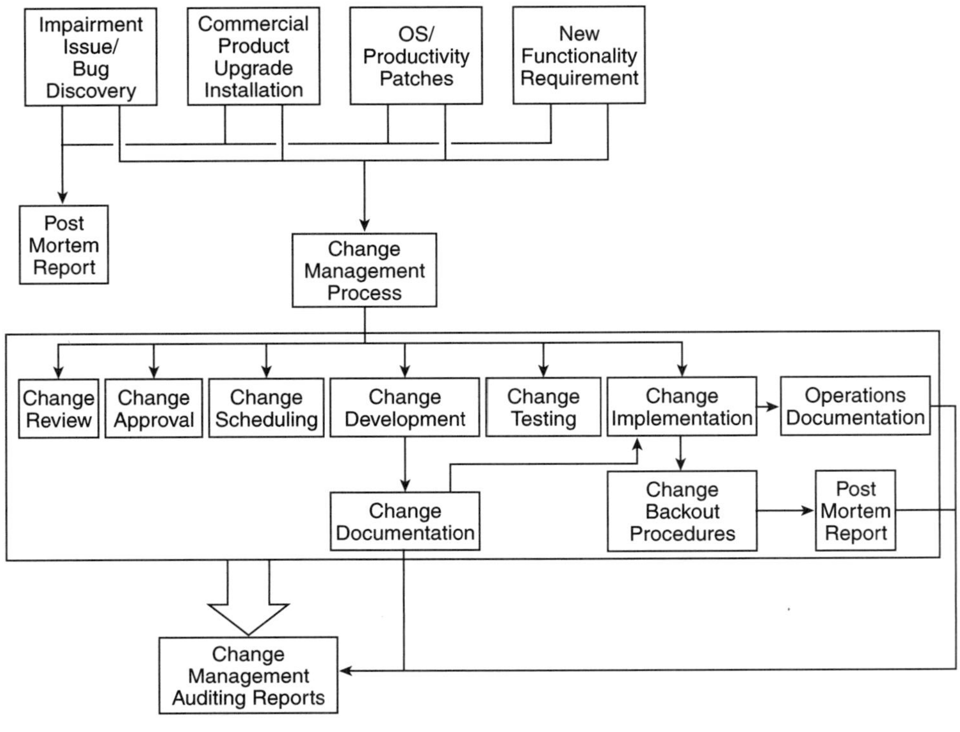

Exhibit 4. A High-Level Overview of a Change Management Process

is dependent upon the organization and how it should deal with the various types of requests. In general, there are a minimum of five steps that must be followed for a Change Management Process to be effective.

1. *A formal Change/Modification Request Form.* This form is required to document and introduce a change request into the process. Change requests can and should be filed by any employee and given to their direct manager. The direct manager should make the formal request to the IT department. The request should clearly identify the issue, all parties affected by the issue, and prioritization of the request. A brief impact analysis of the issue should be performed to determine the scope and expected impact of the request.
2. *An approval process.* An approval process must govern the acceptance of change requests and determine proper scheduling of these requests for production implementation. The approval process should involve the originating client area manager or director, Systems managers, and the vice president of administration. The establishment of a Change Management group should ultimately decide the priority and scheduling of all changes within the environment and communicate the decision back to the client area(s).

3. *A coordination process*. This step begins once thorough preparation and testing of a required change have been completed, verified for accuracy, and passed testing processes. The Change Management group, along with the client area managers, must agree on the completeness of testing in order to schedule the change for implementation and inform the user community as to when that change is expected to be reflected in the production environment.
4. *Implementation process*. This process takes the required change and moves it into the production environment. Ideally, only Systems Operations should have the authority to implement the change into production. Additional resources may be required to assist Systems Operations if necessary. Implementation schedules may vary; however, it is prudent to schedule all change events on Fridays in order to allow for a 48- to 72-hour recovery time frame should a catastrophic failure occur with the production systems. Implementing changes on a Friday should have the least impact on the user community should failure arise.
5. *Follow-up audit process*. This process is used to perform a review of the change that had been carried out. Any discrepancies from the original change request to the actual change implemented will be addressed here. All implementation documentation must be completed, and any problems or unforeseen issues will be documented for future reference. Change logs will be updated to reflect changes to the system for audit purposes.

In addition to the above steps, a regular report of change control activities should be distributed to all managers, directors, and vice presidents. All areas of an organization should be aware of impending change(s) in the environment, even if it does not directly affect all areas. Sometimes, changes can have undesirable overlapping effects that appear immediately after, or perhaps days after, a change has been implemented. Knowing that something has changed in the environment can help isolate the change that may have caused an unwanted side effect more easily than not knowing what is happening in the production environment.

A sample change request is shown in Exhibit 5.

Operations Control Log

In addition to the Change Management Control Process, an operations control log (see Exhibit 6) should be maintained in the computer room. The log book should provide a means to corroborate change implementation with the change management group's implementation schedules. The operations log book should be a feed into the follow-up audit process to ensure that changes were properly installed when scheduled. This log book will also provide an indication of trends should any problems occur after a change is implemented.

Exhibit 5. Sample Change Request Form

Change Request Reference Number #______

Date Received		Date Required		Actual Installation Date
Target System(s)				
Systems Documentation	End-User Documentation	Operations Documentation	Emergency Patch	Other
(Y/N)	(Y/N)	(Y/N)	(Y/N)	
Risk	Change Code	1 – Communications 2 – Network 3 – Hardware 4 – Security		5 – Commercial Software 6 – In-house Software 7 – OS/Patch Software 8 – Other
(L/M/H)				
Change Request From				
Change Approved By				
Change Implemented By				
Documentation Filed By				
Change Reason				
Users Affected by Change				
Business Impact of Change				
Change Description				
Test Results of Change				
Acceptance Sign-off				
Scheduled Installation Date			Notification of Change Sent	(Y/N)
Operations Back-out Procedures				
Manager Operations Completion Sign-off				
Operator Sign-off				

Exhibit 6. Sample Operations Log

Operations Log Date: dd/mmm/yyyy

System/Device	Function Code: 1 Normal Ops 2 Impaired Ops 3 Critical Impairment	Description of Issue	Users Notified (Y/N)	Estimated Service Downtime	Documented (Y/N)	Operator Initials

System Work Log

A system work log (Exhibit 7) is a form used to document changes that were done for a specific system. A system defined in these terms refers to the physical hardware. For example, applying a security patch to an Internet Information Server or SQL server should be accompanied by a system work

Exhibit 7. Sample Server Work Log

System Work Log Date: DD/MMM/YYYY

System Name: ____________________

Date of Work		Logon Time	
Time of Work		Logoff Time	
Operator			
Action	(General Service/Preventitive Maintenance/Repair-Install/Upgrade/ Patch/Other)		
Vendor Service Request ID			
Problem Description:			
Action Taken:			
Additional Notes:			

log. The work log will identify the problem issue, the action taken to correct the problem, and any additional notes regarding the accomplishment of the given task. (e.g., it is necessary to reboot the system before the desired changes take effect). This detail may seem like overkill; however, six months from the time work was done, one might not remember why patch number 123456 was applied and what it fixed. Only by meticulously documenting every change to a system will one know that patch number 123456 was applied to correct an IEEE floating point division error. Not only is proper system change documentation a necessary evil, but it also guides a newcomer into understanding why a system has evolved in a certain manner. This is analogous to the housing contractor who places a central support beam into the center of a house and does not inform the architect of why it was put there in the first place. As soon as the new owners move in, they determine that they wish to remove the structure only to find out that they have inadvertently compromised the integrity of the house — truly a situation no one would want to be in. This is especially true when trying to figure out why something that works on one machine does not work on another and the person that built the original machine left no blueprint to follow.

Notes

1. Appendix A lists the definitions of these levels as defined by the DoD.
2. See http://cryptome.org/nsa-w2k/nsa-w2k.htm.
3. Recent versions of PC Anywhere support Check Point's VPN technology infrastructure known as Secure VPN.
4. Source: *The Toronto Star,* Tuesday, October 16, 2001, Business section, pages c1 and c10.

Chapter 3

What Is a Security Policy?

A security policy in its basic form is an organization's blueprint for a code of ethics, the policies and procedures used to enforce the operational integrity of a business' operations. A security policy must be adopted by senior management and well-communicated throughout the organization for it to be considered in force and thus effective from a managerial perspective. The role of the security policy is to deter unauthorized activities by staff against internal resources or the use of those resources for anything other than business activities. A security policy provides the generally accepted guidelines for acceptable activities within the organization and introduces accountability for an individual's actions in relation to the policies set forth by the organization. Although it is possible to completely submerge oneself into policy and procedure overload, one must determine what is a reasonable level of bureaucracy to conduct business without impeding it. Unless there is a good reason to introduce a policy against an activity, do not introduce it. Carefully weigh its pros and cons and make sure it does not make someone's job or ability to do that job unbearable or, worse yet, prevent someone from doing it or doing it properly.

Steps to a Security Policy

Defining a corporate security policy can be a challenging task even for the most seasoned information technology (IT) professional. If one has been given the responsibility of creating this document, then this has happened because (1) higher powers that be have decreed it, (2) one has been audited, or (3) one has been hacked. If you do not fall into any of these categories, then one is ahead of the game and has been patted on the back for coming up with a great idea. In any event, how does one go about defining such a document?

Who should be involved and have input? Where does one get ideas for drafting the document? How formal does it have to be?

To begin a monumental task such as defining the corporate security policy, one has to break down the areas of concern. There are four main areas of concern when addressing an organization's security policy: hardware, software, operational, and communications.

Each of these subject areas is used to address specific issues surrounding the environment. Areas of concern that do not fall into these categories can be detailed in a miscellaneous category. By evaluating each of the categories and listing specific points for each, it is possible to create a skeleton for a document (refer to Exhibit 1). *Note:* Refer to Appendix G and Appendix H for samples of two different approaches to a corporate security policy. Both cover the same material, but from different approaches.

Along with these topics there should be a contact list for general staff; one such list should be separately maintained by the information technology (IT) group. The IT list should contain roles and responsibilities for the IT group, up-to-date listings of supported hardware and software, and general public access facilities within the organization.

It will be necessary to have senior management involvement as well as Human Resources involvement. In some cases, it will also be necessary to seek legal counsel when creating a security policy. All parties involved need to work together in completing the policy. In addition, it will be critical to the success of the security policy deployment that senior management buy-in be present from the corporate stakeholders. The formation of a Systems Steering Committee should be established to develop and maintain future integrity of the security policy as well as other corporate IT directives.

By having open discussions with managers, directors, and vice presidents, one will be able to assemble a number of common and specific areas to address in the security policy. Each department will undoubtedly have its own specific requirements that only affect or pertain to that department's needs. These items should be quickly noted and addressed as items for departmental procedures manuals. Only items of a global nature to the organization should be itemized. The formality of the document will ultimately depend on the environment in which one operates. Small companies may wish to exercise a simple, easy-to-follow document, whereas medium-sized organizations will tend to be a bit more formal and stringent. Large organizations tend to get very bloated in this area and will have policies and procedures for just about every conceivable option and issue. Policies of this nature tend to be too restrictive for small office/medium office environments. There are too many areas of concern that most staff will find difficult to follow, yet alone interpret. These types of policies are fine for large corporations or ISO 900x-compliant organizations, the military, government, and research and development organizations. An example of such security policies can be seen at www.nist.gov — Internet Security Policy: A Technical Guide, RFC1244, or Site Security Handbook RFC 1296. The focus of this text is on a security policy that can be utilized throughout small, medium, and large corporations that do not require strict adherence to the Department of

Exhibit 1. Areas of Concern

Item	*Points*
Hardware	Purchasing Configuration Equipment handling Equipment at employees homes Equipment used by the mobile workforce Encryption of data, etc. Employees leaving the company
Software	Standard software Evaluation software Non-standard software Workstation environment Licensing
Operational	Backup procedures (local workstations and server based) Password procedures Confidentiality Virus prevention Computer room access Resource access
Communication	Privileged communications Copyright Access and disclosure Internet e-mail Prohibited use
Miscellaneous	Service requests Documentation Training and education Help line Business continuity plan

Defense's security guidelines, although it can accommodate them if necessary. The nature of this document is to prevent unnecessary exposure, maintain adequate levels of security, and keep the business environment operating at optimum efficiency levels. The interest lies not in the assignment of additional work, but in obtaining integrity through process controls and procedures that require proper validation.

Why Is a Security Policy Needed?

At this point one may be wondering why a security policy is required. Everyone behaves properly, no one abuses the environment, and people know how to do their jobs. Why should one complicate matters and cause an uproar in the environment? It is the realization that one must protect both the corporation and its employees. Everyone needs to know the working guidelines for the environment. Verbal commitments to conduct are not enough; they need to be written down, stated so as not to be misinterpreted or subject to alternate interpretation. Policies affect all individuals within an organization and everyone is subject to them. Not having a security policy allows people to establish their own ethics on what can and cannot be done — an obviously undesirable condition because everyone's ethics are not the same and most likely not those of the organization. Take, for example, a fictional employee Sam. Sam is a good employee, a team player, and always gets his work done. In fact, Sam is the ideal employee. Sam uses the company's Internet connection after work to converse with his friends and is an active member of many newsgroups. In fact, Sam is a popular member of a few of the newsgroups because he is knowledgeable about and supportive of his company's line of products. One day, Sam reads a message in one of the groups condemning his company's product line. Sam, being the good employee that he is, quickly replies to defend his company and, in doing so, compares his company's products with competitor products and unintentionally slanders the competitor's products. But, Sam, being the good employee that he is, has just placed the company in a very precarious position. Not only did he slander the competitor's products, but he also did it using an e-mail address that identifies his company as the source of the slander. If lucky, the message may go unnoticed; if not Sam's company may be in for a lawsuit. If a well-communicated security policy is in place, situations such as the one described above can be avoided; or then again, maybe not. At least a security policy is active proof that the company does not condone unethical behavior or actions. This provides the organization with the ability to reprimand the employee for not following corporate guidelines and harbor some protection from a lawsuit.

In any event, a corporate security policy makes sense because it provides ethical guidelines that all employees must follow. Some individuals may not like or agree with the guidelines set forth by the policy, but such a policy will provide protection to both the company and its employees.

What Does a Security Policy Do?

As noted previously, a security policy is used to formally communicate the ethical operating conduct that the staff of a corporation must follow. It provides a basis of procedure for operational areas of the company to follow in clear and certain terms. It is used to inform staff on the political stand of specific areas that affect the corporation's visibility and, from a legal perspective, it protects the corporation from employee misconduct.

Who should be involved in defining a security policy? To effectively implement a corporatewide security policy, the following individuals within the corporation must be on the same side.

- CEO or stakeholder
- CFO or controller
- CIO or IT manager
- COO or administrative manager

These individuals will provide the driving force necessary to introduce the concept of the security policy throughout the enterprise. Once a preliminary introduction has been accomplished, Human Resources will need to be brought into the picture, along with legal counsel. Human Resources and legal counsel will be able to provide a framework in which to operate, the what can and cannot be done, and how to approach sensitive topics such as corporate communications. Additional senior managers and departmental managers will need to be brought on board once the preliminary groundwork is complete and a first draft of the policy has been created. A meeting to discuss the implications of policies, as well as items that may have been overlooked, will need to take place. These items will need to be ironed out, and redrafted if necessary, to accommodate operational procedures. As with any organization, these will be unique to the organization and, as such, specific departmental operational guidelines should be separated into individual departmental policies and procedures guides. Any disagreements should be well-documented and resolved by senior management. Finally, the senior management group must appoint an individual to be the Corporate Security Administrator. The Corporate Security Administrator will be responsible for maintaining the security policies; helping all levels of the organization meet their responsibility to attain these policies; keeping on top of security vulnerabilities that might affect the operating integrity of the organization, and from time to time, performing audits of the security infrastructure as it relates to corporate policy. This last item is of particular interest because, as companies grow, the ability to effectively audit processes becomes increasingly more difficult to accomplish. Introduction of a corporate security stance in the early growth phase of a corporation will help alleviate the task of struggling to come to grips with one when the company has grown three or four times its current size. Of course, it is also possible to enlist the help of one of the big five accounting firms. They will be more than happy to court your organization into developing a corporate security policy.

Additional References

Peltier, T., *Information Security Policies and Procedures: A Practitioner's Reference*, Auerbach Publications, 1998.

Peltier, T., *Information Security Policies, Procedures, and Standards Guidelines for Effective Information Security Management*, Auerbach Publications, New York, 2002.

Chapter 4

Implementing a Security Policy

Implementing a security policy is not an easy task. It requires careful planning and careful execution to ensure effectiveness. Once senior management has been brought onboard and understands the need for a more secure environment, policy planning can commence. Assuming that a preliminary risk assessment has already been carried out, it will need to be refined and documented. External risks and internal risks will need to be graded and classified by risk factor. An application inventory should be carried out to get a detailed definition of the operating environment. These details should be used as a guide for a supported applications directory for a corporate help desk, and also provide the necessary information to segregate these applications between user departments. The operating requirements of these applications can be used to effectively secure the applications properly by securing the necessary access rights by each individual department. Applications should be accessed based on departmental or group rights — not by individual rights. Although there will be cases in which this may not apply, it should be handled by the security policy. In any event, the application inventory will allow for a more secure internal operating environment by preventing abuse from within. Securing internal resources and servers will also be required and should be done in tandem with the application inventory. It will be necessary to capture the required rights and permissions to properly access and execute corporate applications and restrict unauthorized use by narrowing network access to these resources and applications. The introduction of auditing access to these network resources should also be defined and set up. Tracking access failures to these resources will provide intuitive insight into what is happening, and perhaps why. Breaches in security can be classified as either a true access violation or an apparent access violation. Auditing will help uncover these events. The fewer privileges available to a user, the less likely damage can be caused by the user, by either error or account breach. In essence, one needs to avoid the likelihood of a situation such as, "Oh, I wonder what

Exhibit 1. Stages of Implementation

Stage	*Process*
1	Discovery
2	Reporting and documentation
3	Implementation
4	Testing
5	Training and deployment
6	Review

would happen if I ran this program, or click on this, etc." Defining the project will require at least six fundamental stages of implementation (see Exhibit 1). Like any project, these stages depend on one's environment and are only recommendations. A sample project plan is provided in Exhibit 2. It clearly defines each of the stages for a project, as well as the management support for the project.

1. *Discovery stage:* As precisely noted, the discovery stage deals with risk assessment and operating environment issues such as application cataloging or inventory and internal server security. The discovery process will define the nature and implementation details of the project. During this stage, the items and depth of the project will vary as new items or areas of concern are discovered. In all likelihood, securing an environment will have to be implemented in stages, such as external security, physical security, and internal security.
2. *Reporting and documenting stage:* This stage of the project is critical because it is carried on for the life of the project and even after the project ends. All inputs from the discovery process will lead to the compilation of security documents, formats, and templates, including the security policy. Documents such as System Operations Procedures, Departmental Procedures, and other operating procedure manuals will be developed during this stage.
3. *Implementation stage:* This stage defines the tasks that will be carried out in the environment. It is the list of processes that must be carried out to achieve the goals of the security policy mandate. Each step defined within this stage gradually tightens corporate security within the required operating parameters.
4. *Testing stage:* As each task of an implementation is achieved, it must be tested to determine its effectiveness. Not only does the individual area of concern require testing, but the entire system or operational platform must also be tested together. It is always possible to cancel out one change with another, and it is proper practice to ensure that this does not happen. Known as "regression testing" in the development arena for testing programmatic modifications, operations must also adopt a similar perspective in testing. User acceptance testing will also

be required to verify that departmental functionality is maintained and not lost during the process of introducing security.

5. *Training and deployment stage:* Once a task passes its testing phase, it can be deployed. A gradual introduction of deliverables can be rolled out without affecting or impacting the operating environment too abruptly. A gradual rollout will also allow one to monitor the effects of such changes on the environment and perceive their true impact. A "slam-dunk" approach can be too much too fast, causing havoc in the environment; but beware that a too little, too late approach is also not desirable. In addition to deployment, training is required, because staff will need to know what to expect and how new procedures and processes will affect their job functions.
6. *Review stage:* The review stage is used to gauge the overall effectiveness of the project. It is used to assess the success of the project and contributes to a corporation's overall project management methodology. Techniques or processes learned during the project should be documented for future projects, as well as things to avoid. In essence, this is a self-check stage to see how well everyone has adjusted to the outcome of the project (see Exhibit 2).

Involving and Informing Management

During the project, it is critical that management be kept abreast of progress and changing requirements. New areas of concern and risk may surface that will require immediate attention and resolution. As phases of the project reach completion, testing and training will have to be scheduled. Departmental managers will need to let staff know what, when, who, and where things will happen, as well as in what sequence. Regular project status meetings should be held on a weekly basis for management to review where everyone is in the scope of things. A project status brief should be provided that lists accomplishments achieved since the last meeting, goals to achieve for the next meeting, explanations of missed goals or expectations, and possibly a revised or updated project plan. Exhibit 3 provides a sample project status brief.

In addition to the project status brief, a master project status report should be used to track all projects within a department. This report would provide an overall picture of what work is, or is not, in progress. The project status report (Exhibit 4) provides an excellent indicator of workload and workover load. As project work piles up and completion dates slip by, management can use this mechanism to quickly and efficiently re-prioritize project work that is of a critical nature to the organization's continued success. If work is not properly cataloged and kept track of, important tasks might be forgotten; work might be delayed due to inter-project dependencies; or worse, the introduction of work duplication.

A Project Control Committee (PCC) should also be established to manage and coordinate the efforts of all projects that may be carried out in an

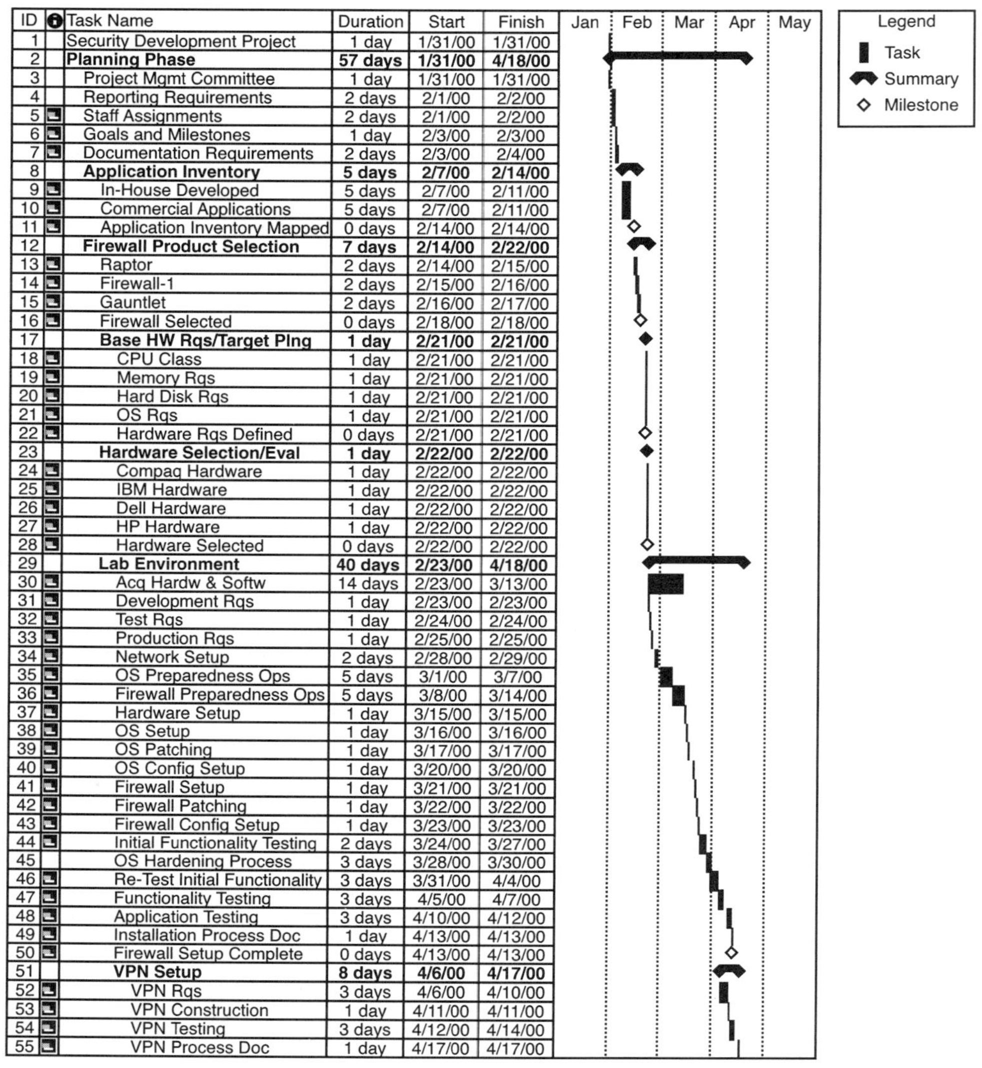

ID	Task Name	Duration	Start	Finish
1	Security Development Project	1 day	1/31/00	1/31/00
2	**Planning Phase**	**57 days**	**1/31/00**	**4/18/00**
3	Project Mgmt Committee	1 day	1/31/00	1/31/00
4	Reporting Requirements	2 days	2/1/00	2/2/00
5	Staff Assignments	2 days	2/1/00	2/2/00
6	Goals and Milestones	1 day	2/3/00	2/3/00
7	Documentation Requirements	2 days	2/3/00	2/4/00
8	**Application Inventory**	**5 days**	**2/7/00**	**2/14/00**
9	In-House Developed	5 days	2/7/00	2/11/00
10	Commercial Applications	5 days	2/7/00	2/11/00
11	Application Inventory Mapped	0 days	2/14/00	2/14/00
12	**Firewall Product Selection**	**7 days**	**2/14/00**	**2/22/00**
13	Raptor	2 days	2/14/00	2/15/00
14	Firewall-1	2 days	2/15/00	2/16/00
15	Gauntlet	2 days	2/16/00	2/17/00
16	Firewall Selected	0 days	2/18/00	2/18/00
17	**Base HW Rqs/Target Plng**	**1 day**	**2/21/00**	**2/21/00**
18	CPU Class	1 day	2/21/00	2/21/00
19	Memory Rqs	1 day	2/21/00	2/21/00
20	Hard Disk Rqs	1 day	2/21/00	2/21/00
21	OS Rqs	1 day	2/21/00	2/21/00
22	Hardware Rqs Defined	0 days	2/21/00	2/21/00
23	**Hardware Selection/Eval**	**1 day**	**2/22/00**	**2/22/00**
24	Compaq Hardware	1 day	2/22/00	2/22/00
25	IBM Hardware	1 day	2/22/00	2/22/00
26	Dell Hardware	1 day	2/22/00	2/22/00
27	HP Hardware	1 day	2/22/00	2/22/00
28	Hardware Selected	0 days	2/22/00	2/22/00
29	**Lab Environment**	**40 days**	**2/23/00**	**4/18/00**
30	Acq Hardw & Softw	14 days	2/23/00	3/13/00
31	Development Rqs	1 day	2/23/00	2/23/00
32	Test Rqs	1 day	2/24/00	2/24/00
33	Production Rqs	1 day	2/25/00	2/25/00
34	Network Setup	2 days	2/28/00	2/29/00
35	OS Preparedness Ops	5 days	3/1/00	3/7/00
36	Firewall Preparedness Ops	5 days	3/8/00	3/14/00
37	Hardware Setup	1 day	3/15/00	3/15/00
38	OS Setup	1 day	3/16/00	3/16/00
39	OS Patching	1 day	3/17/00	3/17/00
40	OS Config Setup	1 day	3/20/00	3/20/00
41	Firewall Setup	1 day	3/21/00	3/21/00
42	Firewall Patching	1 day	3/22/00	3/22/00
43	Firewall Config Setup	1 day	3/23/00	3/23/00
44	Initial Functionality Testing	2 days	3/24/00	3/27/00
45	OS Hardening Process	3 days	3/28/00	3/30/00
46	Re-Test Initial Functionality	3 days	3/31/00	4/4/00
47	Functionality Testing	3 days	4/5/00	4/7/00
48	Application Testing	3 days	4/10/00	4/12/00
49	Installation Process Doc	1 day	4/13/00	4/13/00
50	Firewall Setup Complete	0 days	4/13/00	4/13/00
51	**VPN Setup**	**8 days**	**4/6/00**	**4/17/00**
52	VPN Rqs	3 days	4/6/00	4/10/00
53	VPN Construction	1 day	4/11/00	4/11/00
54	VPN Testing	3 days	4/12/00	4/14/00
55	VPN Process Doc	1 day	4/17/00	4/17/00

Exhibit 2. Sample Project Plan

organization. A managing director should be appointed as a delegate to senior management to communicate overall progress on all fronts. Because senior management does not have the time to get bogged down with the details of a project, someone will be required to keep the top levels of the organization informed. Summary progress reporting to senior management is the function of the PCC. This committee is responsible for informing senior management of progress and issues, and obtaining additional resources for a project when required. The PCC is also required to act as a liason to departmental managers to make sure their needs are being met with respect to projects. It is not necessary to have everyone involved in a meeting all the time. A proper reporting structure will minimize meeting times and keep things moving productively.

Exhibit 3. Sample Project Status Brief

Date: dd mmm yy

Project Identification:

Project Team:

Accomplishments During Last Reporting Period:

Current Issues/Considerations:

Issue No.	*Issue Name*	*Requester*	*Date Identified*	*Assigned To*	*Issue Status*	*Date Resolved*

Milestones:

Date	*Deliverable*	*Estimated Date*	*Actual Date*	*Assigned To*	*Comments*
Current Actions Planned for Next Period					
Key Decisions					

Communication of the Security Policy

Communication of the corporate security policy should be handled by either Human Resources or a Corporate Services department. When the policy is communicated throughout the organization, a cover letter from the executive management team should accompany it. This letter should express the concerns and issues of the executive management team and why this action is necessary. Delivery of the policy itself can be done via an internal Web server or by other conventional means, as long as every staff member can get a copy.

Human Resources or Corporate Services should be able to create a new employee orientation package that contains a copy of the security policy. They should also draft employee contracts with the assistance of corporate legal counsel that binds an employee to adhere to the conduct of such a

Exhibit 4. Sample Project Status Report

Projects/Tasks — Status Report

As of Day Month Year

Project	*Required Completion Date*	*Estimated/ Actual Start Date*	*Resources Assigned*	*Status*[a]	*Comments*	*Priority*[b]

[a] Status codes: WIP — work in progress; P — pending; C — completed; O — open, no progress; NS — not started; D — dependency.

[b] Priority codes: L — low; M — medium; H — high; U — urgent; and R — rush.

policy. Regular updates and additions to the corporate security policy will also need to be communicated on a regular basis. Environments and technology change; a security policy must also change.

Internal Controls

To effectively and efficiently maintain and operate a production environment, internal controls are required. If everyone has the ability to manage their own computing needs and desires and can install whatever software they need to be more productive or creative, the environment will quickly run out of control. The costs to administer such an environment will be high and spin out of control because every computer or system will have its own unique requirements and personality. If the environment is running out of control, one needs to pull in the reins as quickly as possible. An environment that is out of control can be a haven to a hacker or disgruntled employee. If one notices that Systems staff is always fighting fires and that new functionality introduces more fires, then one is already in the downward spin cycle that will eventually lead to full-time firefighting mode.

Businesses do not have the time, money, or resources to operate under such conditions. Although some firefighting is always apparent in any environment, if properly controlled it should not impact the business by increasing support burdens. Along with a change management control process, application inventories on a per-department basis will provide a means to begin standardizing the desktop environment and lock it down for centralized and controlled management (Exhibit 5). In addition to the application inventory, an asset inventory is also necessary to cross reference individuals, assets, and their access profiles (Appendix B).

The establishment of hardware and software standards reduces configuration management overhead and at least provides ample known variables with which to work. Knowing the hardware and software combinations and how they interact with each other removes a tremendous amount of problem-resolution overhead from the support staff because one is dealing with known entities. Any change management controls will involve proper testing procedures, which will allow changes to flow into the environment at a rate conducive to that environment. The days of just applying software upgrades without testing the effect on the environment are over. Businesses cannot afford to beta-test new product releases at the expense of the business, nor can they cater to the unique and individual needs of staff. Business systems are meant to run the business; in no way are they meant for personal use.

When working toward a standardized environment, the application inventory should capture all relevant operating characteristics of a department. These characteristics can then be applied to a departmental operating profile that allows all users within a department to operate in a uniform fashion. Once a standardized profile strategy has been achieved, it will be fairly simple to test changes against that standard. A profile is also much simpler to tailor custom requirements for varying authority within a department. One may have a need for clerical, supervisory, and managerial profiles. It also allows for the rollout of changes in an environment by allowing functionality to enter the environment only where it is required. Refer to Exhibit 6 for a sample profile strategy.

It is imperative that change be focused on the area that is required: change must be localized, not globalized. If changes are of a global nature, they should be introduced into the environment in a staged fashion. One should not approach a global change with a simultaneous rollout. Remember that all changes have an effect. Think of your Physics 101 rule of cause and effect. One needs to bend this rule a little bit to fit the Information Age because any change may not have an equal effect. Subtle differences in hardware can cause a world of difference. Software can also have undesired effects on a change; what works on one system does not automatically guarantee its successful operation on another machine.

Other items to consider in compiling an application inventory include determining if the applications will be required remotely and what TCP/IP ports may be required to run those applications remotely. This, however, heavily depends on the internal production applications architecture. True thin-client or Web-based remote access will require only basic TCP/IP ports (see Exhibit 7 for a listing of defined TCP/IP ports).[1] Highly customized or

Exhibit 5. Sample Application Inventory

Program Group	*Application Item(s)*	*Item Properties (if network)*	*Applies to*	*Yes*	*Applies to*	*Yes*	*Applies to*	*Yes*
Program group name A	Application Identifier	#:\\server\share\executable	Department A	☐	Department G	☐	Department M	☐
	Application Identifier	#:\\server\share\executable	Department B	☐	Department H	☐	Department N	☐
	Application Identifier	#:\\server\share\executable	Department C	☐	Department I	☐	Department O	☐
	Application Identifier	#:\\server\share\executable	Department D	☐	Department J	☐	Department P	☐
	Application Identifier	#:\\server\share\executable	Department E	☐	Department K	☐	Department Q	☐
	Application Identifier	#:\\server\share\executable	Department F	☐	Department L	☐	Department R	☐
Program group name B	Application Identifier	#:\\server\share\executable	Department A	☐	Department G	☐	Department M	☐
	Application Identifier	#:\\server\share\executable	Department B	☐	Department H	☐	Department N	☐
	Application Identifier	#:\\server\share\executable	Department C	☐	Department I	☐	Department O	☐
	Application Identifier	#:\\server\share\executable	Department D	☐	Department J	☐	Department P	☐
	Application Identifier	#:\\server\share\executable	Department E	☐	Department K	☐	Department Q	☐
	Application Identifier	#:\\server\share\executable	Department F	☐	Department L	☐	Department R	☐
Program group name C	Application Identifier	#:\\server\share\executable	Department A	☐	Department G	☐	Department M	☐
	Application Identifier	#:\\server\share\executable	Department B	☐	Department H	☐	Department N	☐
	Application Identifier	#:\\server\share\executable	Department C	☐	Department I	☐	Department O	☐
	Application Identifier	#:\\server\share\executable	Department D	☐	Department J	☐	Department P	☐
	Application Identifier	#:\\server\share\executable	Department E	☐	Department K	☐	Department Q	☐
	Application Identifier	#:\\server\share\executable	Department F	☐	Department L	☐	Department R	☐
Program group name D	Application Identifier	#:\\server\share\executable	Department A	☐	Department G	☐	Department M	☐
	Application Identifier	#:\\server\share\executable	Department B	☐	Department H	☐	Department N	☐

	Application Identifier	#:\\server\share\executable	Department C	☐	Department I	☐	Department O	☐
	Application Identifier	#:\\server\share\executable	Department D	☐	Department J	☐	Department P	☐
	Application Identifier	#:\\server\share\executable	Department E	☐	Department K	☐	Department Q	☐
	Application Identifier	#:\\server\share\executable	Department F	☐	Department L	☐	Department R	☐
Future Groups are added below								
			Department A	☐	Department G	☐	Department M	☐
			Department B	☐	Department H	☐	Department N	☐
			Department C	☐	Department I	☐	Department O	☐
			Department D	☐	Department J	☐	Department P	☐
			Department E	☐	Department K	☐	Department Q	☐
			Department F	☐	Department L	☐	Department R	☐
			Department A	☐	Department G	☐	Department M	☐
			Department B	☐	Department H	☐	Department N	☐
			Department C	☐	Department I	☐	Department O	☐
			Department D	☐	Department J	☐	Department P	☐
			Department E	☐	Department K	☐	Department Q	☐
			Department F	☐	Department L	☐	Department R	☐
			Department A	☐	Department G	☐	Department M	☐
			Department B	☐	Department H	☐	Department N	☐
			Department C	☐	Department I	☐	Department O	☐
			Department D	☐	Department J	☐	Department P	☐
			Department E	☐	Department K	☐	Department Q	☐
			Department F	☐	Department L	☐	Department R	☐

Exhibit 6. Sample Profile Strategy

Operating System	Windows NT 4.0
Policy Name	NTConfig.pol / Department_B
Policy Location	\\server\share\Department_B
NT User Group	Department_B
NT Login Script	COMPANY.BAT

User Policy

Component	*Option*	*Available Restrictions*	*Enabled*	*Comments*
Control panel	Display	Restrict display control panel	✔	Allowed screensaver only
	Network	Restrict network control panel	✔	
	Passwords	Restrict passwords control panel	✔	
	Printers	Restrict printers control panel		
	System	Restrict system control panel	✔	
Desktop	Wallpaper	N/A	✔	Corporate-Deparment-B.BMP
	Color scheme	N/A	✔	TEAL
Network	Sharing	Disable file sharing controls	✔	
		Disable print sharing controls		
Shell	Custom folders	Custom program folders	✔	\\server\share\department_B\programs
		Custom desktop folders		
		Hide Start menu subfolders	✔	
		Custom start-up folder		
		Custom network neighborhood		
		Custom Start menu		
	Restrictions	Remove "RUN" command		
		Remove folders from "SETTINGS" on Start menu		
		Remove Taskbar from "SETTINGS" on Start menu	✔	
		Remove Find command		
		Hide drives in My Computer		
		Hide Network Neighborhood		
		No "Entire Network" in Network Neighborhood		

		No workgroup contents in Network Neighborhood		
		Hide all items on desktop		
		Disable Shut Down command		
		Don't save settings on exit	✔	
System	Restrictions	Disable Registry editing tools	✔	
		Only run allowed Windows applications		
		Disable MS-DOS prompt		
		Disable single-mode MS-DOS application		
Computer Policy				
Network	Access Control	User level access control	✔	
	Logon	Logon banner	✔	
		Require validation by network	✔	
	MS-Client for Windows network	Log on to Windows NT	✔	
		Workgroup		
		Alternate workgroup		
	Passwords	Hide share passwords with asterisks	✔	
		Disable password caching	✔	
		Require alphanumeric Windows password		
		Minimum Windows password length		
	Dial-up networking	Disable dial-in	✔	
	Sharing	Disable file sharing	✔	
		Disable print sharing	✔	
	SNMP	Communities		
		Permitted managers		
		Traps for public community		
		Internet MIB (RFC1156)		
	Update	Remote update		
System		Enable user profiles	✔	
		Network path for Windows setup		
		Network path for Windows "Tour"		
		Run		
		Run once		
		Run services		

fat-client application technology will require more ports and increase the security risk to the environment. In any event, remote access should provide strong authentication and the use of virtual private networking to provide some level of confidence in allowing only authorized individuals to access production systems remotely.

From a system operations perspective, the help desk will benefit greatly. The majority of issues will be resolved during testing before anything reaches the production environment. Problems or issues that do penetrate into the production environment can receive focused attention in order to be resolved. If necessary, they can also be backed out more easily. Once problem issues have been documented, future testing should incorporate testing of the newly discovered issue so as not to introduce it into the production environment again. This concept is known as regression testing. Ensure that new changes do not regress the system to a previous operating state.

When internal controls seem restrictive and end-user departments complain that such controls reduce their ability to respond to their customers, you need to let department managers know that the addition of functionality should not be introduced at the expense of the company's ability to conduct business. A rapid introduction of change sometimes cannot be so rapidly backed out of. For example, take a simple change that affects the ability to report on data from the database. Clients really want to know this information and it has been pushed through to get it into production. It has been poorly tested because the change has gone to a junior programmer and that programmer only tested retrieval functionality. The first time some one tries to enter data into the field and save it, boom! The system goes down. Worse, when the system comes back online, the database has been corrupted. Now, not only does the simple change need to be removed from the production system, but the database must be restored. Is this conducive to customer service? No! Usually IT will take the brunt of a disaster like this; however, it is typically a poor end-user management decision that forces rapid change into the environment until it hits them right in the face. Management needs to recognize that change requires time to implement, no matter how simple it may seem or be. Many companies have tried to run by the seat of their pants. The short-term effects are immediate change and the ability to turn on a dime. The long-term effects are much worse. Ad hoc procedures, firefighting, and poor documentation of systems can be devastating when disaster strikes, and disaster always strikes at the most inopportune moment.

Scenario Example

For demonstration purposes, a fictitious corporation is used to demonstrate the impact of securing the perimeter of an organization. Having discussed many aspects of external and internal security measures, this scenario example only touches upon areas relating to perimeter security.

Exhibit 7a. Known TCP Port Assignments

Port No.	Protocol	Service Name	Aliases	Comment
7	TCP	echo		Echo
7	UDP	echo		Echo
9	TCP	discard	sink null	Discard
9	UDP	discard	sink null	Discard
13	TCP	daytime		Daytime
13	UDP	daytime		Daytime
17	TCP	qotd	quote	Quote of the day
17	UDP	qotd	quote	Quote of the day
19	TCP	chargen	ttytst source	Character generator
19	UDP	chargen	ttytst source	Character generator
20	TCP	ftp-data		File Transfer
21	TCP	ftp		FTP Control
23	TCP	telnet		Telnet
25	TCP	smtp	mail	Simple Mail Transfer
37	TCP	time		Time
37	UDP	time		Time
39	UDP	rlp	resource	Resource Location Protocol
42	TCP	nameserver	name	Host Name Server
42	UDP	nameserver	name	Host Name Server
43	TCP	nicname	whois	Who Is
53	TCP	domain		Domain Name
53	UDP	domain		Domain Name Server
67	UDP	bootps	dhcps	Bootstrap Protocol Server
68	UDP	bootpc	dhcpc	Bootstrap Protocol Client
69	UDP	tftp		Trivial File Transfer
70	TCP	gopher		Gopher
79	TCP	finger		Finger
80	TCP	http	www, http	World Wide Web
88	TCP	kerberos	krb5	Kerberos
88	UDP	kerberos	krb5	Kerberos
101	TCP	hostname	hostnames	NIC Host Name Server
102	TCP	iso-tsap		ISO-TSAP Class 0
107	TCP	rtelnet		Remote Telnet Service
109	TCP	pop2	postoffice	Post Office Protocol - Version 2
110	TCP	pop3	postoffice	Post Office Protocol - Version 3
111	TCP	sunrpc	rpcbind portmap	SUN Remote Procedure Call
111	UDP	sunrpc	rpcbind portmap	SUN Remote Procedure Call
113	TCP	auth	ident tap	Authentication Sevice
117	TCP	uucp-path		UUCP Path Service
119	TCP	nntp	usenet	Network News Transfer Protocol

Exhibit 7a. (Continued) Known TCP Port Assignments

Port No.	Protocol	Service Name	Aliases	Comment
123	UDP	ntp		Network Time Protocol
135	TCP	epmap	loc-srv	DCE endpoint resolution
135	UDP	epmap	loc-srv	DCE endpoint resolution
137	TCP	netbios-ns	nbname	NetBIOS Name Service
137	UDP	netbios-ns	nbname	NetBIOS Name Service
138	UDP	netbios-dgm	nbdatagram	NetBIOS Datagram Service
139	TCP	netbios-ssn	nbsession	NetBIOS Session Service
143	TCP	imap	imap4	Internet Message Access Protocol
158	TCP	pcmail-srv	repository	PC Mail Server
161	UDP	snmp	snmp	SNMP
162	UDP	snmptrap	snmp-trap	SNMP TRAP
170	TCP	print-srv		Network PostScript
179	TCP	Bgp		Border Gateway Protocol
194	TCP	irc		Internet Relay Chat Protocol
213	UDP	ipx		IPX over IP
389	TCP	ldap		Lightweight Directory Access Protocol
443	TCP	https	MCom	
443	UDP	https	MCom	
445	TCP			Microsoft CIFS
445	UDP			Microsoft CIFS
464	TCP	kpasswd		Kerberos (v5)
464	UDP	kpasswd		Kerberos (v5)
500	UDP	isakmp	ike	Internet Key Exchange (IPSec)
512	TCP	exec		Remote Process Execution
512	UDP	biff	comsat	Notifies users of new mail
513	TCP	login		Remote Login
513	UDP	who	whod	Database of who is logged on, average load
514	TCP	cmd	shell	Automatic authentication
514	UDP	syslog		
515	TCP	printer	spooler	Listens for incoming connections
517	UDP	talk		Establishes TCP connection
518	UDP	ntalk		
520	TCP	efs		Extended File Name Server
520	UDP	router	router routed	RIPv.1, RIPv.2
525	UDP	timed	timeserver	Timeserver
526	TCP	tempo	newdate	Newdate
530	TCP,UDP	courier	rpc	RPC
531	TCP	conference	chat	IRC Chat
532	TCP	netnews	readnews	Readnews

Exhibit 7a. (Continued) Known TCP Port Assignments

Port No.	Protocol	Service Name	Aliases	Comment
533	UDP	netwall		For emergency broadcasts
540	TCP	uucp	uucpd	Uucpd
543	TCP	klogin		Kerberos login
544	TCP	kshell	krcmd	Kerberos remote shell
550	UDP	new-rwho	new-who	New-who
556	TCP	remotefs	rfs rfs_server	Rfs Server
560	UDP	rmonitor	rmonitord	Rmonitor
561	UDP	monitor		
636	TCP	ldaps	sldap	LDAP over TLS/SSL
749	TCP	kerberos-adm		Kerberos administration
749	UDP	kerberos-adm		Kerberos administration

Note: For a current list of protocol numbers and TCP and UDP ports, see the Internet Assigned Numbers Authority (IANA).

Source: Microsoft Corporation

Exhibit 7b. Registered TCP Port Assignments

Port No.	Protocol	Service Name	Aliases	Comment
1109	TCP	kpop		Kerberos POP
1167	UDP	phone		Conference calling
1433	TCP	ms-sql-s		Microsoft-SQL-Server
1433	UDP	ms-sql-s		Microsoft-SQL-Server
1434	TCP	ms-sql-m		Microsoft-SQL-Monitor
1434	UDP	ms-sql-m		Microsoft-SQL-Monitor
1512	TCP	wins		Microsoft Windows Internet Name Service
1512	UDP	wins		Microsoft Windows Internet Name Service
1524	TCP	ingreslock	ingres	Ingres
1701	UDP	l2tp		Layer Two Tunneling Protocol
1723	TCP	pptp		Point-to-Point Tunneling Protocol
1812	UDP	radiusauth		RRAS (RADIUS Authentication Protocol)
1813	UDP	radacct		RRAS (RADIUS Accounting Protocol)
2049	UDP	nfsd	nfs	Sun NFS server
2053	TCP	knetd		Kerberos demultiplexer
2504	UDP	nlbs		Network load balancing
9535	TCP	man		Remote man server

Exhibit 7c. Common Service Ports

Service Name	*UDP*	*TCP*
Browsing datagram responses of NetBIOS over TCP/IP	138	
Browsing requests of NetBIOS over TCP/IP	137	
Client/Server Communication		135
Common Internet File System (CIFS)	445	139, 445
Content Replication Service		560
Cybercash Administration		8001
Cybercash Coin Gateway		8002
Cybercash Credit Gateway		8000
DCOM (SCM uses udp/tcp to dynamically assign ports for DCOM)	135	135
DHCP client		67
DHCP server		68
DHCP Manager		135
DNS Administration		139
DNS client to server lookup (varies)	53	53
Exchange Server 5.0		
Client/Server Communication		135
Exchange Administrator		135
IMAP		143
IMAP (SSL)		993
LDAP		389
LDAP (SSL)		636
MTA - X.400 over TCP/IP		102
POP3		110
POP3 (SSL)		995
RPC		135
SMTP		25
NNTP		119
NNTP (SSL)		563
File shares name lookup	137	
File shares session		139
FTP		21
FTP-data		20
HTTP		80
HTTP-Secure Sockets Layer (SSL)		443
Internet Information Services (IIS)		80
IMAP		143
IMAP (SSL)		993
IKE	500	
IRC		531
ISPMOD (SBS 2nd tier DNS registration wizard)		1234
Kerberos demultiplexer		2053
Kerberos klogin		543
Kerberos kpasswd (v5)	464	464
Kerberos krb5	88	88

Exhibit 7c. (Continued) Common Service Ports

Service Name	*UDP*	*TCP*
Kerberos kshell		544
L2TP	1701	
LDAP		389
LDAP (SSL)		636
Login Sequence	137, 138	139
Macintosh, File Services (AFP/IP)		548
Membership DPA		568
Membership MSN		569
Microsoft Chat client to server		6667
Microsoft Chat server to server		6665
Microsoft Message Queue Server	1801	1801
Microsoft Message Queue Server	3527	135, 2101
Microsoft Message Queue Server		2103, 2105
MTA - X.400 over TCP/IP		102
NetBT datagrams	138	
NetBT name lookups	137	
NetBT service sessions		139
NetLogon	138	
NetMeeting Audio Call Control		1731
NetMeeting H.323 call setup		1720
NetMeeting H.323 streaming RTP over UDP	Dynamic	
NetMeeting Internet Locator Server ILS		389
NetMeeting RTP audio stream	Dynamic	
NetMeeting T.120		1503
NetMeeting User Location Service		522
NetMeeting user location service ULS		522
Network Load Balancing	2504	
NNTP		119
NNTP (SSL)		563
Outlook (see "Exchange" for ports)		
Pass Through Verification	137, 138	139
POP3		110
POP3 (SSL)		995
PPTP control		1723
PPTP data		
Printer sharing name lookup	137	
Printer sharing session		139
Radius accounting (Routing and Remote Access)	1646 or 1813	
Radius authentication (Routing and Remote Access)	1645 or 1812	
Remote Install TFTP		69
RPC client fixed port session queries		1500
RPC client using a fixed port session replication		2500
RPC session ports		Dynamic
RPC user manager, service manager, port mapper		135
SCM used by DCOM	135	135

Exhibit 7c. (Continued) Common Service Ports

Service Name	UDP	TCP
SMTP		25
SNMP	161	
SNMP Trap	162	
SQL Named Pipes encryption over other protocols name lookup	137	
SQL RPC encryption over other protocols name lookup	137	
SQL session		139
SQL session		1433
SQL session		1024–5000
SQL session mapper		135
SQL TCP client name lookup	53	53
Telnet		23
Terminal Server		3389
UNIX Printing		515
WINS Manager		135
WINS NetBios over TCP/IP name service	137	
WINS Proxy	137	
WINS Registration		137
WINS Replication		42
X400		102

The XYZ Company

The XYZ Company is a well-established insurance firm that currently employs approximately 75 individuals. It has been operating for a period of 15 years with an average growth rate of 12 percent. Exhibit 8 shows the corporate hierarchy for this fictitious organization. The company itself is quite innovative and staffs a team of eleven developers and operations staff, including two managers and one director. The information technology (IT) director/manager reports to the vice president of IT, who in turn reports to the CEO of the company. The IT group is broken down into two separate groups for application development and systems operations. Although the IT management group has been fairly good at maintaining change and scheduling activities in the environment, some issues have been identified as security risks to the company during a recent audit.

The company's current Internet connectivity is running through a dual-homed server, which also supports remote access users for dial-in purposes. In addition, the server supports file sharing and acts as a login server for the environment. During a recent security audit, this machine was identified and determined to be a major security risk for the organization for two main reasons: (1) it provided too many points of access into the environment, and (2) it was not dedicated to the singular task of securing the organization from the internet. In addition, a number of other topics were identified, one of which was the lack of a corporate security policy.

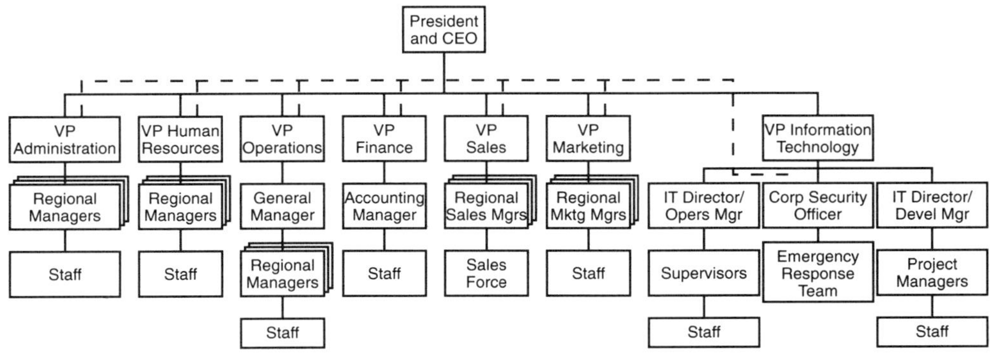

Exhibit 8. Sample Corporate Hierarchy

Corporate Security Mandate

To maintain the integrity of the computing environment, senior management mandated that the following be accomplished by the information technology group.

- Enhance or replace any and all systems that directly connect the companies internal systems to the outside world. These can be either Internet connections or other public/private information systems that provide a pathway into the company network.
- Introduce a corporate security policy that explains proper and acceptable procedures within the computing environment.
- Introduce control procedures and regular reporting to monitor the computing environment through the introduction of a change management cycle. The change management process will be used to accurately control and monitor all changes that will affect the computing environment.
- Introduce formal development procedures and standards for all in-house systems applications development.
- Introduce a standard operating procedures manual for the Systems Operations group.
- Introduce help desk procedures to effectively deal with computing environment issues. (Refer to Appendix F for a sample outline of an operations manual.)
- Provide defensive measures against common computing environment threats such as worms or virus infection.

Sample Security Policies

The following examples provide two simple ways to deliver a corporate security policy into the environment. The first sample is designed to be as unobtrusive as possible. It is specifically designed for smaller organizations that require a simple yet effective policy statement. The second sample is a more formal rendition of the first and is designed for medium to large organizations. Each policy type can obviously be expanded and amended, depending on the nature of the organization's computing environment. This policy structure will be effective for most organizations; however, organizations that require strict compliance with government standards may wish to review RFC 1244 and RFC 2196. These are complete, point-by-point detail-oriented corporate security policies.

Refer to Appendix G and Appendix H for samples of the two security policy formats.

Security Return on Investment

The return on investment in a security solution is equal to the amount of time invested in establishing what needs to be accomplished. Placing a firewall into the picture is costly; however, not maintaining it can be even more costly. The simple approach of just throwing money at the problem does not work well in this case. Unfortunately, security cannot be defined or solved by a simple or even complex mathematical equation. Security is a complex beast with many heads. The hydra comes to mind when dealing with security: for every head you sever, three more pop up. The standard approach of purchasing the best security solution in the world will have little effect if one does not know what one needs to protect. One might just purchase a very efficient gate that lets intruders in anyway.

Keep in mind that what one is trying to protect includes both public and private data assets in order to maintain strong corporate integrity. The fear of dealing with an organization that has been attacked and breached is real. It is difficult to maintain a loyal customer base when their private information may have been pilfered. One needs to protect private internal data assets such as trade/operating secrets, customer lists, pricing information, accounting or financial data, as well as human resources data. One also needs to protect publicly available data resources such as Web servers, FTP servers, and mail servers. These systems constitute a large portion of an organization's visibility to the world. In either case, a breach against either the public or private data resources of an organization would be potentially devastating to the corporation's bottom line and its effectiveness to conduct business. Imagine an intruder gaining access to employee salary records and, for entertainment, sending a corporatewide e-mail message listing all the gory details for everyone to see. Imagine the uproar and chaos that would echo throughout the company. Remember that the intruder can be either external or internal to the organization. It does not matter where the breach comes from; the fact that it was able to take place is the issue at hand. The fact that layers of security could have been in place to prevent the breach will be the sentiment question. Take another example, where the corporate Web site is the target of a hacker or even an activist group. Imagine customers surfing to that corporate Web site and finding explicit pornographic material or details of how that corporation's manufacturing process pollutes the environment. Web site defacement is a real threat and no one is immune to the art. Think it cannot happen to your site? Guess again; it can happen to anyone at anytime if one is not careful to (1) secure the system and (2) practice monitoring techniques.

When determining what is necessary for setting up perimeter security, it will be necessary to figure the following into the equation.

- Internet connection type and speed
- Router between the ISP and the facility
- Hardware class to act as the firewall
- Software for the firewall
- Staff training
- Software and hardware support
- External service monitoring and management

Each of these items can easily cost thousands of dollars. It makes a great deal of sense to investigate each item accordingly. Remember the *caveat emptor*: buyer beware. Cheaper is not necessarily better. Find out why the product is cheaper; there are always reasons and they may be either operational or hidden.

Internet Connection Type and Speed

Internet connection connectivity exists in two basic flavors: landlines and wireless. Landlines exist as either copper or fiber media and range from plain old telephone (POTS) lines to xDSL, ISDN, cable, T(n), OC(n), and SONET. Wireless includes point-to-point laser, satellite, and microwave technologies. Speed, of course, can be purchased for a price. Landlines are always more expensive than wireless solutions because they cost more to install and maintain. In addition, they are also more mature and more reliable than wireless technology because they are not susceptible to atmospheric conditions. Wireless solutions are, however, priced to compete and offer higher bandwidth for cost-conscious customers. As previously noted, reliability is an issue during adverse weather conditions; it becomes fairly difficult to get bandwidth during a storm and sometimes, even after a storm, realignment must be done to achieve optimal transmission conditions. On average, one can expect to pay about $100 a month for a cable or xDSL connection or $1500 to $2000 for a T-1 connection. Wireless connections will cost between $500 and $1000 for a T-3 connection.

Router and Communications Support Equipment

Whichever ISP is chosen, one will most likely be given the option of selecting a basic router. Some ISPs will even provide a list of routers that are available given one's bandwidth and application requirements. For some ISPs, the cost is included with the service; other ISPs will charge additional fees for the router. In any event, one will need to find out if the ISP can secure the router for you and manage it with your security expectations, or at least help out.

If the ISP turns around and says there is no need to secure a router, one should not be talking to them. Most ISPs will request a list of TCP/IP ports to be filtered out and apply the changes. Make sure to get a copy of the template the ISP applied to the router and some sort of confirmation that it actually was applied. Some ISPs will not allow one to directly modify the router configuration because they cannot guarantee reliability of the connection, and network fabric modifications pushed by the ISP may purge modifications done by one's own technical staff. The ISP will not assume responsibility for the equipment or warranty its operation under these conditions. If you wish to control your router, purchase your own; they range in price from $1500 to $7500 for a small to medium-sized corporation. Leasing is another option; this will allow one to start small and eventually right-size to a router that fits the environment and its needs.

When investigating potential ISPs, one should find out how they protect their infrastructure. Do they deploy firewalls? Offer content filtering? Offer virus protection services? Do they employ intrusion detection systems to help identify attacks? If they do, what kind of monitoring is available, and how does reporting of significant events take place? What are significant events and how are they prioritized? If the ISP's perimeter is protected by firewalls, find out if it is possible to set up point-to-point encryption of the communications channel by way of a virtual private network (VPN).

Hardware Selection

There are basically three types of hardware classes that will fit the needs of a firewall: a desktop unit, a tower unit, or a rack mount unit. Of these classes, it is best to stick with a dependable brand-name hardware manufacturer — if only because there will be a better chance of obtaining a high level of operational integrity from the machine. If at all possible, stick to a server class machine as these are typically built for endurance and offer a wider range of options. Typically, a fast processor, 256 MB of RAM, and hardware duplexed and mirrored SCSI hard disks are recommended. Stay away from IDE disks because they will hog valuable CPU resources from the systems that would be better off servicing the firewalls need to filter packets. If the solution demands the highest level of fault tolerance available, make sure that whatever firewall software is purchased can support the hardware it will be deployed on. Budget between $3000 and $7000 for a dependable hardware platform. Remember that this system will be protecting your environment, so make sure it is a reliable platform.

Software Selection

Choosing a firewall software package depends on one's needs and requirements. Keep in mind that all firewall products perform the same basic filtering functions. It is how and how well they perform these functions that differentiates one from the other. A proxy firewall works differently than a firewall that uses stateful inspection. The end results are the same but the algorithms used are different. They either allow or disallow packets to flow into or out of the organization's computing environment, depending on what one allows the firewall to do. Cost will be a factor for most organizations. The typical entry-level enterprise-class firewall software package starts at around $2500 and rapidly rises depending on the number of users to support and the options required.

Training

Staff training is not cheap. Most commercial firewall products on the market have corresponding training courses available. Depending on availability within one's city, this may add additional travel expense costs to the training budget. If considering training a team of five or more staff members, it may be cost-effective to pursue an on-site training course. The typical training course will run $1500 to$2500 per person. Depending on the nature of one's needs, staff members may require both entry-level and advanced training courses.

Software and Hardware Support

Software and hardware support is a necessary evil in order to maintain sanity. Should any one thing fail or not work out to your expectations, it is always prudent to have a support agreement in place to help both you and your staff. Depending on the support level chosen to purchase from the vendor, this will determine cost. Typically budget from $2500 to $10,000 for software support. More exotic support agreements will cost in excess of $20,000 for a Primer Support Agreement from Microsoft. Hardware support agreements are not as expensive as software support agreements. However, one should determine if it is more advantageous to have a spare machine on site to pilfer for parts rather than play a waiting game when a component fails.

Monitoring and Management Services

These are services that can be offered by either the ISP or a third-party support provider. Most firewall vendors can also recommend a network operations center for these services. The service typically requires the installation of a small SNMP management agent on the system to be monitored.

Monitoring typically just checks to make sure the device is alive and on the network. Should the device fail or drop off the network, one will either be informed of the outage and one's staff will be required to correct the situation, or the monitoring company will correct the problem. Management services provide additional help by taking the support burden away. One will need to define one's needs and requirements to the company hired to manage

Exhibit 9. Sample Costs

Service/Item	*Entry-Level Range*
Internet connection	\$100–\$2000 per month
Router	\$1500–\$7500 one-time cost or included in the cost of the ISP connection charge
Hardware	\$3000–\$7000
Software	\$2500 and up, depending on the number of IP addresses to be protected
Training	\$1500–\$2000 per course
Software support	\$2500–\$10,000
Hardware support	\$100–\$450 for extended warranty
Monitoring/management	\$200–\$2000 per month
Staff salary	\$50,000 and up

the device or devices. One will also need to determine what kinds of services are available in a management services contract. Support for intrusion detection is a valuable service and lets one know how often the site is being probed and attacked. For these types of services, plan to budget from \$200 per month for a single device in a monitoring service, to approximately \$1000 to \$2000 per month for a single device under a management contract (see Exhibit 9).

These costs may seem high but it is possible to offset costs by leasing hardware and outsourcing the management of the firewall. In the grand scheme of things, the cost can be considered an insurance policy that protects the organization. The cost may seem a little high during the initial security setup phase but the maintenance will keep further costs in check. Not implementing any security leaves one running the risk of being hacked and having the business brought to its knees. Add up the cost required for systems to recover and rebuild the production environment and then figure out how much business would be lost during that time frame. Finally, calculate the time frame the business can survive without its production systems and without the ability to conduct business. These factors will determine if the company will survive an attack. The cost of implementing a firewall and security practices pales in comparison to the noted costs. In addition, there are other costs to be considered, such as facilities costs that add to the overall downtime costs. Ultimately, it is a senior management decision to choose the type and quality of protection for the organization. Make sure the risks are clearly identified and defined and get sign-off on any decision that comes down the pipe.

Note

1. The IANA maintains up-to-date listings of protocol numbers and TCP and UDP port numbers.

Chapter 5

Perimeter Security Scenarios

There are a number of perimeter security scenarios that can be deployed in an organization. Again, it depends on what the organization requires to meet its immediate security concerns and allow for future growth. There are three levels of firewall deployment: (1) the basic bastion host or dual-homed system, (2) a multi-homed bastion host, and (3) a hybrid solution, which is still considered a multi-homed bastion host. Think of each of these as small, medium, and large-scale deployment strategies, respectively. They also range in complexity from simple, to moderate, to complex, and are priced accordingly.

Basic Bastion Host (Dual-Homed Host)

The basic bastion host scenario is ideal for small organizations that require basic filtering capabilities and want an immediate enterprise level of security protection. Implementation is fairly simple and straightforward. Information can flow into the environment and out of the environment based on a set of rules that allows or disallows the flow of data. The rules should be based on the corporate security policy, which should define the type of data and communications acceptable to the organization. Any data or communications that do not fall into a specific authorized category is stopped from entering or leaving the environment.

Traffic can be filtered at the router (Exhibit 1) to keep unwanted communications from reaching the firewall. Although the firewall rule base would filter undesirable traffic anyway, it only reduces the amount of work it has to do to block that traffic. The router in this case acts as an additional layer of security, with, of course, added management overhead. The router will have to be configured to also log information because the firewall will not see the majority of unwanted traffic. The router, in this case, can be thought of as a

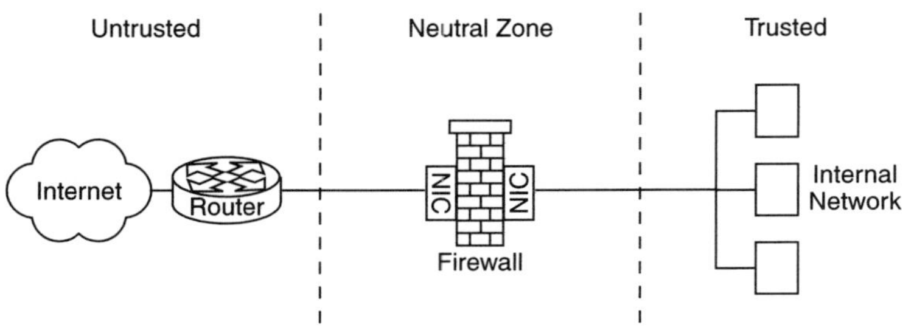

Exhibit 1. Dual-Homed Bastion Host

customs officer, detaining 90 percent of illegal traffic and allowing the other ten percent to filter through or be stopped by the firewall. The firewall uses rules (filters) to allow or disallow types of communications traffic into and out of the corporate network. Just about any type of communications traffic can exist on the trusted side of the firewall.

The advantages of a dual-homed host include the following.

- The staff and skills required to implement this type of firewall can usually be found internally or can be externally sourced.
- This is a good entry-level approach to begin securing the corporate environment and is also a good strong solution for an organization with a low risk profile.
- This solution is typically not difficult to implement.
- This solution has a lower operating cost and is easier to manage with respect to rules and configuration.
- This solution can be easily modified to operate as a multi-homed firewall solution to accommodate future corporate growth and requirements.

The disadvantages of a dual-homed host include the following.

- It does not address internal security threats.
- Initial training costs for staff can be high for smaller organizations.
- Initial hardware costs and software costs can be high for smaller organizations.
- This solution may not be suitable for medium to large enterprises with a low risk profile.
- Inadequate training of administrative staff can lead to misconfiguration, which can allow access into the corporate network.
- Contracted employees skilled in this field are expensive, and a properly defined project plan and task list will be required to minimize extraneous costs.

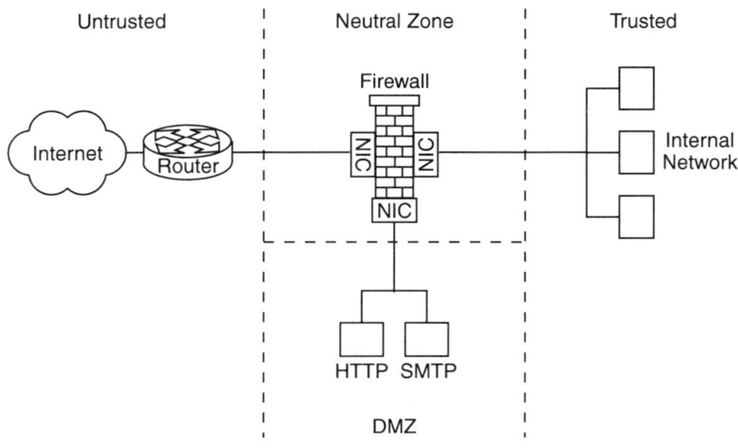

Exhibit 2. Multi-Homed Bastion Host

Multi-Homed Bastion Host

The multi-homed bastion host is a typical deployment scenario for most organizations that require the additional layers of access security for their publicly available resources as well as internal intranet resources. This solution addresses both internal and external security threats against common and restricted resources. The additional layer of security is provided by placing public access servers or intranet servers on a private subnet, commonly known as a demilitarized zone (DMZ). The multi-homed bastion host configuration provides an added layer of security that most organizations want in a perimeter security model.

The DMZ can contain both public and private servers if necessary (Exhibit 2). This additional network segment is typically used to protect access to publicly available HTTP, SMTP, FTP, or applications servers that would otherwise be exposed over the Internet if deployed in the untrusted network. Additional servers can be deployed within the DMZ without exposing them to Internet access but yet allow internal network access. Again, just about any type of communications traffic can exist on the trusted side of the firewall.

The advantages of a multi-homed bastion host include the following.

- It addresses both internal and external security threats.
- It is an excellent approach for organizations with a higher risk profile and larger visibility.
- It allows for finer access control to server resources.
- All traffic to and from the controlled server resources is logged.

The disadvantages of a multi-homed bastion host include the following.

- It has a higher operating cost than a dual-homed solution.
- It has additional management overhead due to the complexity of the rule base.
- Security filters are more complex and require extensive testing to ensure required operating results.
- Anti-spoofing rules can interfere in desired rule-based operation and testing of rules if not properly configured.

Hybrid Multi-Homed Bastion Host

The hybrid multi-homed bastion host is typically required for organizations that have a very-high-risk security profile, both internally and externally. These types of systems not only serve as perimeter defense systems but also serve to isolate internal departmental networks and service resources between the varying departments of an organization. For example, it would be possible to segregate departments and services such as accounting or human resources into their own security domains. They can even be used to isolate systems development and testing from the rest of the corporate network. Although the resources are isolated from each other, public corporate resources such as e-mail can be shared without having to expose all the resources of an organization internally. This type of solution provides a very granular level of control over the entire corporate network. Departmental information can be secured while allowing unhindered access to public corporate services and resources without compromising security. This type of deployment scenario is well-suited to financial, insurance, health, governmental, and educational facilities where high levels of security must be maintained.

In Exhibit 3, a corporate backbone switch is employed for general departmental access to the Internet and public corporate services and applications.

The advantages of a hybrid multi-homed bastion host include the following.

- It has a very high level of granular security control.
- Each resource access is logged.
- It provides for inter-departmental and corporatewide security layering.
- It is well-suited for large organizations with a high risk profile.

The disadvantages of a hybrid multi-homes bastion host include the following.

- At a minimum, two internal staff members will be required for regular maintenance and tuning operations.
- Additional log analysis tools should be purchased for reporting.
- External support and management costs can be expensive, depending on the complexity of the security model.
- Implementation is difficult and rule testing is both difficult and tedious.

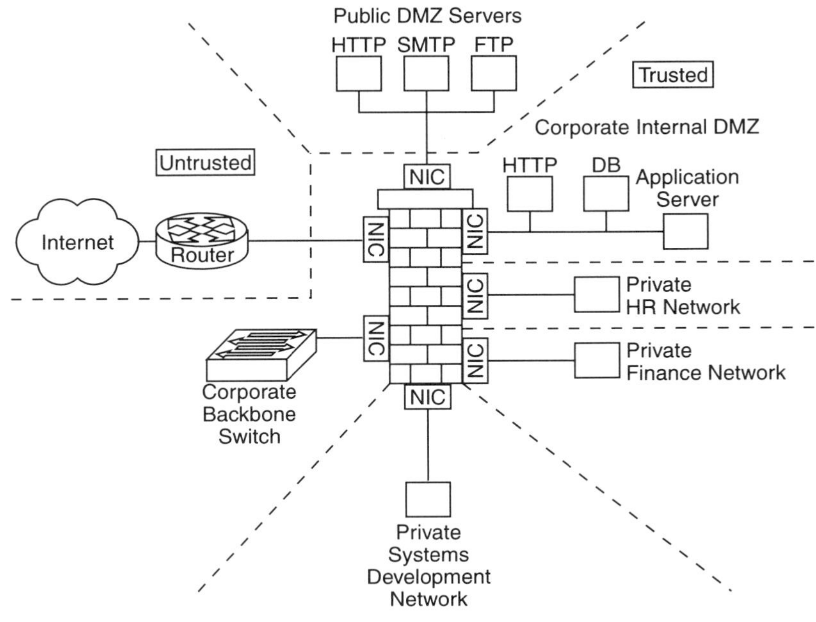

Exhibit 3. Multi-Homed Hybrid Bastion Host

Each of these security models can provide for a multitude of security scenarios. With the proper hardware selection, any deployment scenario can be adapted to a more complex security model. Other security models can be achieved by placing dual- or multi-homed firewalls between departmental boundaries. This can simplify a complex security model best suited by a hybrid security model. For example, consider an office building where each floor houses a different department. A high-speed network backbone is used to link the floors together back to the computer room. Each floor is equipped with a locked wiring closet that can house a firewall. These firewalls protect the local resources from exposure to other areas of the company but allow access to internal public resources that are centrally located in the computer room. The main perimeter defense firewall can then be set up as a simple multi-homed firewall, as opposed to a more complex hybrid multi-homed firewall.

Chapter 6

Directions in Security

As security systems evolve, new products and services will become available to help protect organizations against threats from the outside world as well as those from disgruntled employees and corporate spies. As with most industries, specialized security products offer the best features: dependability and comfort level. However, one must remember that not even these specialized security products can protect us from all vulnerabilities, especially those that have not yet been discovered. Nor are these products without flaws. This class of product does, however, offer some level of comfort in securing the computing environment if the product is properly configured.

With any increase in security comes an increase in management responsibility and administrative overhead. New security products that are emerging on the market must integrate and work with existing security frameworks. Most legacy frameworks that have withstood the test of time, and taken a pounding, have developed extendible frameworks that allow the primitive workings of the firewall to embrace additional areas of security such as virus scanning or content filtering. As long as application complexity increases, so will security complexity. In essence, we must continually adapt to the threats imposed upon us by the environment we create and layer security around the environment we wish to protect.

Perimeter Security

What is perimeter security? Is it a lame attempt to place a lock on a door and keep honest people out? Well, if everyone was honest, there would be no requirements for security. The fact is that people are not always honest, and some are extremely dangerous. Perimeter security will act as a deterrent for most people, much the same way a casual thief is deterred from breaking into a house with a security system. The primary advantage to perimeter security is the prevention of script kiddies or unskilled and casual hackers from penetrating an organization's network infrastructure and wreaking havoc. Perimeter security can keep out professional hackers to some extent. Professional hackers and crackers typically will not target the firewall itself, but they will probe for vulnerabilities behind the firewall by determining what systems and software are exposed by it. Once they know what is running as the corporate Web server or mail server, they will begin to probe for a weakness or a misconfiguration in the system. Should they find any potential holes, they will write their own scripts and executable code and forward requests to the system to attempt to gain control of the machine. Once they attain control, they will root themselves deeper and deeper into the environment until they achieve their objective. Professional hackers and crackers perform their work over an extended period of time to avoid detection. Their style is very different from the casual hacker or layman who will use a brute-force approach.

Any perimeter defense network must be well-monitored, and regular reporting of any or all incidents must be established to detect incursion attempts and determine use-trend analysis. Security administrators need to have a baseline of operational characteristics from which to view and detect anomalies. One thing to keep in mind is that a firewall is not a 100 percent guarantee against perimeter penetration. A firewall is not without flaws. System configuration is half the battle in protecting a network infrastructure and its resources. Opening doorways for nonbusiness-related applications is a hazard. Music, movie, video, and other entertainment-related TCP/IP ports are considered nonessential or immaterial data to the organization. This also violates copyright protection laws and could place a business in jeopardy if found to be distributing copyrighted material. In addition, opening up basic Internet service ports does not automatically mean that systems behind the firewall listening on those ports are secure. Take, for example, the CodeRed worm, which takes advantage of a buffer overflow vulnerability in Microsoft's Internet Information Server (IIS). The CodeRed worm uses a masked HTTP request to deliver its payload to an unsuspecting and unprotected Web server (see Exhibit 1); Simple Mail Transfer (SMTP) servers can also be at risk, as can File Transfer Protocol (FTP) or Domain Name Servers (DNS).

```
134.231.19 229.16.45.34 - [11/Aug/2001:16:44:49 +0500] "GET/
default.ida?XXXXXXXXXXXXXXXXXXXXXXXXXXXXXXXXXXXXXXXXXXXXXX
XXXXXXXXXXXXXXXXXXXXXXXXXXXXXXXXXXXXXXXXXXXXXXXXXXXXXXXXXX
XXXXXXXXXXXXXXXXXXXXXXXXXXXXXXXXXXXXXXXXXXXXXXXXXXXXXXXXXX
XXXXXXXXXXXXXXXXXXXXXXXXXXXXXXXXXXXXXXXXXXXXXXXXXXXXXXXXXX
%u9090%u6858%ucbd3%u7801%u9090%u6858%ucbd3%u7801%u9090%u68
58%ucbd3%u7801%u9090%u9090%u8190%u00c3%u0003%u8b00%u531b%u
53ff%u0078%u0000%u00=a HTTP/1.0" 404 252
```

Exhibit 1. Sample Attack Pattern of the CodeRed Worm

To combat the CodeRed worm, it is possible to block the *get* command on Check Point FireWall-1 by setting up a rule and URI resource. For more information, refer to the following technical notification from Check Point: http://support.checkpoint.com/public/publisher.asp?hotid=a0ff902e-7d65-11d5-97ed-080020a7af00&number=1.

The CodeRed worm can be blocked from Internet Information Servers (IIS) until one can patch them. Or, if the servers are infected, one can also invoke the rule to prevent further infection from occurring to other IIS Web servers on the Internet.

All machines behind the firewall need to be properly secured and kept up-to-date with respect to patches at both the product level and the operating system level. It is highly recommended that security administrators be on alert/bulletin mailing lists from all the vendors used in their environment. Vulnerabilities in all kinds of products are found all the time; and if not aware of an issue, someone else may take advantage of it at your expense. Today, all vendors have their own security mailing lists and Web sites in order to inform and alert their customer base to potential issues and real threats. Work-around instructions and product patches will automatically be sent out as proactively as possible to prevent large-scale breaches or denial-of-service (DoS) attacks from taking place.

In addition, it is always a good idea to read through and surf the "black hat"materials on the Internet. Some are a good source of education and others provide the details and tool kits used to mount attacks. Regular use of port scanners against a system to test for vulnerabilities in the perimeter defense fabric is a necessary evil. It is recommended that a port scan be initiated after each successful modification to a perimeter security model. These scans should be dated, filed, and logged by the operator who performed the operation. In addition, a regular maintenance schedule should include a port scan on a monthly basis. These scans should be cross-referenced against the previous scan and the scan of the last known modification or baseline scan. Any deviation in the scan from the baseline or previous scan should be flagged and immediately corrected. A deviation can be caused by either (1) an attack and successful penetration or (2) a flaw in change management procedures. The majority of instances will fall into the second category. It will then be necessary to trace back through the logs to determine when a change was applied to the system or if malicious activity is present.

Trusted Systems

As briefly mentioned at the beginning of this book, trusted systems use heavily layered and segregated security mechanisms to protect an operating system. In a trusted system, there is no global, god-like administrator that assumes total control over the system. Administrative privileges are assigned to a variety of groups and individual accounts. These can be considered as demigods or minor deities that collectively have all administrative capability. Being able to segregate administrative duties across a group of individual accounts is a major accomplishment in the scope of information security. Not only are individuals restricted in their own capabilities, but also the subsystems they administer. In essence, each individual account and process subsystem has its own "sandbox" in which to work. Communication between process sandboxes is handled by a supervisor process that requires proper authentication and permissions to be granted in order to carry out inter-process communications. Process A that has administrative capabilities over its own domain cannot request process B to perform a task that process A does not have the authority to do — even if both process A and process B have administrative capabilities.

Although a trusted security system leap-frogs current operating environment security, it comes so at a cost. The costs of administering a trusted security environment is steep in terms of resource costs. The administrative costs of maintaining and defining a trusted environment, as well as the added staff requirements, lead to higher operating costs, although the trade-off in cost is an extremely secure operating environment.[1]

Intrusion Detection Systems

Intrusion detection systems (IDSs) are early warning systems, similar in nature to the early warning detection systems of NORAD to counter an impending attack by unfriendly foes. Intrusion detection systems use software monitoring agents that are deployed on network equipment throughout the enterprise in both trusted and untrusted networks. A master console monitors all data feeds from the agents to determine network activity and classify the activity by comparing the data streams to known attack patterns. The data streams are also compared to an acceptable activity rule base that tracks and alerts administrators to the use of tools such as Telnet or FTP. IDSs are also used to detect network sniffing, the ability to siphon network traffic and view the contents of the traffic to capture data, user ids, and passwords. IDSs detect snooping by monitoring low-level network activity. Network interface cards will announce themselves on the network when active and in what is termed a promiscuous state. A note of caution: IDSs can be fooled with network snooping. The Sun Solaris operating system allows one to set up a network interface and not bring the interface online or up. The Sun Solaris Operating System *snoop* command can then be used to view network traffic in an inactive state that would not trigger an alert on the IDS console. To prevent such activity from occurring, client-to-server encryption should be deployed in high-risk environments. If an IDS detects a suspect data stream in the environment, it typically notifies the console with an alert status. Network administrators can then determine if the alert is valid or not. Should the IDS detect malicious activity occurring from an external source against an internal or public resource, the system will alert and attempt to block the source of the attack. Distributed attacks are a little more difficult to detect and counter than a single source.

Intrusion detection systems are typically expensive to design and deploy in a network environment. The operating cost of an IDS is also high, again due to the administration and staffing aspects to keep the system tuned and operating efficiently. When considering an IDS, design and deployment should be conducted by an experienced networking professional who is familiar with the product that is to be deployed throughout the enterprise. This network professional will help set up the system to avoid and prevent an IDS from arbitrarily issuing alerts and warnings of valid network activity. Any early warning system that acts out the "Peter and the Wolf" syndrome is useless. Warnings and alerts must have meaning; otherwise, potentially fatal network activity can be overlooked, which defeats the ultimate purpose of deploying an IDS. Check Point Technologies, Inc. has teamed together with Internet Security Systems, Inc. (ISS) to develop an intrusion detection system that is marketed as a product known as Real Secure.

IDSs should be deployed in organizations in which extremely strong threats of attack and misuse are real. Financial institutions, health care facilities, Internet service providers, and network operations centers should use IDSs to protect their networks and minimize threats.

Intrinsic Security

A new security model that has emerged and is known as Intrinsic Security (Okena, Inc.) promises to provide a proactive approach to network security. Developed by the founders of the Raptor™ firewall, Okena has taken a proactive approach in implementing enterprisewide security. Similar in nature to the constructs of an IDS with a rule base and anti-virus protection capabilities, the Stormwatch™ product relies on intelligent agents that are deployed throughout the organization. These intelligent agents maintain a set of rules that define acceptable activities within the domain of an application. The agents gather their rules of activity from a central management console at regular intervals. These agents, sometimes known as interceptors, act as a preprocessor for the system by analyzing activities before allowing them to be implemented on the system. If an activity is detected that does not conform to the rule set defined for a particular application, then the agent informs the users of the impending actions and requests confirmation to carry out or cancel the request. If the operation is found to be valid, fine; if it is found to be invalid, then an alert is sent back to the system console, where the issue is identified as a hostile undesirable act and blocked out. Actions are compared against the rule base and are either allowed or denied, based on definitions of the rule base.

The Okena Stormwatch™ product ships with predefined security policies for managing both servers and workstations. Policies are provided for the protection of mail servers, SQL Database Servers, and Internet Information Servers (IIS). Workstation policies are available to protect both Microsoft Office and the operating systems registry from malicious conduct. Operations and security staff can create or modify existing rules at any time, and at specified intervals, the intelligent agents will contact the console and retrieve the new or modified rule definitions and apply them. For example, rules can be applied to the existing rule sets that only allow an HTTP developers group to have write access to specific resources on the corporate web server. The agents will prevent any other users, groups, or process from gaining write access to those resources, thereby proactively protecting the system from undesirable activities.

Honey Pots

The concept of a honey pot has been around for a few years now, mostly floating in conversations on the firewalls lists. Only recently has this topic surfaced from its obscure beginnings. The concept is much the same as luring a fly to flypaper. The deployment of a server is used in an environment to allow hackers to penetrate a system. The decoy system is configured with just enough vulnerability that a hacker is lured away from other systems to attack this seemingly potential victim. The system provides enough bait to get a hacker to vigorously attack the system and thereby allows such actions to be logged and examined. There are currently no products available on the market that can be used to deploy decoy servers because this is purely a research project. We can only take a wait-and-see approach that this may eventually lead to a new suite of security products that diverts hackers and crackers away from the production system by way of deception or countermeasures. For more information on this exciting new research topic, refer to project.honeynet.org.

Note

1. A B-level security study was conducted by Trusted Systems Services Inc. (www.trustedsystems.com).

Chapter 7

Corporate Security Requirements for Conducting Business over the Internet

Conducting business over the Internet is not as safe as conducting business over secured private lines. Contrary to popular belief, conducting business over the Internet is a very hazardous undertaking. Placing a Web server on the Internet and exposing business applications over 128-bit Secure Socket Layer (SSL) is not considered a highly secure solution. One might think that 128-bit SSL is secure enough, so why do banks not use it? Everyone else does. For most intents and purposes, 128-bit SSL suffices for encrypting trivial transactions. However, keep in mind that although the banks use SSL to provide transaction security to the consumer, they do not use it internally to protect their monetary transactions. Military-grade encryption systems are known to use key lengths on the order of 1024K and up. The previous government standard of 56-bit Data Encryption Standard (DES) was broken in 1997 and recently again in 1999 in less than 24 hours by using a distributed algorithm from www.distributed.net. Currently, the challenge to break RC5 SSL is underway and has been for some time. It is only a matter of time before the key will be cracked via a brute-force method. In general, the longer the encryption key length, the greater the time required to crack the key. The Federal Information Processing Office requirements in the United States have standardized on 3DES, also known as the Triple DES algorithm. 3DES uses dual encryption keys and a three-phase mechanism to encrypt and decrypt a data stream. 3DES is a 168-bit encryption standard that is available in all security-capable devices manufactured and sold in North America. 3DES is

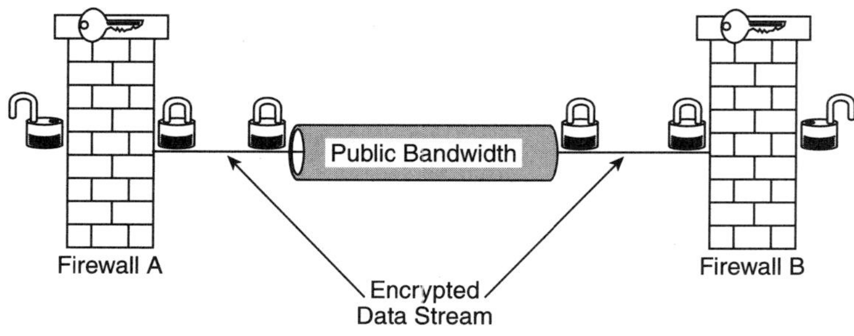

Exhibit 1. VPN Data Stream on Public Medium

not considered a highly secure encryption mechanism but it is the standard set forth by the Federal Information Processing Office (http://ccf.arc.nasa.gov/fipmo/index.html). For the majority of business transactions over the Internet, SSL and 3DES are acceptable. For others that demand higher levels of security that support greater key encryption lengths, proprietary encryption hardware or software will be required. A note of caution, however: the greater the encryption key length, the more time required to encrypt and decrypt the data. As such, encryption will increase the average latency time for completing a transaction between two points.

Virtual private networking (VPNing) had a slow and painful acceptance process among vendors during the mid- to late 1990s. Today, it is a fairly routine task to set up and maintain VPNs between dissimilar product lines that use IP Security (IPSec) standards.[1] However, there are still those vendors that make VPNing a trying task to perform. In any event, it is usually best to implement a VPN using similar products when possible. The future of secured business and inter-business transactions is within the realm of the virtual private network (Exhibit 1).

A virtual private network (VPN) is a virtual implementation of a private dedicated data line. The use of public communications lines and facilities is required for the communications fabric. Encryption technology is used to establish a point-to-point private channel between the two endpoints of the VPN. Should more endpoints be required, further negotiation is performed to expand the VPN to additional sites when required. Once key exchange and negotiation have been performed and the desired encryption channel established, communications between all sites of the VPN can be conducted in complete privacy.

In the example VPN in Exhibit 2, the business partner security domain should include the firewall, the network object for the shared business network, and the network object for the shared business resource. The sample rule base depicts two separate VPNs with entirely different security domains, which isolates VPN traffic.

Virtual private networks have allowed us to shed the high costs of private dedicated lines in favor of cheaper Internet bandwidth. The costs of VPNing are negligible in comparison with the monthly operating costs of dedicated data lines. Unless your situation demands the use of private dedicated lines,

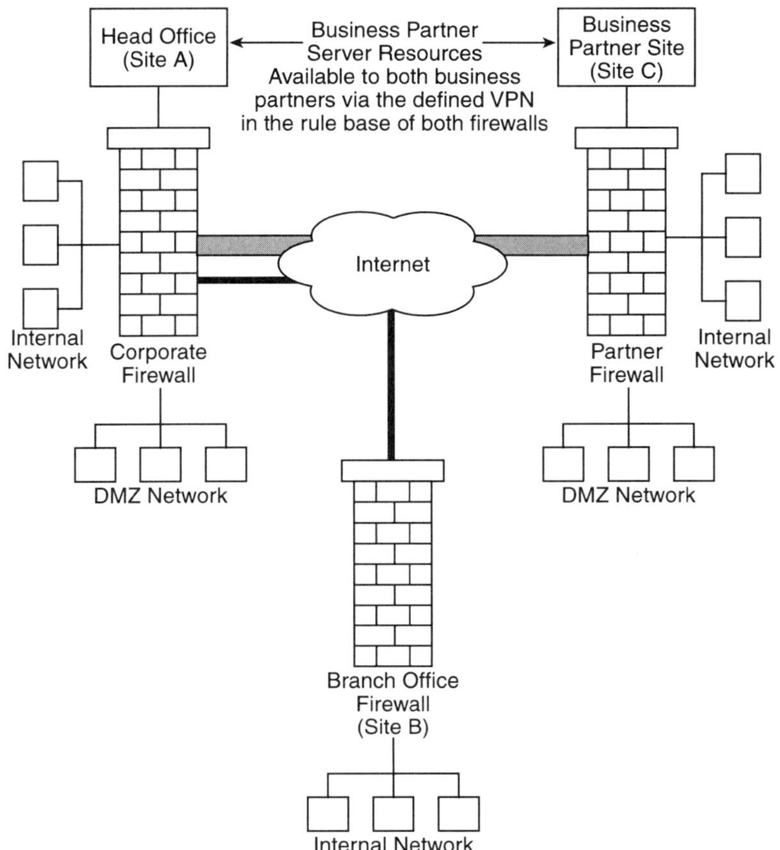

Source	Destination	Service	Action	Track	Comment
Site A	Site C	Business Apps	Encrypt	Long	Site A to Site C
Site C	Site A	Business Apps	Encrypt	Long	Site C to Site A
Site A	Site B	Any	Encrypt	Short	Site A to Site B
Site B	Site A	Any	Encrypt	Short	Site B to Site A

Exhibit 2. Example VPN

a VPN is the most effective, cost-efficient way to ensure data privacy in a potentially hazardous environment such as the Internet.

Internal Corporate VPNs

Probably the first deployment of a virtual private network (VPN) in an organization will be to deliver head-office applications to subsidiary offices across the country or across the globe. VPNs have given new life to legacy applications that would cost a small fortune to migrate to a Web interface. Even client/server applications can be delivered over a VPN.

Virtual private networks can be set up for point-to-point and multi-point access. Corporate applications that were once only available over expensive

Frame Relay networks can now be accessed securely over the Internet via point-to-point VPN technology. The mere fact that a communications channel can be established over insecure public communications media in a secured fashion can save an organization a tremendous amount of money. Not only are there monetary gains with the deployment of a VPN, but also productivity gains. A centralized computing environment can be mastered without the need to retool and rebuild in order to create a centralized computing environment. Technology aside, the VPN allows IT and business professionals to work safely within the confines of their own network. Corporate communications systems, databases, and applications are available to everyone in a secure manner. It is no longer necessary to send privileged corporate communications over the back of an Internet postcard or FTP a database to another office.

Business Partner VPNs

Today, one can interface dissimilar VPN equipment together to establish secure communications channels with one's business partners. Order processing and stock replenishment can also be achieved via business partner VPNs. The possibilities are endless. Exchanging inventory data, automating order processing, quotation management for new purchases, and even more can be set up and integrated into a business partner VPN. Making portions of one's production systems available to one's business partners is an ideal way to streamline timelines and shave percentages on costs when purchasing or selling products. Although the idea of business partner integration is wonderful, it still requires some forethought in setup. It is important that one's internal systems contain proper security mechanisms that will allow business partners to see only what one wants them to see and also to make sure that multiple business partners cannot view each other's data. Opening up services to one's business partners is a great idea, as well as an opportunity to capture more business; however, one must be cautious in pursuit of this idea and determine exactly what one wants to deliver.

The Mobile Workforce and VPNs

Virtual private networks (VPNs) are an excellent mechanism to extend the reaches of the corporate network to the mobile workforce. Everyone can benefit from a well-architected VPN. Traveling executives and salespeople only need an access point to the Internet to securely access their own data files or access pricing and stock level information. Best of all, the connection is completely secure. All data packets exchanged from the remote client to the firewall are completely encrypted; and to the user, it merely seems that he or she is actually on the corporate network.

This, however, also opens up a new level of security and end-user training issues. Staff members will have to be trained in proper use and security protocol when using their laptops to access the corporate office and its resources. The loss or theft of a laptop computer with a user's logon id and password taped to the bottom of the machine poses a serious threat to any corporate security policy.

Systems Management and Security

As previously noted in this chapter, remote users can be a serious threat to a corporate security model if they are not adequately trained. The end users of any remote access system must be made aware of the issues and must be held accountable for their corporate access credentials, the standard principle being that any action conducted from the use of a user id/password pair is assumed to be an act of the authenticated user to which that user id/password pair is assigned. This is a very important issue that must be addressed. Without clarification of this point to the end-user community, there will be no way to combat abuse of the system or potential unauthorized access. This is especially true in cases where general global access mechanisms are used, for which a shared user id/password pair is commonly used by a large group of users.

Corporate network management of the VPN can be established in a variety of ways and utilizing a wide array of techniques. At the low end of the spectrum lies the Check Point FireWall-1 user database. With this user database, it is possible to define user groups and create users that belong to those groups. It is then possible to define access rules in the FireWall-1 rule base, which allows members of the groups to gain internal corporate network access. The use of the Secure Remote Client or Secure Client authentication package allows remote users to gain access to the corporate network by way of a user id and password combination. Once the client has been authenticated, the communications between the firewall and the client are encrypted. (See Exhibit 3.)

When dealing with a small number of users, the Check Point user database can be very effective in delivering a secured remote access solution. However, when dealing with a large number of remote access users, typically 50 or more, this can become a cumbersome approach to management. In such cases, it is recommended to use an approach that allows one to tap into an existing user definition such as LDAP (Lightweight Directory Access Protocol) or RADIUS (Remote Authentication Dial-In User Service). In addition, the following authentication schemes are supported by Check Point FireWall-1.

If the environment is currently set up to use any of the authentication models in Exhibit 4, it will be possible to use those services to drive the Check Point FireWall-1 Remote Client or Secure Client authentication services. It will still be necessary to define groups in the FireWall-1 user database for the remote users that will gain access through the firewall. Although the users will not be defined within the Check Point user database, the group will point to the external resource database that is referenced for that group. The users must be defined within the external reference group to gain internal network access. Optionally, one can use the Check Point Account Management Client for managing users in an external LDAP directory. The group definitions will

Exhibit 3. Sample Secure Client Authentication

No.	*Date*	*Time*	*Inter.*	*Origin*	*Type*	*Action*	*Service*	*Source*
12861	20Aug2001	19:58:19	daemon	PDFW0001	log	keyinst		24.43.134.30
12862	20Aug2001	19:58:19	daemon	PDFW0001	log	keyinst		24.43.134.30
12863	20Aug2001	19:58:20	daemon	PDFW0001	log	decrypt	Nbsession	24.43.134.30

Destination	*Prot.*	*Rule*	*Sport*	*User*	*SrcKey*	*DstKey*	*Elapsed*	*Bytes*	*Xlat*
PDFW0001									
PDFW0001	ip	0			*0x30c4600f*	*0x4c31efaa*			
192.168.1.10	tcp	4	*1063*	*msmith*	*0x30c4600f*				

XlateD	*XlateSP*	*XlateDP*	*Product*	*Info*
			firewall	IKE Log: Phase 1 (aggressive) completion. 3DES/SHA1/Pre shared secrets Negotiation Id: 878d69e4233df66a-097a3ea11b3afc0a
			firewall	scheme: IKE methods: Combined ESP: 3DES + SHA1 (phase 2 completion) for host: 24.43.134.30 and for subnet: 0.0.0.0 (mask = 0.0.0.0)
			firewall	scheme: IKE methods: Combined ESP: 3DES + SHA1

"12861" "20Aug2001" "19:58:19" "daemon" "PDFW0001" "log" "keyinst" "" "24.43.134.30" "PDFW0001" "" "" "" "" "" "" "" "" "" "" "" "" "firewall" " IKE Log: Phase 1 (aggressive) completion. 3DES/SHA1/Pre shared secrets Negotiation Id: 878d69e4233df66a-097a3ea11b3afc0a"

"12862" "20Aug2001" "19:58:19" "daemon" "PDFW0001" "log" "keyinst" "" "24.43.134.30" "PDFW0001" "ip" "0" "" "" "0x30c4600f" "0x4c31efaa" "" "" "" "" "" "" "firewall" " scheme: IKE methods: Combined ESP: 3DES + SHA1 (phase 2 completion) for host: 24.43.134.30 and for subnet: 0.0.0.0 (mask = 0.0.0.0)"

"12863" "20Aug2001" "19:58:20" "daemon" "PDFW0001" "log" "decrypt" "nbsession" "24.43.134.30" "192.168.1.10" "tcp" "4" "1063" "msmith" "0x30c4600f" "" "" "" "" "" "" "" "firewall" " scheme: IKE methods: Combined ESP: 3DES + SHA1"

Exhibit 4. Supported Authentication Schemes in Check Point FireWall-1/VPN-1

Firewall-1 supported authentication schemes include:

- S/key
- SecureID
- VPN-1/FireWall-1
- OS password
- RADIUS
- Axent Pathways Defender
- TACACS

be the only requirement to interface with the external user database. This will elevate Systems Operations from the need to maintain duplicate user databases across dissimilar systems. The end users will also be grateful because they will not have to memorize two sets of user id and password combinations or, worse, write them down on a piece of paper and tape them to the back of the laptop computer.

Apart from the obvious benefits of lowered communications costs, the VPN allows the Systems Operations group to centralize its operations and staff within the heart of the corporate data center. The need for system and data duplication to remote subsidiary sites is not required, except for the need of a disaster recovery site used in business resumption planning. The ease with which remote access over the VPN delivers corporate resources to the remote user or remote site is exceptionally secure. With properly defined pipes to the Internet, remote sites can actively access and participate on the corporate network as if they were just on another floor connected to the network backbone switch.

Setting up a High Available VPN-1/FireWall-1 server pair at the remote sites will reduce the risks of failure and remote site disconnection. Centralized IT operations staff can remotely manage and administer these systems securely to adjust parameters of the remote firewall cluster via the management console without leaving the data center. Should a catastrophic failure occur, personnel can be dispatched to the remote site or local vendors can be sent on site to correct the issues at hand to bring the site back online. In any event, being able to centralize both staff and resource management is an immense cost-saving measure.

Finally, all corporate VPN access events are monitored and logged to allow for the auditing of activities. Every successful access attempt and failure to access the systems protected by the firewalled VPN are recorded. This data can then be filtered using reporting tools to generate usage patterns and determine if there is any malicious activity directed toward the VPN from inside or outside the corporate network. With the release of Check Point FireWall-1 V4.1 SP2, Check Point has introduced the Malicious Activity Detection (MAD) module. The configuration file (*cpmad_config.conf*), found in the

Exhibit 5. Malicious Activity Detection (MAD) Features

Attack Type	*Description*
successive_alerts	Detects when an excessive number of alerts have been generated
port_scanning[a]	Detects when an excessive number of connection attempts to the ports of a specific IP address occur; related to blocked_connection_port_scanning
blocked_connection_port_scanning[b]	This is related to port_scanning; however, only rejected and dropped connection attempts will trigger this alert; the inverse of port_scanning
login_failure	Detects an excessive amount of failed log-in attempts
successive_multiple_connections	Detects an excessive amount of opened connections to a specific destination IP address and port from a specific IP address
land_attack	Detection pattern for the "land attack"
syn_attack	Detection of TCP SYN flooding attack; must be activiated in the Properties tab of SYNDefender
anti_spoofing	Detects anti-spoofing activities; logging must be set in the Security tab of the interface properties

[a] Either use port_scanning or blocked_connection_port_scanning, but not both options. See page 26 of the Check Point Getting Started Guide for more information.

[b] Source: Check Point FireWall-1 Getting Started Guide.

C:\winnt\fw1\4.1\conf directory, can be tuned to detect malicious activity of known attack patterns. To invoke the MAD facility, the file must be edited and the parameter *MAD_system_mode* must be set to "ON". The MAD facility can be used to detect and report the activities shown in Exhibit 5.

A sample of the *cpmad_config.conf* file is shown in Exhibit 6. This file defines what actions to take when certain activities have been detected by the firewall logging facility (e.g., port scanning). Should this feature be enabled and a port scan takes place, the system will automatically log the event and an alert can be sent. This is the detail that an audit log needs to allow the systems group to respond to threats against the organization. Without these basic tools, an organization is helpless to prevent attacks against the organization and cannot retaliate by using preventative techniques or reporting the activity to the authorities.

The Virtual Workforce

Not only is the field force a benefactor of remote VPN technology, but so are the stationary employees. Typically locked in a cubicle at the office, it becomes

Exhibit 6. Sample *cpmad_config.conf* File

```
                                        # MAD Configuration file

# A comment starts with "#" .Anything written in that line after the
"#" is considered as comment.
# Blanks and tabs are ignored.

                                              # MAD mode

MAD_system_mode = on

                                              # MAD global
                                                parameters

MAD_memory                                = 75000 # in KBytes
MAD_clean_interval                        = 60    # in seconds
MAD_number_of_connection_attempts         = 10
MAD_interval_between_connection_attempts  = 60    # in seconds

                                              # MAD attacks

# syn_attack

MAD_syn_attack_mode = on
MAD_syn_attack_resolution = 10
MAD_syn_attack_time_interval = 60
MAD_syn_attack_repetitions = 100
MAD_syn_attack_action = alert

# anti_spoofing

MAD_anti_spoofing_mode = on
MAD_anti_spoofing_resolution = 300
MAD_anti_spoofing_time_interval = 3600
MAD_anti_spoofing_repetitions = 10
MAD_anti_spoofing_action = alert

# successive_alerts

MAD_successive_alerts_mode = on

MAD_successive_alerts_resolution = 60
MAD_successive_alerts_time_interval = 600
MAD_successive_alerts_repetitions = 100
MAD_successive_alerts_action = alert

# port_scanning

MAD_port_scanning_mode = off
MAD_port_scanning_time_interval = 60
MAD_port_scanning_repetitions = 100
MAD_port_scanning_action = alert
# blocked_connection_port_scanning

MAD_blocked_connection_port_scanning_mode = on
MAD_blocked_connection_port_scanning_time_interval = 600
MAD_blocked_connection_port_scanning_repetitions = 50
MAD_blocked_connection_port_scanning_action = alert
```

Exhibit 6. (Continued) Sample *cpmad_config.conf* File

```
# login_failure

MAD_login_failure_mode = on
MAD_login_failure_resolution = 5
MAD_login_failure_time_interval = 600
MAD_login_failure_repetitions = 30
MAD_login_failure_action = alert

# successive_multiple_connections

MAD_successive_multiple_connections_mode = off
MAD_successive_multiple_connections_resolution = 10
MAD_successive_multiple_connections_time_interval = 60
MAD_successive_multiple_connections_repetitions = 50
MAD_successive_multiple_connections_action = alert

# land_attack

MAD_land_attack_mode = on
MAD_land_attack_resolution = 10
MAD_land_attack_time_interval = 60
MAD_land_attack_repetitions = 5
MAD_land_attack_action = alert
```

possible to allow staff in key positions to work from the comfort of their own home from time to time. It also allows key staff members to support ongoing business operations when adverse weather conditions make travel to the office impractical. Traveling managers and executives can also benefit from the use of the remote VPN to access their own corporate libraries during extensive business trips when packing hundreds of documents and files is not considered practical. Even application developers can utilize the framework of the VPN when developing applications for the field. Third-party access can be granted to allow organizations to offload services such as the help desk or other support functions.

Preparing to run an organization in this fashion is still a long way off. There are many nontechnical obstacles that must be overcome and resolved in the realm of Human Resources. Deliverables and expectations need detailed definitions for this to be effective for both the business and its employees. Project management and workplan details will require more sampling and monitoring to gauge the effectiveness of progress. Only then will an approach to the "virtual workforce" become effective in running a business.

Note

1. The IP Security standards can be found at http://www.ietf.org/html.charters/ipsec-charter.html.

Chapter 8

Implementing Check Point FireWall-1/VPN-1 with Windows NT and Windows 2000

Performing a system build is a time-consuming process. To make sure that the setup of the machine will be reliable throughout the machine's operational lifespan, a step-by-step approach should be followed. This allows one to repeat a known process in the future or create additional systems for deployment. Ideally, the system should be configured to withstand failure. Hardware selection is important because the machine will perform a critical function within the environment.

When selecting hardware and sizing potential hardware for the environment, the following are critical to the proper operation of a Check Point FireWall-1 system: (1) CPU, (2) memory, and (3) disk subsystem. These items will determine how well the system will perform in the environment. When selecting a system, try to find one that will allow for the easy upgrade of a CPU from an entry-level speed to a high-performance processor. The system should support a minimum 256 MB of RAM; larger environments may require more memory. Recent test results from Check Point show that a system with 330 MB+ RAM can support a million simultaneous connections, Exhibit 1.

In addition to CPU and memory, it is highly recommended to use a fast SCSI-based disk subsystem. SCSI-based disk subsystems do not place additional load and stress on the CPU, as do IDE-based disk subsystems. This is important and will determine the impact of event logging for the system. In the end, it all boils down to the number of users, connections, and VPN tunnels that will

Exhibit 1. VPN-1/FireWall-1 Performance Brief

Metric	*Maximum Performance*	*Platform*
Firewall throughput	1.75 Gbps	Nokia IP740
Concurrent firewall connections	1,000,000	Any with greater than 330 MB of memory
AES256 VPN throughput	90 Mbps	Windows NT — 1.7 GHz XEON
3DES VPN throughput w/hardware accel.	154 Mbps	Linux — Windows NT 1.7 GHZ Xeon
Concurrent VPN tunnels	20,000	Any with greater than 256 MB of memory

Source: Check Point (www.checkpoint.com).

be required to support the computing environment. At a bare minimum, one should consider the requirements listed in Exhibit 2 for an entry-level platform.

Selecting a hardware platform that will allow one to upgrade the processor complex is a simple way to approach an upgrade if it is found that the system becomes CPU bound within the environment's specifications. Another alternative is to increase the amount of memory in the system before upgrading the CPU complex to make sure that the system is not starved for memory. Determining the performance characteristics of a machine is well-documented in the Microsoft Windows NT Resource Kit for Windows NT Workstation and Windows NT Server Version 3.5, Volume 4, Optimizing Windows NT.

Network failure is another area of concern that will need to be addressed. Speed between the internal network and the firewall should be optimal; a switch is recommended to keep the subnets from experiencing saturation. The external interface of the firewall should be matched to the speed of the external Internet connection. In most cases, a 10/100 MB Ethernet card will suffice.

Performing Background Preparation

Before beginning any project, it is generally good practice to know what one is up against. Assembling all the needed materials for the project is a prudent

Exhibit 2. Recommended Entry-Level Requirements

Option	*Recommendation*
CPU	300 MHz Pentium II
Memory	256 MB
Disk space	9 GB
Disk subsystem	RAID 0 or 1
Network interface cards	10/100

step. Reading the material may be a great leap; however, it will save in frustration when things just do not seem to work properly — and sometimes they just do not work properly. Firewalls are very finicky and no two installations are alike. Even when using hardware from the same manufacturer, it is possible to get a difference in hardware components that can throw a wrench into one's carefully crafted plan.

Performing system hardening for the operating system is a task left for the reader to determine. Check Point advises some form of hardening in its document entitled "Securing/Configuring Windows NT Server." However, it is also a known fact that a properly configured FireWall-1 installation removes the burden of an exhaustive hardening process. Hardening the operating system should be done at one's own risk; if truly paranoid about security, plan for an extended period of time to discover how much hardening can be achieved before the system becomes inoperable. Another thought before one considers hardening is to determine how much of the native operating system services one wishes to disable. All of these services can be safely protected from abuse by carefully inserting a rule in the Check Point rule base to prohibit access to the firewall and specific services. System hardening of the firewall should be left for the Operations staff to consider; use discretion when performing a hardening process against the firewall. Also remember that it is possible to harden a system to the point where a complete system rebuild is required; so exercise caution when doing so.[2] It is highly recommended, however, that a hardening process be performed against any and all publicly exposed systems of a corporation that will be behind the firewall. A firewall can only prevent access to doors that are locked. Doors that are open to servers and services not properly protected are susceptible to attack and compromise. Always secure and maintain any exposed systems behind the firewall. Do not fall into a false sense of security that having a firewall automatically protects the environment. One can still be attacked, so beware. Exhibit 3 lists other hardening resources.

Assembling the Hardware

Determine that all the components required for the installation have proper BIOS revisions and firmware updates. Make sure that any proprietary drivers needed for the operating system are up-to-date. It is usually a good idea to jot down part numbers and serial numbers of all components before assembling them together. This may help in fault isolation should one run into hardware difficulties with the software or operating system. In any event, the information should be useful in planning for disaster recovery. Knowing what goes into a system makes it that much easier to rebuild when the time comes.

Assemble the hardware for the system on an isolated network away from contact with the Internet or any internal networks. Only place the system on the network once it is secured. Never build a system when it is exposed to a live network where it can be easily compromised. Once the hardware is

Exhibit 3. Listing of Hardening Resources

Document	URL
Securing/configuring Windows NT Server Check Point Software Technologies Ltd. May 27, 1999 Jeffrey Fieldman	www.checkpoint.com
Building a Windows NT Bastion Host in Practice HP Consulting September 2, 1999 Stefan Norberg	secinf.net/info/nt/ntbastion
Armoring NT Lance Spitzner April 16, 2000	www.enteract.com/~lspitz/nt.html
Windows NT 4.0 Security Graded Security Configuration Document Intersect Alliance January 16, 2001	www.intersectalliance.com/projects/WinNTConfig.html
Hardening Windows 2000 *Windows 2000 Security Handbook* Copyright Osborne/McGraw-Hill SystemExperts Corporation May 25, 2001	www.windows2000securityhandbook.com www.systemexperts.com

assembled, let it burn-in for approximately 48 hours. If the system survives the burn-in test, the hardware components should be fine.

Materials List

The type of firewall will determine the materials required. A general dual-homed server will require two network interface cards (NICs), and a multi-homed server will require at least three NICs and possibly more, depending on the desired configuration scheme. The sample build will assume a multi-homed configuration with three NICs. Exhibit 4 displays a sample materials list.

Network Settings

Before embarking on the installation of any software, one will need to determine the configuration of the machine, addressing, etc. (see Exhibit 5). An important concept to keep in mind if the system will be part of a VPN network is that all internal and DMZ subnets will require different subnet addressing schemes between the sites. Failure to do so will result in a nonfunctioning VPN. For example, if two internal VPN sites share the same internal subnet address of 192.168.0.0, neither firewall will be able to route

Exhibit 4. Sample Materials List

Item	*Description*
Server class machine	Pentium II 300 MHz or above CD-ROM Floppy Tape backup system Keyboard, mouse, and monitor
Memory	256 MB RAM
Hard disk	9 GB × 2
NICs	Two or three 10/100 cards
RAID controller	Capable of RAID 0 or 1 mirroring for fault tolerance
Operating system	Windows NT Server 4.0 or Windows 2000 Server
Operating system patches	Windows NT 4.0 SP6a and SP6a Security Rollup Windows 2000 SP2
Firewall software	Check Point 4.1
Firewall system patches	Check Point SP4
Hardware patches or drivers	Additional hardware drivers or patches, as needed

Exhibit 5. Address Requirements for Installation

Requirement	*Value*
Internal IP address	www.xxx.yyy.zzz
Internal subnet[a] mask	Leave entry blank
External IP address	www.xxx.yyy.zzz
External subnet mask	www.xxx.yyy.zzz
DMZ IP address	www.xxx.yyy.zzz
DMZ subnet mask	Leave entry blank
DNS server IP addresses	www.xxx.yyy.zzz
Domain model	Stand-alone
Workgroup name	A unique name not currently used in one's environment

[a] Refer to Microsoft Knowledge Base article Q157025.

packets to the other because both the destination and the source are within the same subnet. Check Point will generate the following error message if you try to connect a VPN with similar subnets:

```
"Gateway connected to both endpoints"
```

The external address and DNS server entries will be provided by an Internet service provider (ISP). When determining the server name, use an obscure naming convention (e.g., PDFW0001 for Perimeter Domain Firewall 0001). The workgroup name should be unique to the domain names currently used in the environment (e.g., Security, or something more obscure).

When building the machine, keep an ample supply of floppy disks around to create emergency recovery disks. If hardening the system, make copies of

Exhibit 6. External to DMZ Mapping Table

MAC address of external interface: 00-20-af-a5-c2-12

External IP Address	*DMZ Address*	*System Function*
24.43.134.47	10.10.10.1	SMTP server
24.43.134.48	10.10.10.2	HTTP server

the ERD (emergency repair diskette) before and after every alteration; this makes the task of recovery just a bit more palatable if something goes wrong. If applying the *syskey* utility to the registry, see Microsoft Knowledge Base article Q143475 regarding the backup and recovery of the registry. It is recommended that remote access to the registry be disabled; see Exhibit 9 to apply this procedure and where to reference further hardening procedures. Shutting down remote access to the registry removes the burden of applying the *syskey* utility; however, the ERD disks will need to be stored in a secured area to prevent someone from using utilities to hack the disk for the user id and password of the administrator.

Always properly label ERDs with the server's name, date/time, and the name of the operator who created the ERD. ERDs should be created before and after any hardware or software modifications to a system. This should be considered a mandatory step for back-out procedures. Always construct a back-out plan before performing any maintenance on a system; it may one day save hours of grief.

Determine the IP addresses of all systems that will be publicly exposed to the world from the firewall's DMZ subnet. It will be necessary to map external IP addresses supplied by the ISP to the nonroutable addresses of the DMZ. Make sure to get enough external IP addresses from your ISP before beginning. If there are not sufficient external IP addresses, the ISP may provide an entirely different subnet to accommodate one's needs. If this happens, it will be necessary to regenerate the Check Point firewall product keys for the new IP address of the firewall. In addition, one will need the MAC address of the external network interface card in order to set up the *local.arp* file for Check Point FireWall-1. Windows NT and Windows 2000 require this file to be present in order to forward requests from the virtual IP addresses. In addition to the *local.arp* file, a route will need to be constructed to forward traffic to the correct IP address behind the firewall.

For example, suppose one has an SMTP server in the DMZ with a nonroutable address of 10.10.10.1. One needs to create a *local.arp* file in the c:\winnt\fw1\4.1\state directory with the following format assuming 24.43.134.47 is the external address supplied by the ISP:

```
24.43.134.47 00-20-af-a5-c2-12
```

The MAC address of the external network interface card can be queried by issuing a *route print* command at the command line (see Exhibit 7).

```
C:\>route print
===========================================================================
Interface List
0x1 ........................... MS TCP Loopback interface
0x2 ...00 20 af a5 c2 12 ...... elnk33 ELNK3 Ethernet Adapter
0x3 ...00 80 5f 1a fe 6b ...... CpqNF32 Compaq NetFlex-3 Driver, Version 4.25m SP4
===========================================================================
===========================================================================
Active Routes:
  Network Destination          Netmask          Gateway        Interface  Metric
            0.0.0.0            0.0.0.0     24.43.134.1     24.43.134.46       1
         10.10.10.0      255.255.255.0    10.10.10.100     10.10.10.100       1
         10.10.10.1    255.255.255.255    24.43.134.47     24.43.134.46       1
       10.10.10.100    255.255.255.255       127.0.0.1        127.0.0.1       1
        24.43.134.0    255.255.255.128    24.43.134.46     24.43.134.46       1
       24.43.134.46    255.255.255.255       127.0.0.1        127.0.0.1       1
     24.255.255.255    255.255.255.255    24.43.134.46     24.43.134.46       1
          127.0.0.0          255.0.0.0       127.0.0.1        127.0.0.1       1
          224.0.0.0          224.0.0.0    10.10.10.100     10.10.10.100       1
          224.0.0.0          224.0.0.0    24.43.134.46     24.43.134.46       1
    255.255.255.255    255.255.255.255    24.43.134.46     24.43.134.46       1
===========================================================================
```

Exhibit 7. Sample Output from the *route print* Command

Create a table to list all the DMZ systems that map to external IP addresses and label their function. The information captured in such a table will be necessary for creating the route and *local.arp* file. The *route* commands will appear as follows:

```
C:>route add 10.10.10.1 24.43.134.47 -p
C:>route add 10.10.10.2 24.43.134.48 -p
```

The `-p` option permanently adds the route to the registry. Upon a system restart, routes are automatically set up.

Password Selection

Make password selections for the system prior to installation to avoid entering a simple password when prompted during the installation. Keyboard walks make for the best password selection process because they are truly random in nature. However, try to avoid using control characters; they typically do not work out very well. The following are acceptable character sets for password selection:

```
Numeric character set: ( 0 - 9 )
Alpha character set:   (A, a - Z, z)
Special characters:    (~!@#$%^&*()_+{}|:"<>?,./;'[]\=-`)
```

Because Windows NT passwords can be a maximum of 14 characters in length, referring back to the sample security policy in Appendixes G and H, the recommended password length for an administrative password is 14 characters. A sample password would thus be as follows:

```
!QAZ-pl,XSW@.;
```

This is a perfectly valid password and difficult to predict because it is not based on any personal motifs, such as the name of one's cat or dog.

It is highly recommended that one use at least two characters from each set to randomize the password string. In any case, a minimum password length of eight characters should be mandatory. It is also prudent to enable password protection on the system's screen saver if the system is to be left unattended for a period of time. Set the timeout to a reasonable time frame (from five to ten minutes). Even if the system is in a secured location, other unauthorized Operations staff should not have access to this system.

Documentation

Assemble and review any documentation needed to perform the operating system installation and Check Point FireWall-1 software installation.

Check the patch levels available for all software and examine all release notes. Highlight any areas that may impact the ability to perform any portion of the installation. Review any and all security bulletins from the vendors and also check security sites such as www.cert.org. (See Appendix I for a listing of other sites that carry security-related information.)

Software Patches

Assemble patches and other necessary driver software for the installation. Perform all downloads to a machine capable of virus scanning the downloaded files and creating a CD-ROM. All patches and drivers should be virus scanned and then collectively written to a CD-ROM. The CD-ROM can then be used in building the system in isolation and then, for future reference, be filed with the other materials that were necessary to build the system.

Refer to Appendix C for a listing of patches included with the Windows NT 4.0 SP6a Security Rollup and a list of post-Windows 2000 SP2 patches.

Communications and Protocol Selections

The system should only support the TCP/IP protocol suite. Do not install NetBIOS services over TCP/IP. Do not configure WINS, DHCP, or DNS services on the machine destined to become the firewall. The firewall should only provide the required filtering services to keep authorized traffic open while closing the doors to all unauthorized traffic. By default, a number of services are installed that are at one's discretion to remove; these services are listed in Exhibit 8.

Exhibit 8. Default Services for Windows NT 4.0

Computer browser
RPC configuration
NetBIOS interface
Server
Workstation

One can safely remove all the listed services if desired. Note that it is just as easy to block all NetBIOS-related traffic to the firewall. This, in effect, will provide the same results as removing the services. Again, it is left to one's own discretion to remove these services. Removing these services will remove a level of risk associated with these services. If these services are removed, one should also remove WINS binding from all network interface cards and disable the service TCP/IP NetBIOS Helper. One correction that should be noted in the work by Lance Spitzner in Armoring Windows NT in the section entitled Eliminating Services and Tweaking: "I like to keep Workstation because it allows useful things like AT to run." Even with the Workstation service removed, the AT command scheduler will remain operational. When using the AT command, one may get a Schedule error message such as:

```
Event ID: 7901
Source: Schedule
Type: Error
Category: none
The system cannot find the file specified.
```

With reference to the Microsoft Knowledge Base, article Q119919 instructs the user to execute the command with the prefix "CMD /C;". For example,

```
At 1:00 /every:M,T,W,TH,F,S,SU CMD /C c:\winnt\fw1\4.1\
bin\fw logswitch
```

Registry Tuning

By default, the registry is unsecured and also requires some additional tuning to help secure the system and prevent certain types of Internet attack profiles (e.g., SYN or arp attacks).

Exhibits 9 and 10 list the articles from the Microsoft Knowledge Base that detail recommended security settings (Exhibit 9) and TCP/IP settings (Exhibit 10).

System Policies

Set up default systemwide policies and restrict ACLs (Access Control List) for directory security. As the system is tightened, it will be necessary to impose account policies, modify user rights, and modify the audit tracking capabilities of the system. The system's ACLs can also be modified, if desired. However, because all remote access capabilities will be disabled to the system, it is left to personal discretion to trim ACL access control on the directory structure. Note that there are documented issues with removing the "everyone" group from the root directory, which can cause a Virtual Memory error. See Microsoft Knowledge Base articles Q130016 and Q140472. In addition, to prevent remote access to the registry, tweaking the registry keys is also left to your discretion. When performing any additional tuning or hardening on the firewall system, remember that should the firewall software come down or crash unexpectedly, the system can potentially be exposed to attack, as can the internal network. Some basic hardening is required; however, any further hardening may be fruitless because the system will be running an enterprise security product.

Installing the Operating System

The basic installation procedure for the operating system consists of three phases. The first phase is the text-based setup phase. This consists of the

Exhibit 9. Registry Tuning Articles and Information for System Security

Article Reference	*Description*
Q101063, Q238148	Display legal notice at logon
Q114463	Do not display last logged on user
Q172931	Disable caching of logon credentials
Q147706	Disable LAN Manager 2.x password support
Q114817	Allow only logged-on users to shut down the machine
1, 2, 3	Disable Remote Registry Access (refer to Q153183 and Q155363 for additional information)
1, 2, 3, 4	Disable remote access to event logs
Q143474	Disable remote listing of accounts and shares
Q124859	Restrict access to scheduler service
Q146906	Restrict access to performance monitor resources
Q218473	Secure base system objects
1, 2, 3	Enable auditing of base system objects
1, 2, 3	Enable auditing of privileges
1, 2, 3	Enable auditing of backup and restore operations
1, 2, 3	Enable auditing of scheduler service
Q140058	Enable system shutdown upon full audit log (use this with discretion)
Q182086	Clear Pagefile contents
Q155217	Disable CD-ROM auto-run feature
1, 2, 3, Q245517	Disable administrative shares
1, 2, 3	Disable the OS/2 subsystem
1, 2, 3	Disable the POSIX subsystem

Note: 1 — Windows NT C2 Configuration Checklist.
2 — C2 Administrator's and User's Guide.
3 — ITSEC FC2-E3 Installation of Windows NT Workstation 4.0 and Windows NT Server 4.0.
4 — Securing Windows NT 4.0 Installation.
5 — Chapter 13, Auditing Windows NT Security Features and Control.

Exhibit 10. TCP/IP Protocol Tuning Articles for System Security

Article	*Description*
Q120642	TCP/IP and NBT configuration parameters for Windows NT and Windows 2000
Q186463	Windows NT replies to address mask requests
Q225344	ICMP redirect attack causes Windows NT Server and workstation to hang
Q139415	New TCP/IP ArpCacheLife parameter in Windows NT
Q150543	TCP/IP ports used by Windows NT
Q142641, 1[a]	Internet server unavailable because of malicious SYN attacks

[a] 1 — "Security Considerations for Network Attacks."

initial load of the operating system, drivers, formatting, and system bootstrap for the hard disk to continue the operating system installation. The second phase is the GUI-based setup phase. This phase consists of selecting the required operating system features and characteristics to bring the system up and operational. The third phase is the tuning phase. This phase consists of patching the operating system from its initial release to a current, updated release level. It also involves the installation of security patches, driver updates if necessary and security tweaking. As previously discussed, the security tweaking for a C2 classification can be accomplished if desired; however, because the system will act as a firewall only, this level of fortification is left to personal discretion (see Exhibit 11). It is recommended, however, that stringent hardening or fortification be done against all publicly accessible systems exposed to the Internet via the firewall. It is not possible to communicate the urgency of this recommendation other than to say that if these systems are protected as much as possible, one will have a higher probability of protection than if left unprotected.

Exhibit 11. Additional Knowledge Base References

Article Reference	*Description*
Q93362	C2 evaluation and certification for Windows NT
Q155363	How to regulate network access to the Windows NT registry
Q130016, Q140472	Removing everyone on RootDir leaves limited virtual memory
—	C2 Administrator's and User's Security Guide
—	Security Windows NT 4.0 Installation
—	Windows 2000 Security Recommendation Guides www.nas.gov http://nsa1.www.conxion.com/win2k/download.htm

The following sections discuss the installation of both the Windows NT 4.0 Server operating environment and the Windows 2000 Server operating environment. This in turn will be followed by a discussion of the installation of Check Point FireWall-1 on top of each of these environments. Although the Check Point FireWall-1 product follows the same installation procedures and setup, there are some subtle differences between the underlying operating environments that will be highlighted. Otherwise, from a configuration perspective, FireWall-1 on NT 4.0 looks and feels just like FireWall-1 on Windows 2000.

Microsoft Windows NT 4.0 Server

The entire installation of the operating system takes place over three distinct phases: (1) initial installation steps for hardware identification and preparation, (2) operating system installation and software selections, and (3) post-installation patching and tuning. Once these phases are complete, the installation of the FireWall product can commence; and once the firewall has become operational, the system can be hardened further if desired.

Before proceeding, the information listed in Exhibit 12 must be gathered.

Exhibit 12. Pre-Installation Requirements

Requirement	*Value*
Router IP address	
Firewall external IP address and interface name	
Firewall internal IP address	
Firewall DMZ IP address	
Server name	
Workgroup name	
Administrator password	
Additional HOST table IP address entries	
ISP DNS server IP addresses	
Display resolution	

Installation Phase 1

The installation of Windows NT 4.0 Server begins with three boot floppies: the software CD-ROM and two additional blank floppies that will become the systems emergency repair diskettes (ERDs) (see Exhibit 13).

Exhibit 13. Windows NT 4.0 Server Installation Notes: Phase 1

1. Place the diskette entitled Windows NT Server Boot Disk 1 into the floppy drive of the machine (Drive A:).
2. Power up the system.
3. The following message will be displayed as the system boots from the floppy diskette.
   ```
   Setup is inspecting your computers hardware configuration...
   ```
4. Then the screen will go blue and a status bar will appear on the bottom of the screen. The following messages will be displayed on the status bar prior to the final display of screen two.
   ```
   Setup is loading files (Windows NT Executive)...
   Setup is loading files (Hardware Abstration Layer)...

   Windows NT Setup
   ================
   Please insert the disk labeled Windows NT Server Setup Disk 2
   into Drive A:
   * Press ENTER When ready.

   ENTER=Continue F3=Exit
   ```
5. Place the diskette titled Windows NT Server Setup Disk 2 into the floppy drive and press the ENTER key to continue the installation process. After pressing the ENTER key, the status line at the bottom of the screen will display a series of messages as follows:

```
Please wait...
Setup is loading files (Windows NT Configuration Data)
Setup is loading files (Loading Font)
Setup is loading files (Locale Specific Data)
Setup is loading files (Windows NT Setup)
Setup is loading files (PCMCIA Support)
Setup is loading files (SCSI Port Driver)
Setup is loading files (Video Driver)
Setup is loading files (Floppy Disk Driver)
Setup is loading files (Keyboard Driver)
Setup is loading files (FAT File System)
```

6. After this series of messages is displayed, a new screen will be temporarily displayed with the following information:

```
Software version, number of processors, installed memory in mega
bytes.

Microsoft(R) Windows NT (TM) Version 4.0 (Build 1381)
1 System Processor [XXMB Memory] MultiProcessor Kernel
```

7. When this screen cycles to the next screen in the installation process, the following messages are displayed on the status bar:

```
Processing Information File
Loading Library file KBDUS.dll ...
Windows NT Server Setup
======================
Welcome to Setup.
The setup program for the Microsoft(R) Windows NT(TM) operating
system version 4.0 prepares Windows NT to run on your computer.
To learn more about Windows NT Setup before continuing, press F1.
To set up Windows NT now, press ENTER
To repair a damaged Windows NT version 4.0 installation, press R.
To quit Setup without installing Windows NT, press F3.
ENTER=Continue R=Repair F1=Help F3=Exit

Press the ENTER key to continue.
```

8. Press the enter key to continue with the installation process.

```
Windows NT Server Setup
======================
Setup automatically detects floppy disk controllers and standard
ESDI/IDE hard disks without user intervention. However, on some
computers, detection of certain other mass storage devices, such
as SCSI adapters and CD-ROM drives, can cause the computer to
become unresponsive or malfunction temporarily.
For this reason, one can bypass Setup's mass storage device
detection and manually select SCSI adapters, CD-ROM drives, and
special disk controllers (such as drive arrays) for installation.
- To continue, Press ENTER.
Setup will attempt to detect mass storage devices in your computer.
- To skip mass storage device detection, press S.
```

```
Setup will allow you to manually select SCSI adapters, CD-ROM
drives, and special disk controllers for installation.
F3=Exit ENTER=Continue S=Skip Detection
```

9. Press the enter key to continue with the installation process.
10. Advanced users can select S to skip detection and manually select devices from the scrollable menu; otherwise, press Enter to continue with the installation process. If one is installating a RAID controller, it will be necessary to press S. In addition, the manufacturer's device drive will be required for the installation process to proceed successfully. It is recommended that the installation documentation be read prior to proceeding with the installation process.
11. Press Enter to continue Step a or Selection S to Skip Detection Step b.
    A. Press ENTER to continue:
       - Press Enter to continue with the installation process. We are assuming standard hardware for the installation sequence.
       - The status bar message will briefly display the Please Wait… message and then the following screen will be displayed.

```
Windows NT Server Setup
=======================
Please insert the disk labeled Windows NT Server Setup Disk
#3 into Drive A:
* Press ENTER When ready.
ENTER=Continue F3=Exit
```

    B. Process SKIP detection
       - Press the S key to skip detection; the following screen will be displayed:

```
Windows NT Server Setup
=======================
Setup has recognized the following mass storage devices in
your computer:
    <none>
To specify additional SCSI adapters, CD-ROM drives, or special
disk controllers for use with Windows NT, including those
for which you have a device support disk from a mass storage
device manufacture, press S.
If you do not have any device support disks from a mass
storage device manufacturer, or do not want to specify
additional mass storage devices for use with Windows NT,
press Enter.
S=Specify Additional Device ENTER=Continue F3=Exit
```

       - Press S to specify the device driver that you wish to load. You will be immediately asked to select the Other option, which requires a disk from a hardware manufacturer. If this is the case, as with RAID devices, you will be prompted to insert the diskette into the floppy A: drive. You will need to retain this diskette as it will also be required during the graphical installation process. Otherwise, you may use the UP arrow key to scroll through the default list of supported mass storage devices. Select the driver that corresponds to your computer. If you select incorrectly, a message will state that the device cannot be found.

```
Windows NT Server Setup
=======================
```

```
You have asked to specify an additional SCSI adapter, CD-
ROM drive, or special disk controller for use with Windows NT.
To select a mass storage device from the following list, use
the UP or DOWN arrow key to move the highlight to the mass
storage device you want, and then press Enter.
To return to the previous screen without specifying an
additional mass storage device for use with Windows NT, press
ESC.
ENTER=SelectContinue F3=Exit ESC=Cancel
```

- You are prompted to now insert the Windows NT Server Diskette Setup Disk 3 into the floppy drive. Proceed to do so and then press the Enter key to continue with the installation process. The next screen will display the selected device driver.

```
Windows NT Server Setup
=======================
Setup has recognized the following mass storage devices in
your computer:
   IBM MCA SCSI Host Adapter
To specify additional SCSI adapters, CD-ROM drives, or special
disk controllers for use with Windows NT, including those
for which you have a device support disk from a mass storage
device manufacture, press S.
If you do not have any device support disks from a mass
storage device manufacturer, or do not want to specify
additional mass storage devices for use with Windows NT,
press Enter.
S=Specify Additional Device ENTER=Continue F3=Exit
```

- If you selected a device that is not in your machine, you will be greeted with the following screen:

```
Windows NT Server Setup
=======================
The SCSI adapter, CD-ROM, or special disk controller you
specified is not installed in your computer.
ENTER=Continue
```

- Press Enter to return to the previous screen.

Both processes continue here:

12. You are prompted to now insert the Windows NT Server Diskette Setup Disk 3 into the floppy drive. Proceed to do so and then press the Enter key to continue with the installation process.
13. The standard blue installation screen will be displayed and the status bar will begin displaying a series of messages that indicate which device drivers are being loaded and scanned for detection. ie:

```
loading device driver (device driver name)...
```

14. Once the mass storage devices have been detected, the Installation screen will display the detected device and allow you to select additional devices if you know that there are additional devices available.

```
Windows NT Server Setup
=======================
Setup has recognized the following mass storage devices in your
computer:
```

```
    IBM MCA SCSI Host Adapter
To specify additional SCSI adapters, CD-ROM drives, or special
disk controllers for use with Windows NT, including those for
which you have a device support disk from a mass storage device
manufacture, press S.
If you do not have any device support disks from a mass storage
device manufacturer, or do not want to specify additional mass
storage devices for use with Windows NT, press Enter.
S=Specify Additional Device ENTER=Continue F3=Exit
```

15. Press the Enter key to continue with the installation process.
16. Again, you will see displayed a number of messages on the status bar. These messages are attributed to the device driver loading and will resemble a similar sequence:

```
Loading Device Driver (Windows NT File System (NTFS))...
Loading Device Driver (SCSI CD-ROM)...
Loading Device Driver (SCSI Floppy)...
Loading Device Driver (SCSI Disk)...
Loading Device Driver (SCSI CD-ROM File System)...
```

17. Then the message bar will display a message that it is examining the drive as follows:

```
Examining xxxx MB Disk 0 at id 1 on bus 0 on spock
```

18. Once the drive has been verified the Windows NT Licensing screen will appear.

```
Windows NT Licensing Agreement
==============================
Windows NT Server
MICROSOFT LICENSE AGREEMENT
SERVER LICENSE FOR MICROSOFT SERVER PRODUCTS

IMPORTANT READ CAREFULLY: This Microsoft End-User License Agree-
ment ("EULA") is a legal agreement between you ...
                 .
                 .
                 .
...lowing rights to the Server Software and Client Software
PAGE DOWN=Next Page
```

19. Press the Page Down key until you reach the bottom of the agreement. Thirteen times to be exact; and then press the F8 key to accept the license agreement.
20. The installation process will continue and the status bar will change to display the message Loading Information File.... During this process, the Windows NT installation process will check the system for a previous installation of Windows NT if you are using an upgrade floppy media; otherwise, if a previous version of NT is found, you will be prompted to overwrite the system. You may need to place the Windows NT 3.1, 3.5, or 3.51 CD into the CD-ROM drive to continue the installation process.
21. Once you have placed the CD-ROM into the drive, press Enter to continue. The next screen will display all the detected and selected options for the machine you are installing upon.

```
Windows NT Server Setup
=======================
```

```
Setup has determined that your computer contains the following
hardware and software components.
        Computer: IBM PS/2 or other Micro Channel-based PC
         Display: Auto Detect
        Keyboard: XT, AT or Enhanced Keyboard (83-104 keys)
 Keyboard Layout: US
Pointing Device: Microsoft Mouse Port Mouse (Including BallPoint)
      No Changes: The above list matches my computer.
If you want to change any item in the list, press the UP or
DOWN arrow key to move the highlight to the item you want to
change. Then press Enter to see alternatives for that item.
When all the items in the list are correct, move the highlight
to "The above list matches my computer" and press Enter.
ENTER=Select F3=Exit
```

22. The next step is to select the partition to install the operating system on. If this is a new system an unformatted partition will be available for selection. If the system was previously used for another purpose, the detection software will try to determine what operating system is on the drive. You may then delete the partition in order to install Windows NT on it instead.

```
Windows NT Server Setup
=======================
The list below shows existing partitions and space available for
creating new partitions.
Use the UP and DOWN arrow keys to move the highlight to an item
in the list.
To install Windows NT on the highlighted partition or unpartitioned
space, press Enter.
To create a partition in the unpartitioned space, Press C.
To delete the highlighted partition, press D.
 xxxx MB Disk 0 at Id 1 on bus 0 on spock
       Unpartitioned space xxxx MB
ENTER=Install C=Create Partition F1=Help F3=Exit
```

23. Press enter to install on the unformatted partition.

```
Windows NT Server Setup
=======================
A new partition for Windows NT has been created on XXXX MB Disk
0 at Id 1 on bus 0 on spock. The partition must now be formatted.
Select a file system for the new partition from the list below.
Use the UP and DOWN arrow keys to move the highlight to the file
system you want and press Enter.
If you want to select a different partition for Windows NT, press
ESC.
Format the partition using the FAT file system
Format the partition using the NTFS file system
ENTER=Continue ESC=Cancel
```

24. This screen allows you to determine the format of the files system for Windows NT. Although the FAT file system can be easily recoverable, it is not secure and is not efficient for handling large files. (i.e., Log files)
25. Use the DOWN arrow to highlight and format the partition for NTFS.

26. Press Enter to begin formatting of the partition. Be patient because the drive is formatted.

```
Windows NT Server Setup
=======================
Please wait while Setup formats the partition
C: New (Unformatted) XXXX MB
on XXXX MB Disk 0 at Id 1 on bus 0 on spock.
ENTER=Continue ESC=Cancel
```

27. Once formatting of the drive has finished, you will be prompted for the location of the operating system. The default is \WINNT. It is highly recommended that this default be left as is. Prior versions of CP have been known to malfunction with alternate path names. In practice, it is usually good form to rename any defaults for a secure system, as this makes an attack difficult to predict.

```
Windows NT Server Setup
=======================
Setup installs Windows NT files onto your hard disk. Choose the
location where you want these files to be installed:
   \WINNT
To change the suggested location, press the Backspace key to
delete characters and then type the directory where you want
Windows NT installed.
ENTER=Continue F3=Exit
Once you confirm the installation directory for Windows NT, the
installation process will prompt you to perform a scan of the
hard disk for corruption. It is recommended that you perform
this test.
Windows NT Server Setup
=======================
Setup will now examine your hard disk(s) for corruption.
In addition to a basic examination, Setup can perform a more
exhaustive secondary examination on some drives. This can be a
time-consuming operation, especially on large or very full drives.
To allow Setup to perform an exhaustive secondary examination of
your hard disk(s), press Enter.
To skip the exhaustive examination, press ESC.
 ENTER=Continue ESC=Skip Operation
```

29. Press Enter to begin the diagnostic of the hard disk(s).
"If you are using an upgrade package you may be prompted for the Windows NT Server CD-ROM."

```
Windows NT Server Setup
=======================
Please insert the compact disk labeled Windows NT Server CD-ROM
into your CD-ROM Drive.
* Press ENTER When ready.
F3=Exit ENTER=Continue
```

30. The scan process has two phases. The first is the physical scan and, as displayed by the screen, a series of messages will be displayed on the status bar as follows:

```
Please Wait...
Checking Drive C:
```

31. Once the initial check is complete, a directory structure will be written to disk:

```
Windows NT Server Setup
=======================
Please wait while Setup copies files to your hard disk.
  |Copying: filename
```

32. The second step is the physical OS transfer from the CD-ROM to the hard disk, as shown in the next screen.

```
Windows NT Server Setup
=======================
Please wait while Setup copies files to your hard disk.
  |Copying: filename
```

33. Once this task is completed, a brief message will appear stating:

```
Please wait while Windows NT initializes your system.
```

34. You will then be prompted to remove all media from Floppy and CD-ROM drives in order to restart your computer.

```
Windows NT Server Setup
=======================
This portion of Setup has been completed successfully.
If there is a floppy disk inserted in drive A:, remove it.
Also remove any compact disk from your CD-ROM drive(s).
Press Enter to restart your computer.
When your computer restarts, Setup will continue.
ENTER=Restart Computer
```

35. The second phase of the installation process will take place after the machine reboots.

We will be installing the operating system from a base version of no service pack, and Check Point FireWall-1 V4.1 SP2 is the most common release in circulation at the time of printing this book. It will be necessary to download and scan the following to accomplish this installation task:

- Windows NT 4.0 Server Service Pack 6a
- Windows NT 4.0 Server security rollup[1]
- Check Point FireWall-1 SP4
- Any additional driver updates from the hardware vendor. Make sure to first check whether the driver is supported under the operating system being installed.

Once the first phase of the installation process has been completed successfully, the second phase will begin once the system reboots.

Installation Phase 2

In this phase of the installation, it will be necessary to carefully remove extraneous portions of the operating system and strip out the Internet Information Server.

1. Once the system reboots and comes back up, one will be greeted with the GUI Windows NT Setup screen. Press the Next button to continue to the next installation screen.
2. When prompted, enter the name and organization for the new system. For example, an abbreviation can be used for the name of the organization in the name field and the full organization name can be placed in the organization field. Press the Next button to continue to the next installation screen.
3. Enter the registration number for the software to activate it. Without a proper registration key, the software will not allow one to continue with the installation. The registration number can be found on the back of the CD jewel case. Press the Next button to continue to the next installation screen.
4. Select either per seat or per server licensing mode. If one selects per server mode, one must have purchased the required number of licenses. Press the Next button to continue to the next installation screen.
5. Enter the computer name that will be used to identify the system on the network (e.g., PDFW0001). Press the Next button to continue to the next installation screen.
6. Select a Standalone installation for the Server Type. This system should not be part of any domain; nor should it be a domain controller. It is not necessary to install additional services that are not required for a firewall's operation.
7. When prompted, enter the password to be used for the administrative account. For example, as per the sample security policy, this would be a 14-character password. Press the Next button to continue to the next installation screen.
8. Select Yes to create an emergency repair diskette (ERD). If desired, one can perform this task manually after the system comes up from the command prompt by executing the *rdisk* command. Press the Next button to continue to the next installation screen.
9. When the default installation components for the Windows NT 4.0 Server screen come up, one should select each component area and deselect all their attributes. We do not wish to install any of these additional items on the firewall. The only selection one may wish to retain is for the standard screen savers. Once done, press the Next button to continue with the installation
10. The Windows NT Network portion of the GUI installation process will not begin until the Next button is pressed.
11. Select the option "This computer will participate on a network" and check the box "Wired to the Network." Press the Next button to continue to the next installation screen.
12. Do not, under any circumstances, select the Internet Information Server option. The firewall should *never* run this service. Press the Next button to continue to the next installation screen.
13. The following screen allows one to detect network interface cards (NICs) in the machine. Select the Start Search button to detect network

interface cards. If one's card is not detected, one will have an opportunity to load the Network Interface card by either selecting a card from a list or loading the driver from diskette, provided one has a driver diskette from the hardware manufacturer (see Exhibit 14).

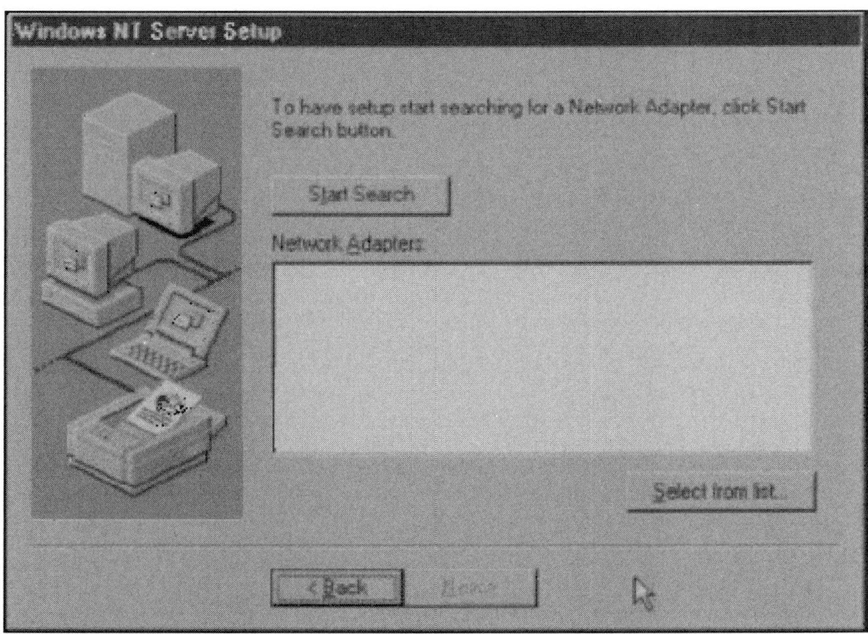

Exhibit 14. Windows NT Setup GUI Screen

14. Once network interface cards (NICs) have been detected, select the Next button to continue with the installation process.
15. When the Networking Communications Protocols screen is displayed, deselect all protocols except for TCP/IP. Press the Next button to continue to the next installation screen.
16. The Services screen is displayed next. It is not possible to remove any of these default services at this time. However, if necessary, one can install the Simple Network Management Protocol (SNMP) if it is required for network management. It can also be added at any time after the installation is complete. Press the Next button to continue to the next installation screen.
17. Select the Next button to continue with the installation process.
18. The network interface cards (NICs) may now require some configuration. Only certain cards will require this and most of the time default values are sufficient. For example, an IBM Token Ring 16/4 PCI adapter will prompt the user for configuration parameters. Refer to the hardware vendor's reference manual for specific instructions on configuration parameters. Press the OK button to continue and save changes.

19. Other network interface cards (NICs) will only display the loading of their drivers.
20. Once all the network adapters have been set up and installed, the system will prompt for DHCP services. Do not select any DHCP services; they are not required for a firewall.
21. The next screens will display the TCP/IP driver installation and its accompanying utilities. Wait for the installation to load these subsystems onto the computer.
22. When prompted, one will be required to set the internal network parameters for the network interface card that will face the inside corporate network. Set the values as follows:
    - IP Address: 192.168.0.1
    - Net Mask : 255.255.255.0
    - The Default Gateway should be left blank.

Note

Generally it is good practice to utilize RFC 1918 addresses within the internal and DMZ portions of the network. This is recommended for two reasons (1) RFC 1918 addresses are nonroutable over the Internet, (unless encapsulated in a VPN data stream); (2) RFC 1918 addresses are usually filtered at an ISP's border router(s) and are discarded, which helps prevent spoofing of internally used RFC 1918 addresses from a distance. It will not protect against a malicious local neighbor within one's own subnet; that is where anti-spoofing rules will be required.

---

23. Select the Routing tab to check the enable IP forwarding feature. It is required for Check Point FireWall-1 operation. If using any other firewall product, check with the vendor's documentation before enabling this feature. (This is an extremely dangerous feature to turn on. Only do so if required, as in the case of FireWall-1).
24. Set the external TCP/IP address settings for the network interface card that faces the outside or untrusted network. This would be the card that will connect one to the ISP and the Internet beyond. Set the values as follows:
    - IP Address: www.xxx.yyy.zzz
    - Net Mask: 255.255.255.zzz
    - Default Gateway: www.xxx.yyy.zzz

Note

www.xxx.yyy.zzz is a representation of a real address that is routable on the Internet. It will be part of the address block defined by one's ISP. The net mask will also be defined by one's ISP, as is the gateway address. For example, a network IP block of eight address (200.100.100.192 – 200.100.100.199 would yield five usable addresses only: .192 and .199 are reserved for broadcast and .193 would be set up as the gateway. This leaves .194 through .198 for systems such as the firewall, Web server, or FTP server.

25. Select the DNS tab and set the ISP's DNS server settings for the firewall so that Domain Name Resolution can take place.
26. Set the TCP/IP address settings for the network interface card that will be used for the DMZ network. Set the values as follows:
    - IP Address: 10.10.10.1
    - Net Mask: 255.255.255.0
    - Leave the default gateway blank

Note

Generally, it is good practice to utilize RFC 1918 addresses within the internal and DMZ portions of the network. This is recommended for two reasons: (1) RFC 1918 addresses are nonroutable over the Internet (unless encapsulated in a VPN data stream); and (2) RFC 1918 addresses are usually filtered at an ISP's border router(s) and are discarded, which helps prevent spoofing of internally used RFC 1918 addresses from a distance. It will not protect one against a malicious local neighbor within one's own subnet; that is were anti-spoofing rules will be required.

27. When done setting all the TCP/IP parameters for the network interface cards, select the Apply button to continue. You will receive a message stating that "At least one of the adapter cards has an empty primary WINS address. Do you want to continue?" Select Yes. One does not want any WINS to be set up on the firewall.
28. The Bindings screen will be displayed next. If one selects to remove WINS bindings from the adapters at this time, an error will occur when the networking components try to detect the network. Do not remove

the WINS components at this time. They can be removed after the installation has been completed.

29. When prompted for a workgroup name, select a name that is not currently utilized within any of the production environments. The use of a cryptic name is a good choice.
30. Select the Next button to continue the installation process.
31. Set the Time and Date parameters for the system according to your time zone.
32. Set the display resolution for the system. The desired resolution of the display adapter and monitor must be tested before they are set — to prevent a poor or unusable display. Once complete, select the OK button to continue.
33. After the display settings have been completed, the final installation touches of the operating system are applied and the system prompts for a reboot. Select Reboot when prompted.

Installation Phase 3

Once the operating system has been installed and the system reboots, and one can successfully log on to the new system destined to become the firewall, one can begin to patch, tune, and configure the system to meet the required fortifications.

1. Execute the Service Pack 6a installation executable. Accept the licence agreement and select Backup Old Files. Reboot the system for the changes to take effect.
2. Once the system has rebooted and you have sucessfully logged back on to the system, apply the Post Service Pack 6a Security Rollup. Once the rollup has been applied, you will have to reboot the system again.

(Refer to Appendix C for details regarding Service Pack 6a and the Service Pack 6a Rollup.)

The post-installation patching process will take a little bit of time. As mentioned earlier, one should have downloaded the service packs and security patches, scanned them, and burned them onto a CD-ROM so they can be applied to the target system.

Once the system comes back up, it is a good idea to run a quick port scan against the system to see what is open and can be attacked (see Exhibit 15). This will give an idea of what the vulnerabilities are with an unprotected operating system.

This port scan shows that there have been significant improvements with the Default Installation of the Windows NT 4.0 Server Operating System with SP6a and the Security Rollup. Only two service ports are open on this machine. However, the two ports that are open are insecure. It is absolutely critical to close off these ports. These ports must be closed off or the entire security infrastructure will be at risk.

Exhibit 15. Post Installation and Patching Port Scan

```
# Nmap (V. nmap) scan initiated 2.53 as: nmap -v -sS -O -P0 -p1-65535
-o PDFW0001.txt 24.43.134.46
Interesting ports on PDFW0001 (24.43.134.46):
(The 65533 ports scanned but not shown below are in state: closed)
Port      State     Service
135/tcp   open      loc-srv
139/tcp   open      netbios-ssn

TCP Sequence Prediction: Class=random positive increments
 Difficulty=14982 (Worthy challenge)

Sequence numbers: D8D4CD68 D8D56DD0 D8D60352 D8D733B7 D8D7CAF9 D8D89068
Remote operating system guess: Microsoft NT 4.0 Server SP5 + 2047 Hotfixes

# Nmap run completed at Thu Aug 09 15:16:48 2001 -- 1 IP address (1
host up) scanned in 36 seconds
```

Installing Check Point FireWall-1

Now one can begin the installation of Check Point FireWall-1/VPN-1. Perform additional system hardening after verifying the proper operation of FireWall-1/VPN-1. One does not want to harden the system prior to the installation of the firewall because there is always a possibility to tweak the system into an inoperable state. This procedure is more of a safety net approach and will save countless hours of aggravation if something goes wrong. Another important point to consider with the application of service packs and patches is that they modify the system's operating kernel and any future service packs that are applied to the system will require one to perform the following:

- Back up the Firewall/conf directory and any files that may have been modified for functionality
- Remove the FireWall-1/VPN-1 software
- Apply the service pack
- Reinstall the FireWall-1/VPN-1 software
- Restore the configuration back into the /conf directory and any modified files back to their directories

This process is necessary because there is a very probable chance of disabling the firewall software by breaking existing functionality with a service pack. As a rule of thumb, always make sure you can back out of any change promptly before beginning any patch, tweak, or upgrade to an operational system.

Environmental Setup

Begin by setting up the environment to make it work more efficiently: remove items from the desktop and add items to make system configuration and maintenance easily attainable, both now and in the future.

1. The initial desktop is not very conducive to a security administrator's needs. Disable the Default dialog box from appearing by deselecting the Checkbox option and closing the window. Remove the following items from the desktop:
   - Install Internet Information Server shortcut
   - Internet Expolorer
   - Inbox
   - My Briefcase

   Also remove the briefcase shortcut from the administrator's SendTo path, C:\winnt\profiles\administrator\sendto. Add Notepad to the SendTo feature.
2. Modify the desktop by adding the following items:
   - Notepad
   - Windows NT Explorer
   - Command Prompt
   - Event Viewer
   - Server Manager
   - User Manager for Domains
   - Windows NT Diagnostics
3. Rename the administrator account. This should be done to prevent the use of a known variable in an attempted attack. Pick a name that is obscure, such as "SAPDFW0001," short for Security Administrator Perimeter Domain Firewall 0001. Also rename the guest account; although it is disabled by default, other people know that it exists (e.g., GPDFW0001).
4. In addition, remove the briefcase shortcut from the administrator's SendTo path, C:\winnt\profiles\administrator\SendTo. Add Notepad to the SendTo path.
5. Set the system account policies from the user manager application; select the Policies menu option and then the Account option. Set the following field values:
   - Minimum password length = 14
   - Lock out after = 3
   - Reset counter after = 60
   - Lockout duration forever = on
   - Select the OK button to accept the new values
6. From the Policies menu, select the User Rights option. Using the right drop-down field, navigate and set the following User Rights options as follows:

- Change the default entries for Access to this Computer from the Network right by removing Administrators, Everyone, and Power Users from the right
- Change the default entries for log on locally right by removing all entries except administrator

7. Right click with the mouse on the Network Neighborhood icon and select the properties option from the list. From the Network dialog screen, select the binding tab. Disable the WINS CLIENT (TCP/IP) options.

Check Point FireWall-1 Installation Process

Once the desktop environment has been cleaned up, one can begin the Check Point FireWall-1 installation process:

1. Insert the Check Point CD-ROM into the CD-ROM drive of the machine. It will automatically launch and come up with the Check Point Installation screen. Select the Next button to continue.
2. The License installation screen will be displayed. Read and make sure you accept the terms of the license agreement by selecting the Yes button.
3. The Product installation screen appears next. Select the radio button corresponding to Server/Gateway Components.
4. The Server/Gateway Components screen appears with default product selections. De-select all except for VPN-1/FireWall-1. *Note:* Only select the components for which a license has been purchased. In this case, only select VPN-1/FireWall-1. The other products are licensed separately.
5. Selecting the type of installation is dependent upon the license that one has purchased. A stand-alone installation usually corresponds to the gateway server products and the distributed option is usually for enterprise products. Only the enterprise product can be set up in a distributed manner.
6. Select the Next button to continue with the desired installation type. A Wait message will appear while the installation components are assembled.
7. Select the radio button for the purchased license type, in this case the VPN-1/FireWall-1 Gateway Module — Limited Hosts (25-250) and then select the Next button to continue.
8. Select the radio button option Install Without Backward Compatibility. Backward compatibility is only required if the environment has pre-4.1 VPN-1/FireWall-1 systems in place. If required, it has a small footprint. Select the Next button to continue the installation process.
9. Choosing the software installation location. It is highly recommended to install the software in the default location. There are known issues with moving this location. Version 4.0 of FireWall-1 has to be in the default location. Select the Next button to continue with the installation.

The following screen will then display installation statistics for the software installation. Once completed, select the OK button to exit this phase of the installation process. It is necessary to reboot the machine at this point.

10. Upon rebooting the system and logging on to the system, the Check Point Configuration Tool will come up. Begin by adding license string information by selecting the Add button. It is required to generate the license information from the Check Point Web site before proceeding with the configuration process. Go to https://usercenter.checkpoint.com/home1/index.jsp. One might be referred to http://license.checkpoint.com/license; however, this site has been replaced by the new user center site, which is a little friendlier than the old site. A blank license screen will be displayed. One can either cut-and-paste the license string data to the required fields, type them in, or read them in from file. Reading them in from file is preferable. The license file from Check Point will fit on a floppy. Click on the Fetch from File button to load the license strings into their proper fields. One should load as many license files as one has and then press the OK button to continue. One will then see the loaded Licenses on the licenses tab of the Check Point Configuration Tool dialog box. It is highly recommended that the floppy diskette with the license files be stored in a safe place, along with the build documentation for the firewall.
11. Select the Administrators tab from the Check Point Configuration Tool dialog box. Select the Add button to begin entering an administrator for the system. Enter the Administrator Name and Password for the administrative account for the firewall. For example, the Administrator Name is sapdfw01. Make sure the Read/Write All radio button is selected in the Management Clients Permissions section. Select the OK button to return to the previous dialog and then select the OK button again to return to the Configuration Tool dialog box.

Note

This section is used to set up and configure multi-level concurrent access to the firewall management console. It is possible to assign various access levels to administrators and operators. Only one administrator with write privileges is allowed access to the console at any one time. A second administrator with write privileges will be warned that the console is already accessed in write mode and will be available only in read-only mode.

---

12. Select the IP Address tab from the Configuration Tool dialog box. Press the Change IP button. Enter the external IP address of the firewall into

the Change IP Address dialog box. Press the OK button to return to the previous screen. The screen should now reflect the IP address entry in the IP Address field. Press the OK button again to return to the Configuration Tool dialog box.

13. From the Configuration Tool dialog box, select the GUI Clients tab. Select the Add button to enter the IP addresses of workstations that will run the Policy Management Client Software against the firewall. Without the IP address entered into the GUI_clients configuration file, no remote system can access the management interface of the firewall. Press the OK button again to return to the Configuration Tool dialog box.
14. From the Configuration Tool dialog box, select the External I/F tab. This field requires the external NIC's interface name to be entered. This can be determined by typing the *ipconfig* command at the command prompt or by using the *route print* command. In any event, the name must correspond to the card that is mapped to the external IP address. This is a requirement for the gateway products only. If it is not set up properly, one may get a message such as:

    ```
    FW-1: too many internal hosts detected
    ```

    This is a well-documented issue with the gateway products and usually a stumbling block for many first-time installations. If such a message is received, it may be legitimate if one has more IP devices on the internal network than allowed for by the license. A good method for debugging this issue is available at www.phoneboy.com. Press the OK button to return to the Configuration Tool dialog box (see Exhibit 16).
15. From the Configuration Tool dialog box, select the IP Forwarding tab. Select the Control IP Forwarding radio button. This option prevents the flow of data between interfaces when the firewall is not loaded, during loading, or if no security policy exists. Press the OK button to return to the Configuration Tool dialog box.

Note

One always wants to be in control of IP Forwarding. Should the firewall be stopped, one wants to make sure that routing between interfaces ceases also.

---

16. From the Configuration Tool dialog box, select the SMTP tab. These fields are used to set the Simple Mail Transfer Protocol (SMTP) settings for the mail server. Leave them as they are. They can be configured at a later time, if required. Press the OK button to return to the Configuration Tool dialog box.

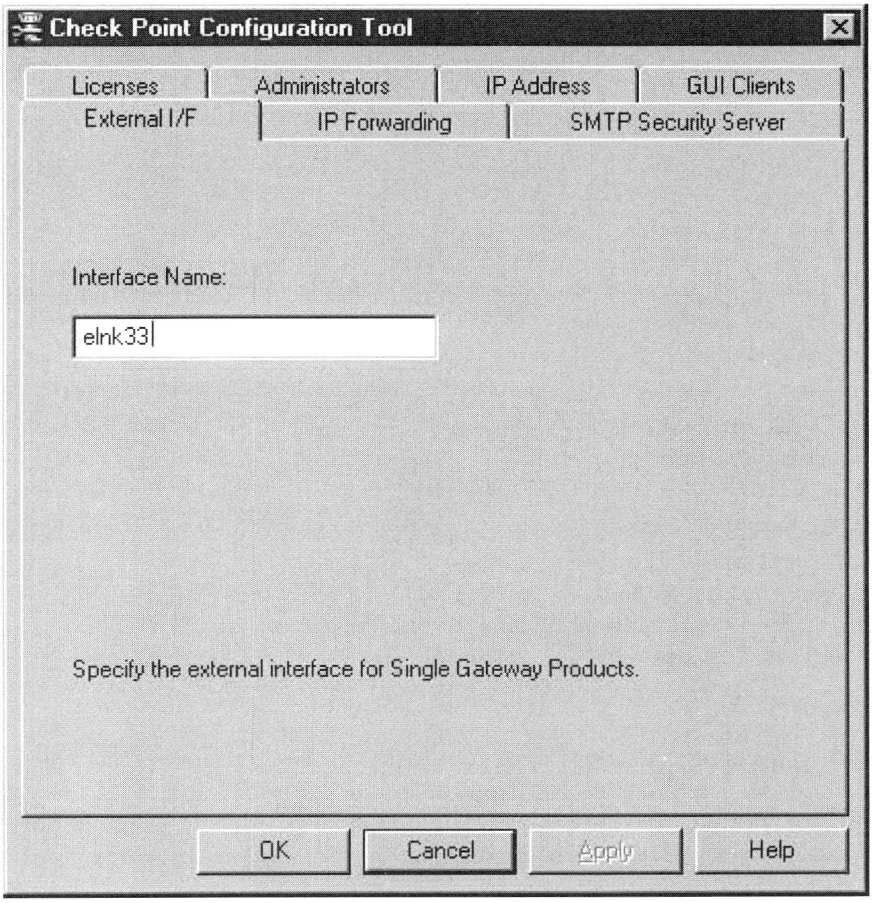

Exhibit 16. External Interface Name Used by FireWall-1 Gateway Products

---

Note

If modifying the SMTP parameters, it is recommended to leave the defaults in effect until one has verified proper operation of the firewall and SMTP mail is routing correctly. Once everything is working properly and as expected, any modifications to this section that disrupt functionality can be easily localized.

---

17. Press the OK button from the Configuration Tool dialog box to process the data entered to configure the firewall. Select the Yes button to restart the VPN-1/FireWall-1 service. This is necessary for the changes to take effect.

This installation process assumes the use of the Check Point 2000 Enterprise Suite V4.1.2 Strong (3DES) Edition. This equates to the SP2 release. Any release grade higher than SP2 is preferable in order to skip a patching process. The following installation instructions include the application of SP4.

After the initial installation of the software from the CD-ROM, one needs to apply SP4:

1. Disable the FireWall-1 services before applying SP4. This can be accomplished by opening the NT service control manager and stopping the firewall services. Place the Check Point SP4 CD-ROM, created by downloading the patch from the Check Point site, into the CD-ROM drive of the firewall machine. Using the explorer, navigate to the directory on the CD-ROM where the files were burned and run the setup application. The Setup dialog box will appear briefly.
2. The Check Point VPN-1/FireWall-1 4.1 Service Pack 4 Installation screen will begin installation of the service pack. The process will finish and then one may continue.
3. Copy and place the *crypt.def* and *table.def* files of the SP4 Hot Fix patch into the C:\winnt\fw1\41\lib directory.
   - Rename the existing *crypt.def* and *table.def* files with an extension of *bak* or with an extension that denotes the original patch level (e.g., *sp2*).
   - Copy the new sp4 file definitions from the burned CD-ROM into the C:\winnt\fw1\41\lib directory. For more information, refer to the Check Point SP4 Hot Fix documentation. Once these files have been copied to there destination, one can restart the FireWall-1 services.

Note

SP4 can be applied at any time after the initial installation, setup, and configuration of Check Point FireWall-1. It is left to personal discretion when to install it; however, it is highly recommended that it be installed. SP4 can only be obtained from the Check Point Web site if a valid software subscription is active.

After the initial Check Point configuration process has been completed, it will be necessary to install the Check Point management clients on the firewall:

1. Place the Check Point CD-ROM into the CD-ROM drive of the firewall machine. If the Auto Run feature is still enabled, one will be greeted

by the Check Point 2000 screen. Exit from this installation process. Using the explorer, navigate to the following directory on the CD-ROM:

\Windows\CPMgmtClnt-41

and run the setup application. The setup dialog box will appear briefly.

2. The Check Point management client 4.1 installation screen will appear. Select the default location for the management clients.
3. Next, one is prompted for component selection. By default, all are checked off. If desired, one can deselect System Status and Real Time Monitor.

Note

The Real Time Monitor option will be available with the next major release of the FireWall-1 product.

---

4. The final screen displays the progress statistics for the installation of the software. Once done, the management clients will be installed on the machine.

The clients can also be installed on any other Windows 9x, Windows NT, or Windows 2000 systems, as long as the IP addresses of the clients were inserted into the *GUI_clients* file. The *GUI_clients* file can always be manually edited to add and remove clients when necessary. The *GUI_clients* file can be found in the C:\Winnt\FW1\4.1\conf directory.

After the initial installation of the management client software from the CD-ROM, one will need to apply SP4 for the Client software:

1. Place the Check Point SP4 CD-ROM created from downloading the patch from Check Point's Web site into the CD-ROM drive of the firewall machine. Using the explorer, navigate to the directory on the CD-ROM where the files were burned and run the Setup application. The Setup dialog box will appear briefly.
2. The Check Point Management Clients 4.1 SP4 installation screen will begin the installation of the service pack. The process will finish and then one can continue.
3. Launch the Policy Editor and verify that the patch was successful. Click Help and About to check the version.

Note

The build number for the GUI client should be 41862.

Note

SP4 can be applied anytime after the initial installation, setup, and configuration of Check Point FireWall-1. It is left to personal discretion when to install it; however, it is highly recommended that it be installed. One must apply the SP4 patch for the GUI management clients if one has applied the SP4 patch for VPN-1/FireWall-1.

Once the Check Point initial configuration has been completed, one can begin by setting up the security environment. Before one begins to set up the environment and define network objects, there needs to be a naming convention for objects and a definition of color schemes for trusted, public systems and untrusted networks and servers. These will help to visually identify objects and also see them in the log files. Use color codes to identify resources, define groups to collectively gather common objects together, and also group the services that one will allow to enter the firewall and to exit the firewall together. This will also help in maintaining a small, tight, and concise rule base that will be easier to manage as one's security needs evolve and change over time.

1. Run the Policy Editor 4.1 application from the Start, Programs, Check Point Management Clients menu. It would be wise to add the management programs as links on the desktop for easier access. Select either the Manage Menu item and then select Network Objects, or select the Manage Network Objects icon from the graphical menu bar. From the Network Objects dialog, one can begin defining objects that make up the computing environment.
2. The first object to define is the firewall object (see Exhibit 17). Set the following fields in the General tab of the workstation object to your required values.
   - Name = the system name: it should also be defined in the host table under the \winnt\system32\drivers\etc directory. It is added by default during the installation; however, always check to make sure that the entry exists, just in case.
   - IP Address = the external IP address of the firewall goes here.
   - Comment = place a good descriptive comment in this field.
   - Select the following radio buttons:
     Location — Internal
     Type — Gateway
     VPN-1 and FireWall-1
     Version 4.1
     Management Station
     Set the color to deep red

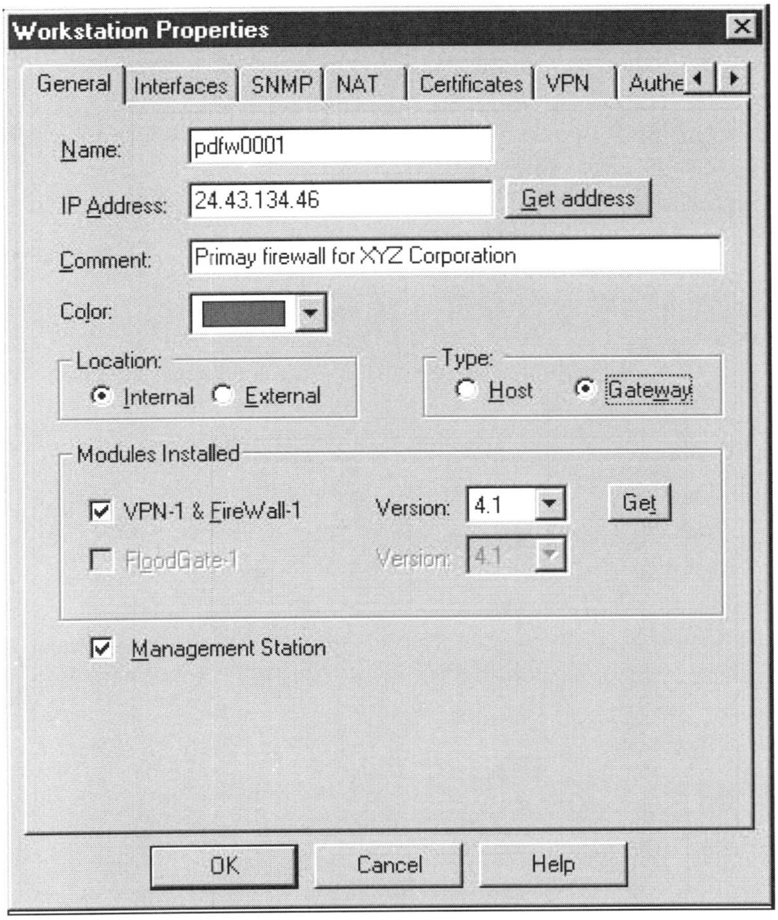

Workstation Properties

General | Interfaces | SNMP | NAT | Certificates | VPN | Authe

Name: pdfw0001

IP Address: 24.43.134.46 Get address

Comment: Primay firewall for XYZ Corporation

Color:

Location: Internal External

Type: Host Gateway

Modules Installed

VPN-1 & FireWall-1 Version: 4.1 Get

FloodGate-1 Version: 4.1

Management Station

OK Cancel Help

Exhibit 17. Workstation Network Object for Firewall pdfw0001

3. Select the Interfaces tab next and then the Get button. If the network interface cards were set up properly, they will be automatically populated. The interface properties will be defined after defining some additional network object groups for anti-spoofing security (see Exhibit 18).
4. Select the Authentication tab (see Exhibit 19) and deselect all checkboxes that do not apply. In the example, only VPN-1 and FireWall-1 Password has been selected. Press the OK button to save the object.
5. Create the Internal Network Object using the Network Objects Add function and select New Network (Exhibit 20).
   - Set the field values as follows:
     Name = Internal_Corporate
     IP Address = Subnet for network
     Net Mask = network mask for above network
     Comment = suitable description
     Color = green
   - Select the radio buttons as follows:
     Location = Internal
     Broadcast = Allowed
   - Select the NAT tab (Exhibit 21) for the object to set up the Network Address Translation of the RFC 1918 address. NAT is required if one's internal network addresses are nonroutable Internet addresses. Set the following fields for NAT on the Internal Network Object as follows:
     Check the Add Automatic Address Translation Rules checkbox.
     Translation Method = hide
     Hiding IP Address = external IP address of firewall
     Install On = All
6. Create the DMZ Network Object using the Network Objects Add function and select New Network (see Exhibit 22). Set the field values as follows:
   Name = dmz
   IP Address = subnet for network
   Net Mask = network mask for above network
   Comment = suitable description
   Color = orange
   - Select the radio buttons as follows:
     Location = Internal
     Broadcast = Allowed
   - Do not set any Network Address Translation (NAT) for this object (Exhibit 23).

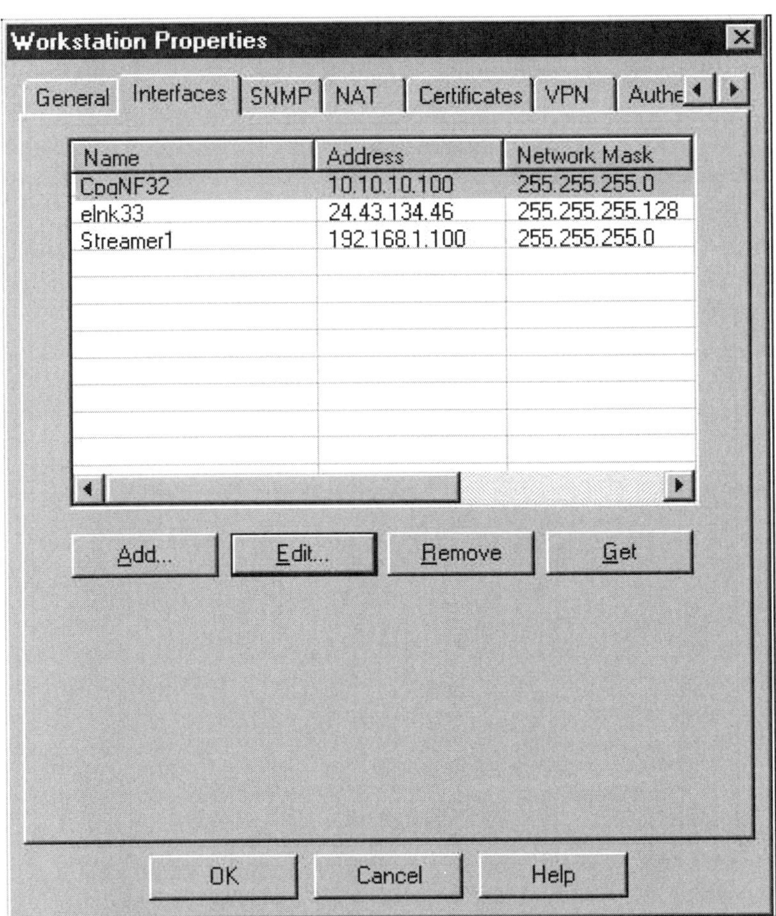

Exhibit 18. Workstation Network Object Interfaces for Firewall pdfw0001

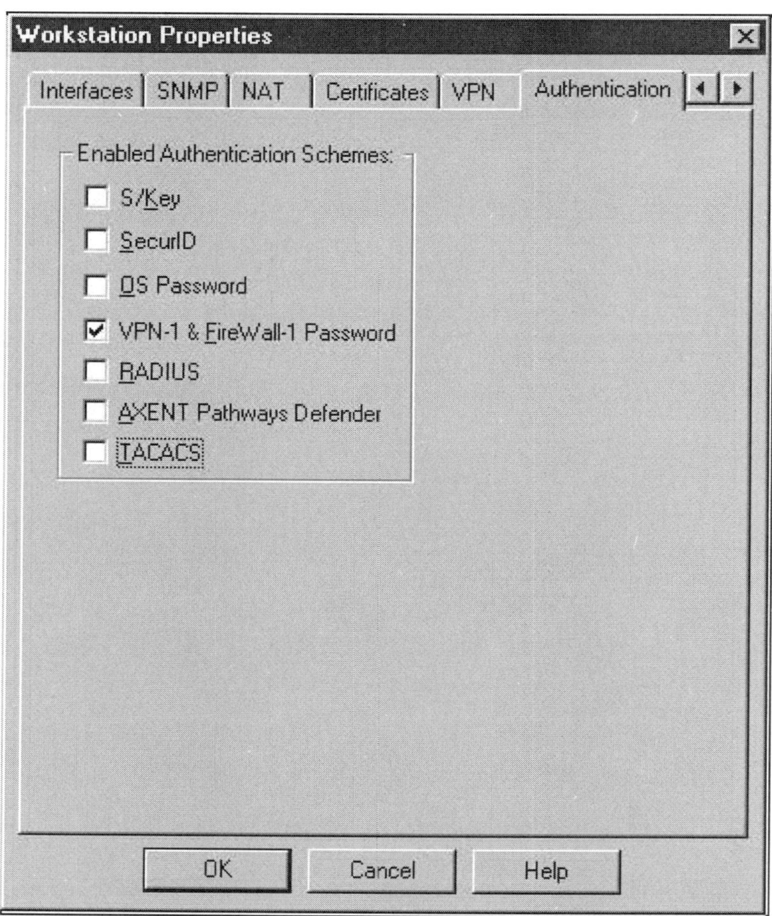

Exhibit 19. Workstation Network Object Authentication for Firewall pdfw0001

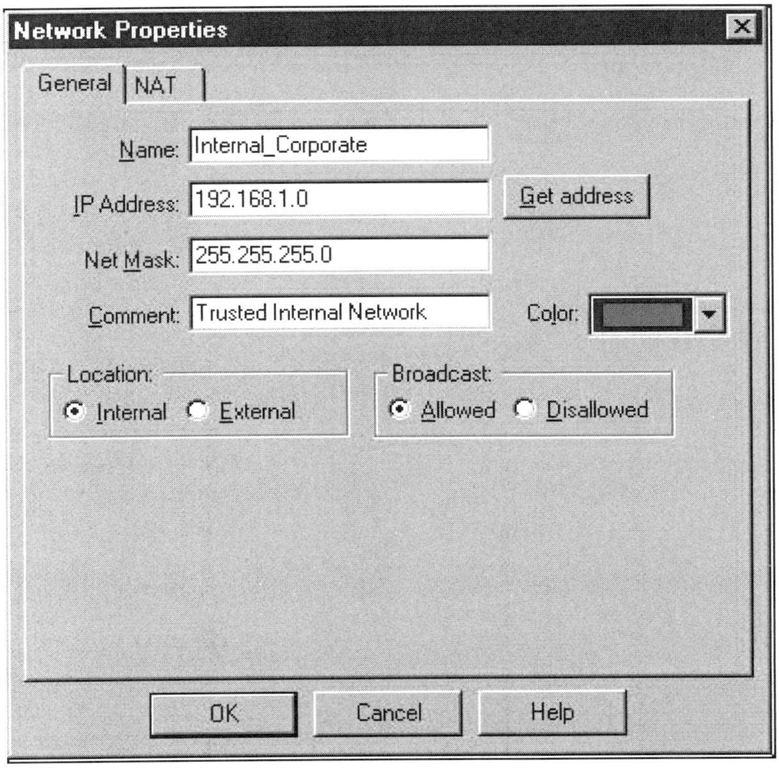

Exhibit 20. Internal Network Definition Screen 1

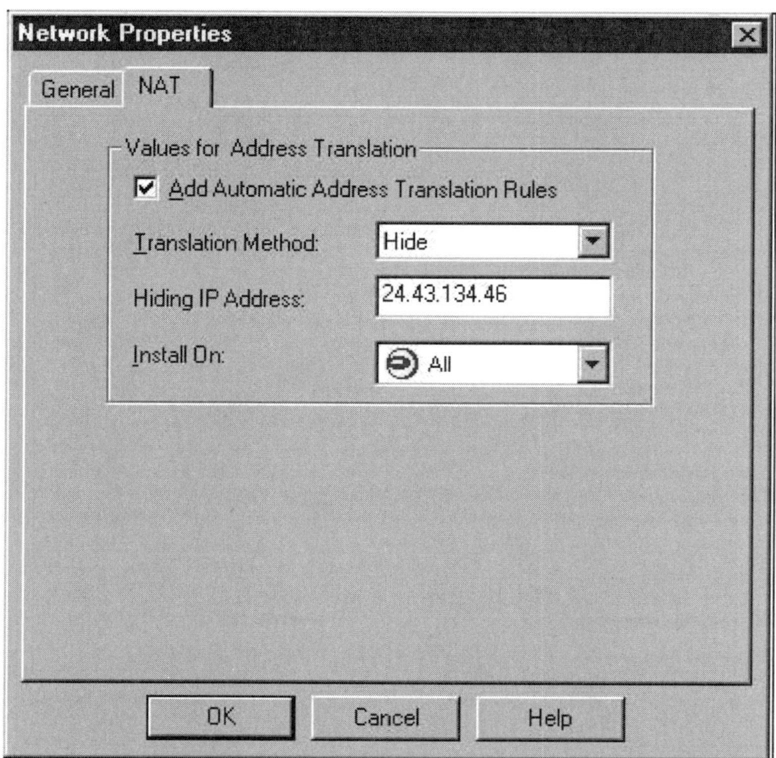

Exhibit 21. Internal Network Definition Screen 2

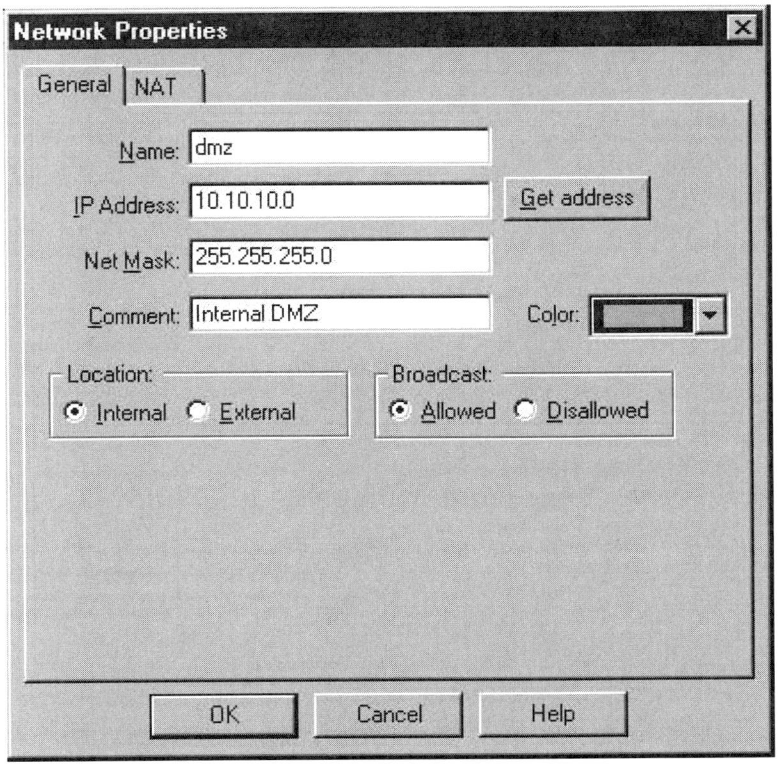

Exhibit 22. DMZ Network Definition Screen 1

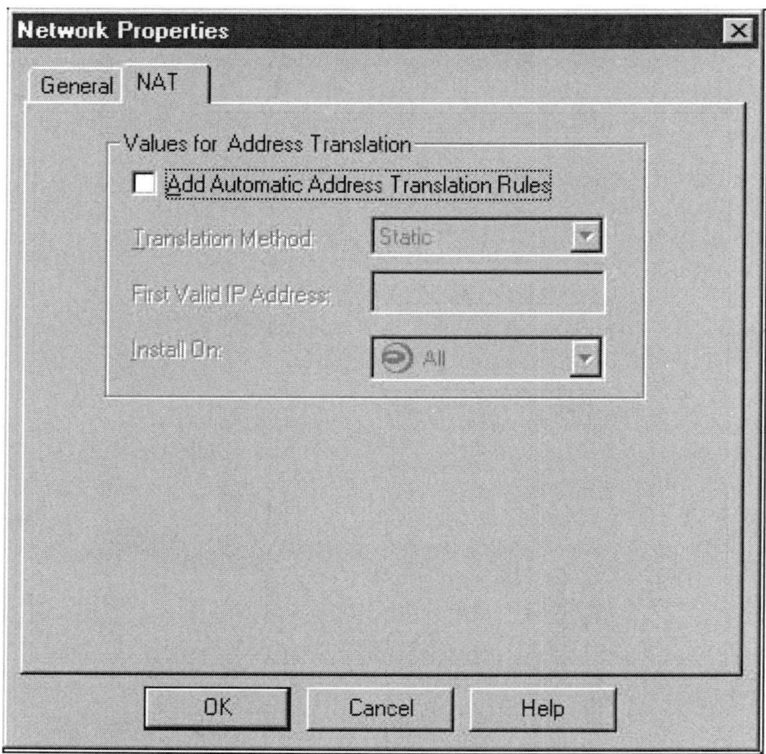

Exhibit 23. DMZ Network Definition Screen 2

7. Create group objects that will be used for anti-spoofing on the interfaces (Exhibit 24). These groups can be created now but should be updated when the network definitions change for the internal and DMZ networks. Create the Group Objects using the Network Objects Add function and select New Group (Exhibit 25). Set the field values as follows:
   - Internal Group Object
     Name = Corporate_Internal_group
     Comment = a suitable description
     Color = green
   - DMZ Group Object
     Name = Corporate_dmz_group
     Comment = a suitable description
     Color = orange
8. Once the Anti-Spoofing group definitions have been defined and saved (Exhibit 26), select the Network Objects icon from the menu bar, highlight the pdfw0001 firewall object, and click Edit to edit the object (Exhibit 27). Click on the Interfaces tab, highlight each interface one at a time, and edit the Interface Properties Security tab.
   - For both the internal network and DMZ network, select the radio button Specific in the Valid Addresses section. Set the Internal Interface to the Corporate_Internal_group and set the DMZ Interface to the Corporate_dmz_group. For the external interface, select the radio button Others in the Valid Addresses section (Exhibit 28). It is recommended that the logging options for each be set to log.
9. Defining the Properties Setup screen for the firewall (see Exhibit 29). The default Security Policy Tab of the Properties Setup needs to be changed in order for testing of the rule base to proceed. It also requires some default timeouts to be reduced to keep the firewall state tables small. Select the following settings for the Security Policy Tab:
   - Set TCP Session Timeout = 300
   - Check the following additional checkboxes:
     Accept Domain Name Over UDP (Queries) = First
     Accept ICMP = First
     Log Implied Rules
   - Check the Access Lists tab and make sure that Accept RIP and Accept Domain Name Over TCP (Zone Transfer) are not checked. Select the SYNDefender tab and set the following entry:
     Select the radio button = Passive SYN Gateway
     Select OK to accept the modifications for the time being

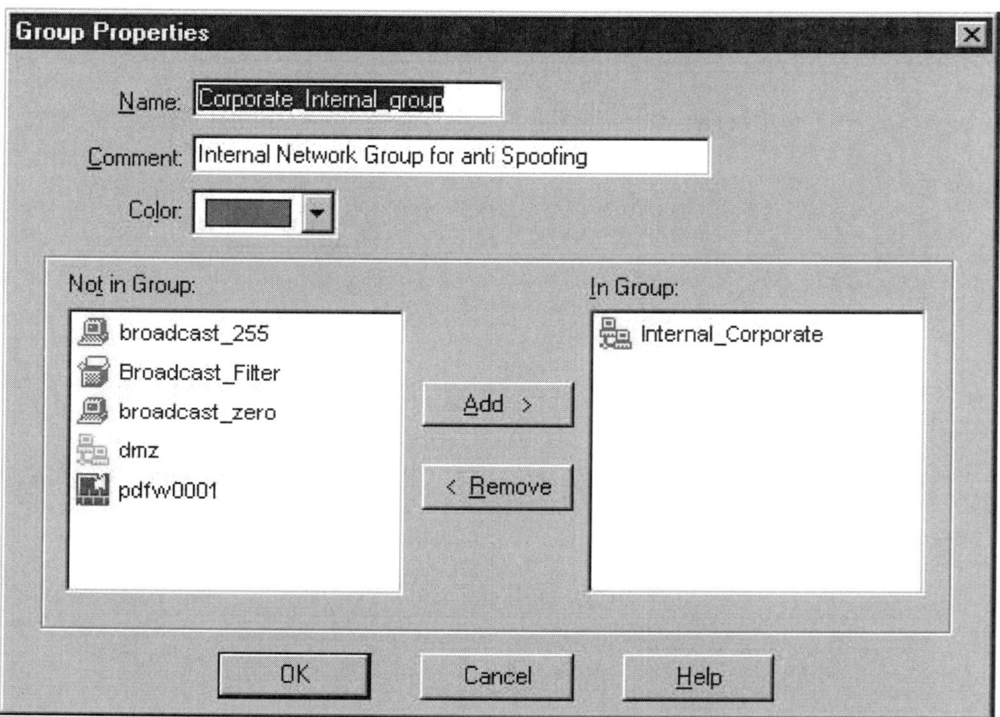

Exhibit 24. Anti-Spoofing Group for Internal Network

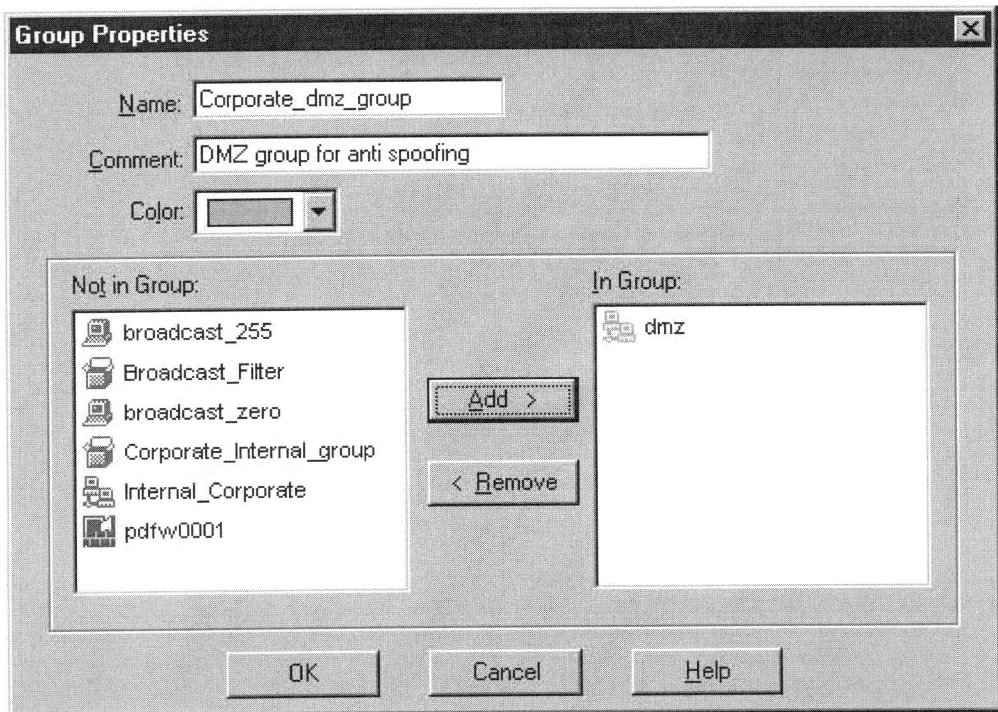

Exhibit 25. Anti-Spoofing Group for DMZ Network

Interface Properties
General
Security
Valid Addresses:
Any
This net
No security policy!
Others
Others +
Specific
Corporate_Internal_g
Spoof Tracking:
None
Log
Alert
OK
Cancel
Help

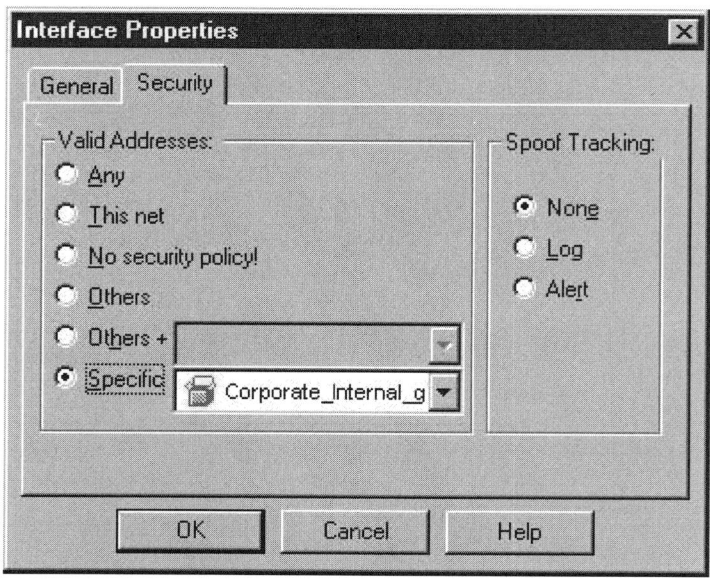

Exhibit 26. Anti-Spoofing for Internal Interface of Firewall pdfw0001

Interface Properties
General
Security
Valid Addresses:
Any
This net
No security policy!
Others
Others +
Specific
Corporate_dmz_grou
Spoof Tracking:
None
Log
Alert
OK
Cancel
Help

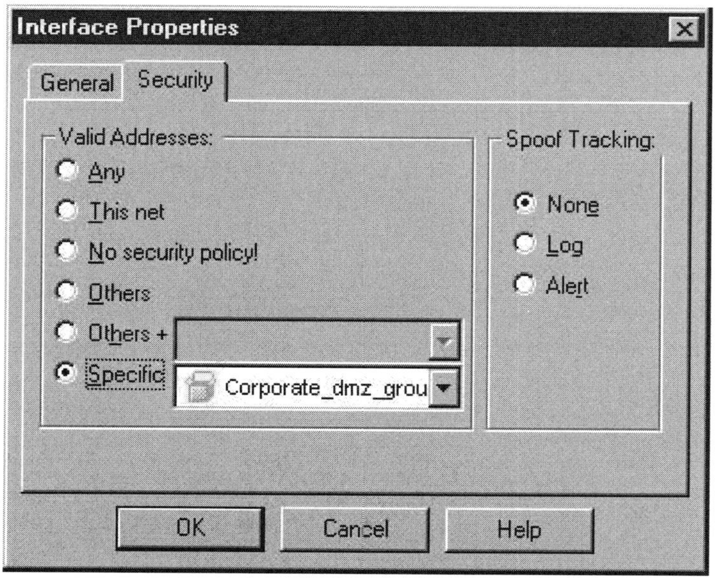

Exhibit 27. Anti-Spoofing for DMZ Interface of Firewall pdfw0001

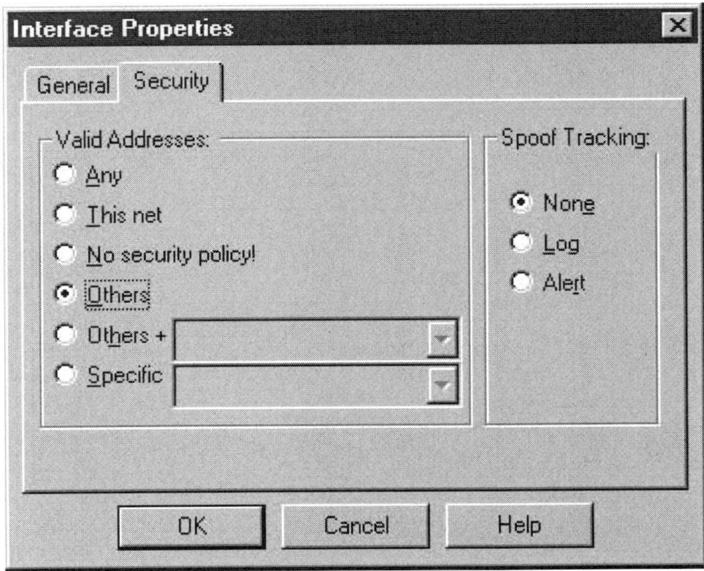

Exhibit 28. Anti-Spoofing for External Network Interface of Firewall pdfw0001

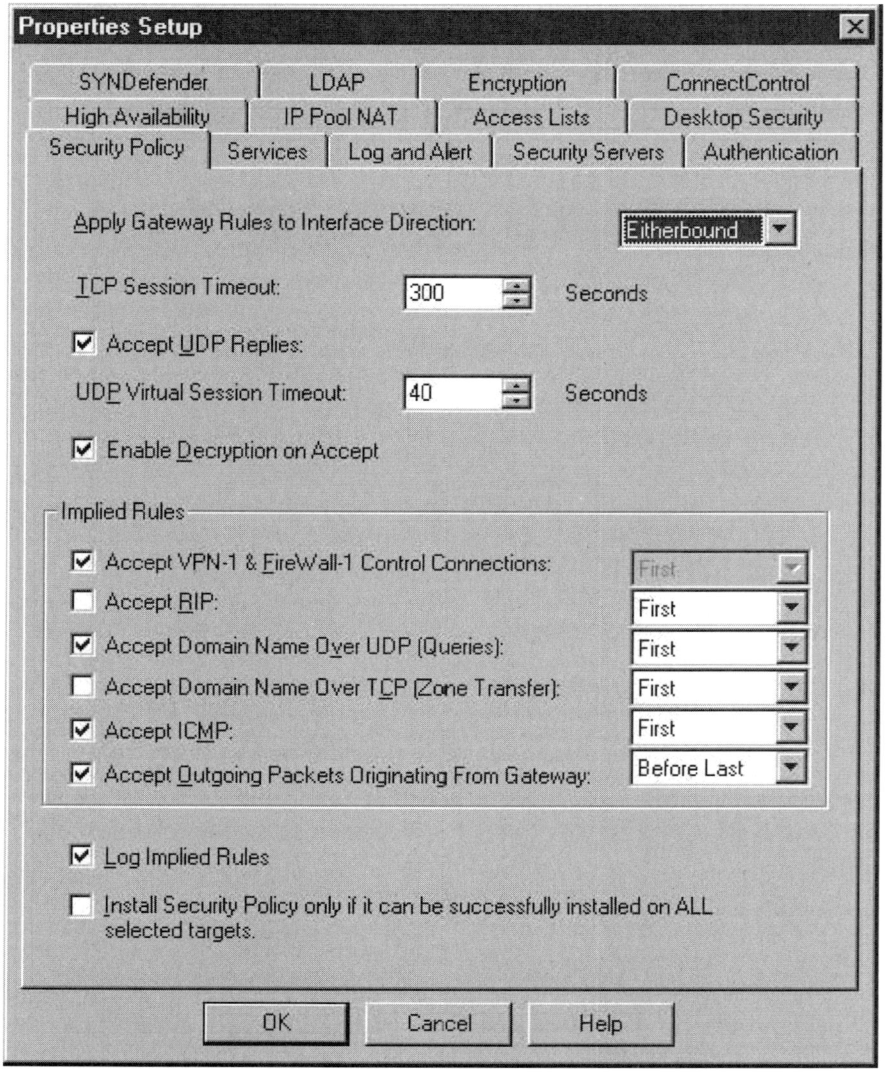

Exhibit 29. Properties Screen Modifed prior to Final Selection

10. The next step is to create a broadcast filter (Exhibit 30) and filter group (Exhibit 31). These objects will be used to filter out broadcast traffic from the log file. Create two new Network Objects using the Manage Network Objects icon from the menu bar and select the New button to create new workstation objects for the following broadcast filters:

    0.0.0.0 and 255.255.255.255

    Once these are defined, create a broadcast filter group consisting of these two objects. It will be used during the rule base definition later in this exercise. Create the filter group by clicking on the New button of Network Objects and selecting Group.
11. Creating a service group for Internet applications or administration is done by selecting the Manage Services icon on the menu bar or by selecting the Manage Menu option and selecting Services. From the Services dialog box, select the New button and select Group. This will allow one to create a group services object that can encapsulate a set of required Internet services. This makes the setup of the rule base easier and simpler. We define a service group for the following activities with the following services assigned to each:
    - *Standard Internet services* (Exhibit 32). These are the basic Internet surfing services: HTTP, HTTPS, FTP, and NNTP.
    - *Administration services* (Exhibit 33). These services are restricted for administrative use only: Telnet and FTP.
    - *Application services* (Exhibit 34). Application services are those that have been identified in an application inventory process. These can range from commercial applications to custom in-house developed applications (e.g., SMTP, POP-3, IMAP, Lotus, or MS-Exchange v5.5).
    - *Filter services* (Exhibit 35). These are services that we wish to filter and remove from the firewall logs. This typically consists of NetBIOS-related traffic (i.e., the NBT Service group).
    - *Diagnostic services.* These are services that are used to enable ICMP diagnostic services such as Ping and Traceroute to work through the firewall without having to modify the Properties Setup to enable ICMP. Enabling and disabling these sets of services is a conscious decision on the security administrator's behalf (e.g., echo request and Traceroute for outbound testing (Exhibit 36) and echo reply, time exceeded and dest-unreach for inbound testing (Exhibit 37).
12. Creating user groups for system administration and remote access is accomplished from the Manage menu item and selecting the User option, or simply click on the Manage User icon on the menu bar. It will be necessary to create an administrative group for use with restrictive services such as Telnet and FTP. If one will require users to have remote access to the internal network, a SecuRemote users' group should be created.

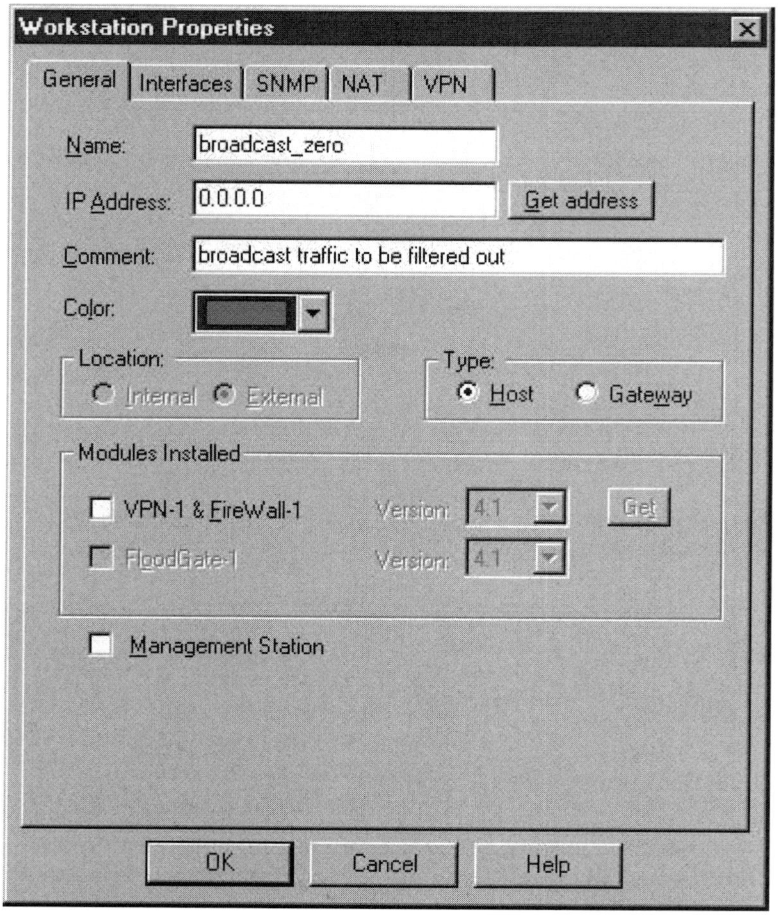

Exhibit 30. Broadcast Filter for 0.0.0

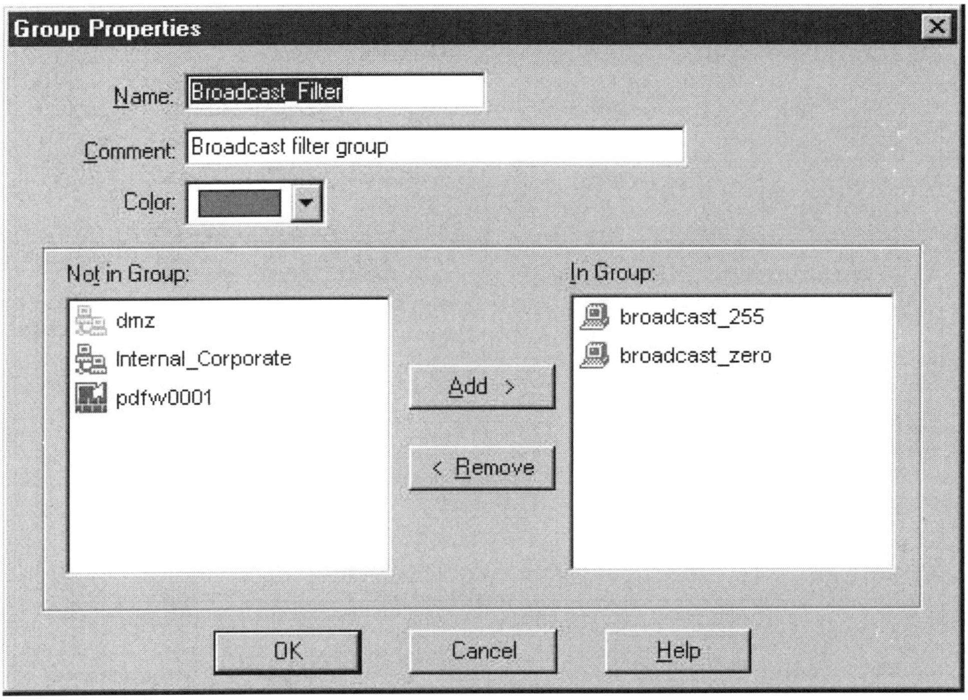

Exhibit 31. Broadcast Filter Group

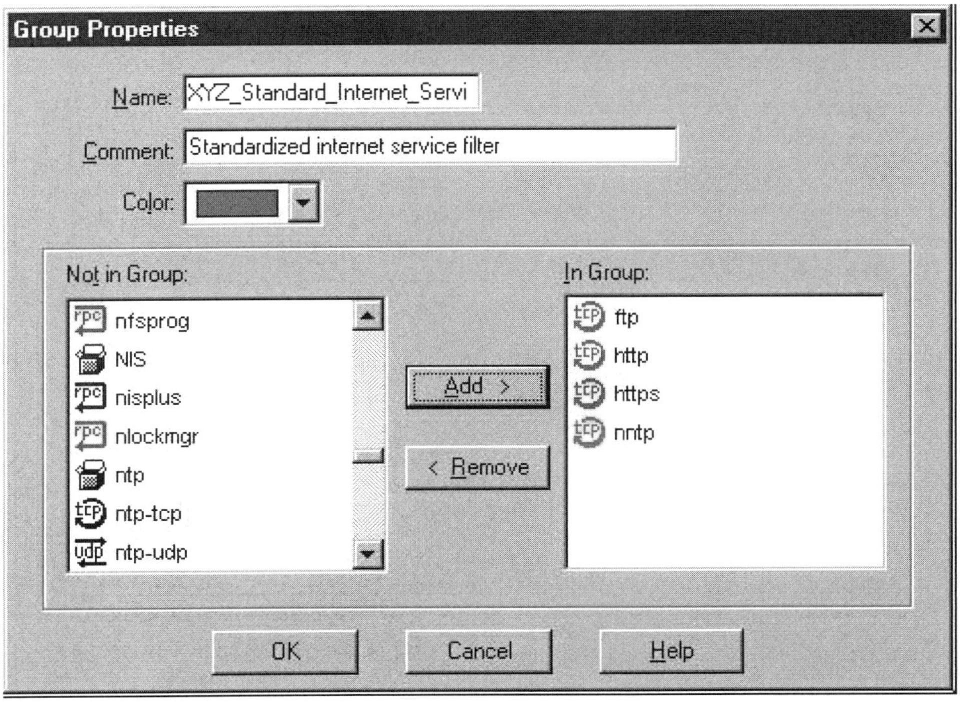

Exhibit 32. Standard Service Group

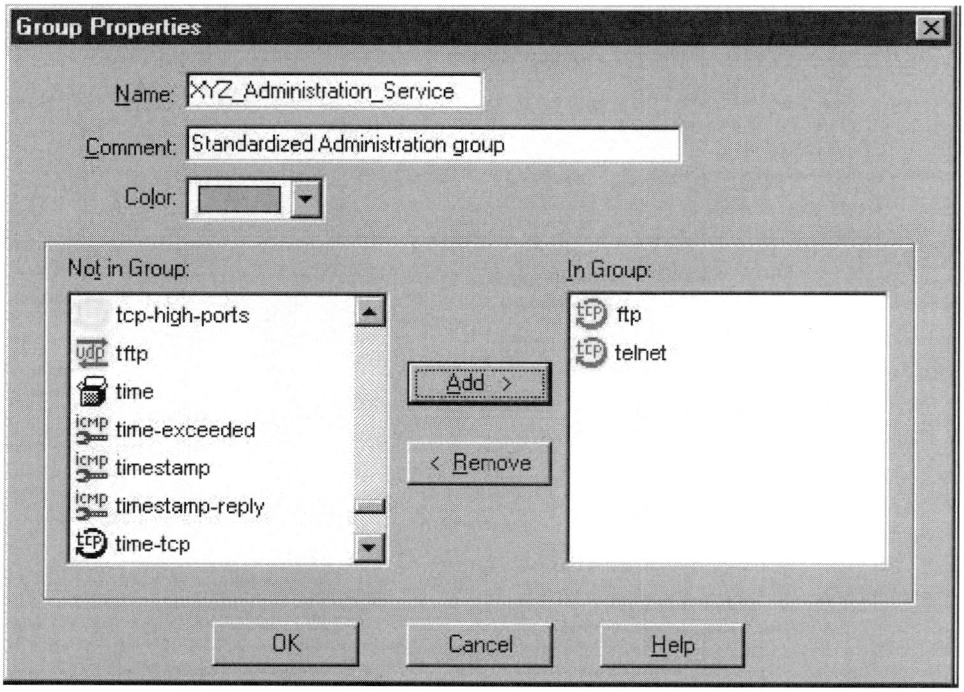

Exhibit 33. Administration Service Group

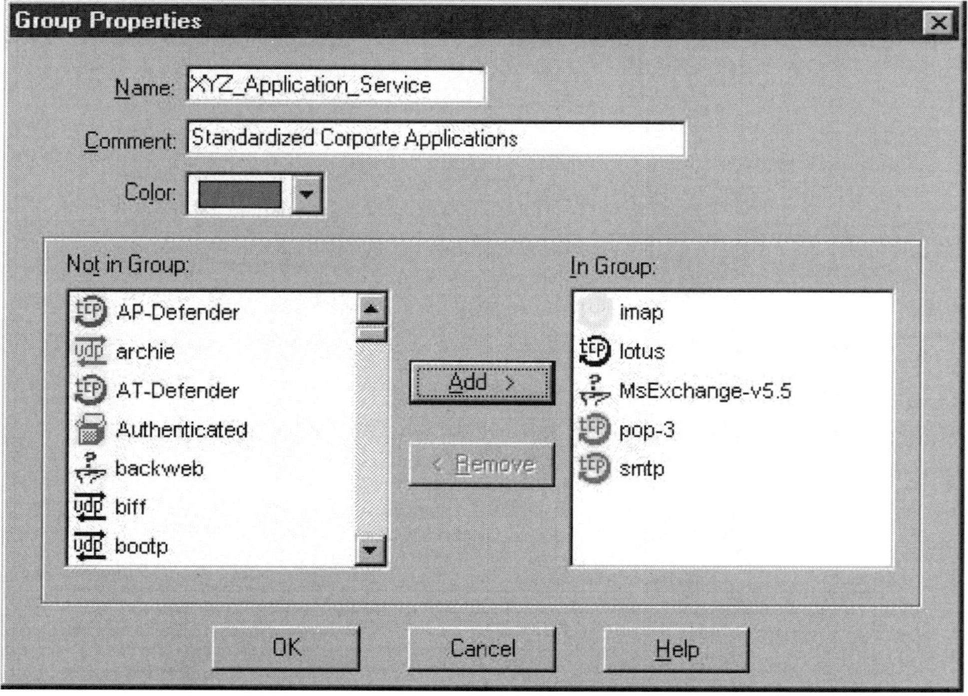

Exhibit 34. Application Service Group

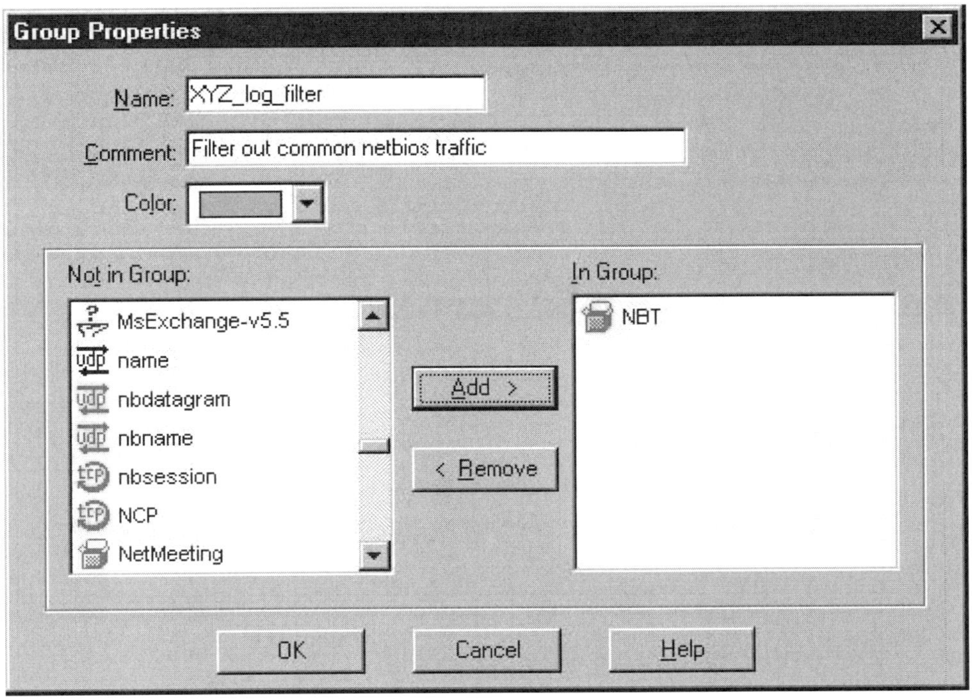

Group Properties

Name: XYZ_log_filter

Comment: Filter out common netbios traffic

Color:

Not in Group:

MsExchange-v5.5
name
nbdatagram
nbname
nbsession
NCP
NetMeeting

Add >

< Remove

In Group:

NBT

OK Cancel Help

Exhibit 35. Filter Service Group

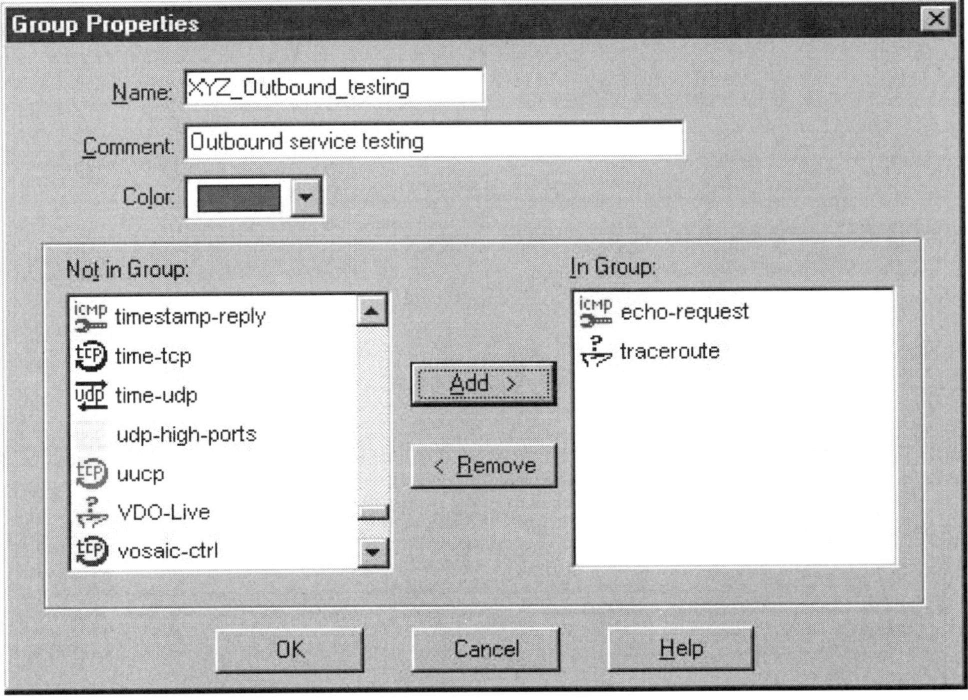

Exhibit 36. Outbound Service Testing Group

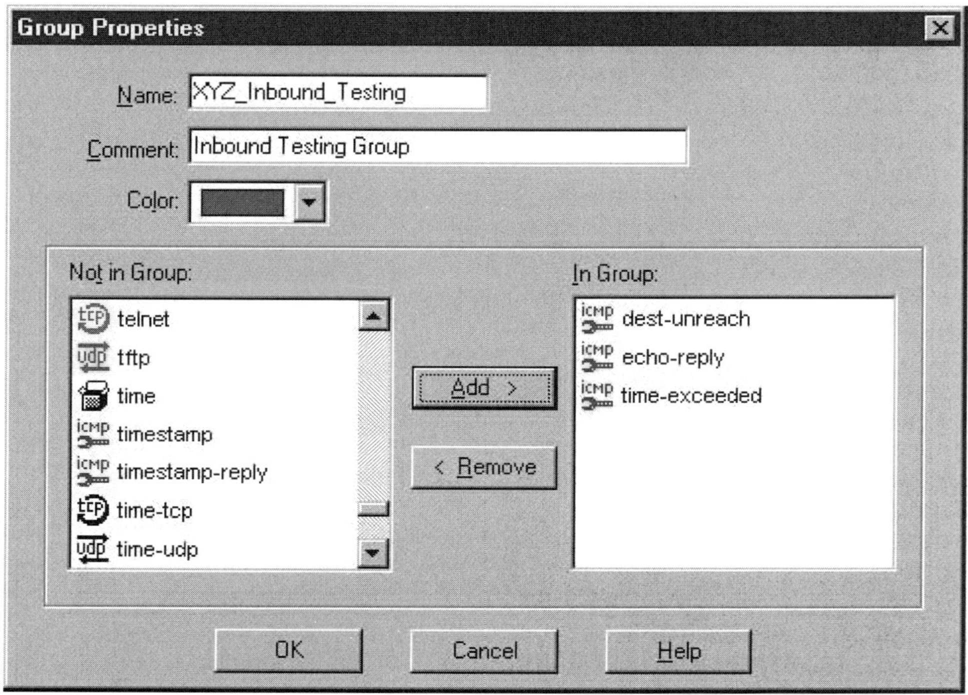

Exhibit 37. Inbound Testing Group

13. Creation of users for each of the above user groups can be accomplished using the same Manage User interface. However, initially one needs to create a new template for the user class. Using the Manage User icon, select the New button and then select the Template option. Set the name for the template, comment, color, and expiry date for users created with this template under the General tab. Under the Groups tab, select the group the users will belong to. Under the Authentication tab, select VPN-1 & FireWall_1 Password. Under the Location tab, select Any for both source and destination. Under the Time tab, select the appropriate settings. Under the Encryption Tab, select IKE for the encryption method. Edit the IKE properties and select Password in the Authentication tab; and under the Encryption tab, select the Encryption and Data Integrity radio button, SHA1 for data integrity and 3DES for the encryption algorithm. Select the Encryption tab to define encryption settings.

Note

Please refer to the following Check Point FireWall-1 manuals for more information on user management: Getting Started Guide, page 217 — Creating Users; Administrators Guide, Chapter 5, page 153 — Managing Users.

---

14. Creating the remote user is done by selecting the Manage menu option and clicking on Manage Users, or one can click on the Manager Users icon. Click on the New button and select RemoteUser. This is the template that was previously created. From the General tab, enter the user name and provide a more descriptive comment for the user if desired. Then select the Authentication tab and enter an eight-character password for the user. Then select the Encryption tab and select the Edit button to enter the encryption password. Note that both the Authentication and Encryption passwords must match or access will be denied to remote users. One will then need to install the user database by selecting the Load option. The user database is automatically installed when one loads the rule base for the firewall.

Note

Refer to the following for more information on user management: Getting Started Guide, page 217 — Creating Users; Administrators Guide, Chapter 5, page 153 — Managing Users.

---

15. Creating the initial rule base for the firewall (Exhibit 38) is accomplished by using either the icon menu bar or the Edit Menus item and selecting Add Rule. Based on the objects that have been created, one can set up a basic rule base to test the functionality of the firewall. Having confirmed that the firewall is operational, one can revisit and tweak the rule base for added security.
    - The first rule will be to set up a log filter for NetBIOS traffic. Set the following options for rule 1:
      Source = Any
      Destination = Any
      Service = XYZ_log_filter
      Action = drop
      Track = leave blank
      Install On = Gateways
      Time = Any
      Comment = Drop and do not log NetBIOS traffic
    - The second rule will be used to filter broadcast traffic.
      Source = Any
      Destination = Broadcast_Filter
      Service = Any
      Action = drop
      Track = leave blank
      Install On = Gateways
      Time = Any
      Comment = Drop and do not log Broadcast traffic
    - The third rule is used to block all communications to the firewall. This is sometimes called the Stealth rule. One uses this rule to hide the firewall from the majority of intruders.
      Source = Any
      Destination = pdfw0001
      Service = Any
      Action = drop
      Track = Long
      Install On = Gateways
      Time = Any
      Comment = Drop all direct communication to the firewall and log it. Listen on FW-1 services only.

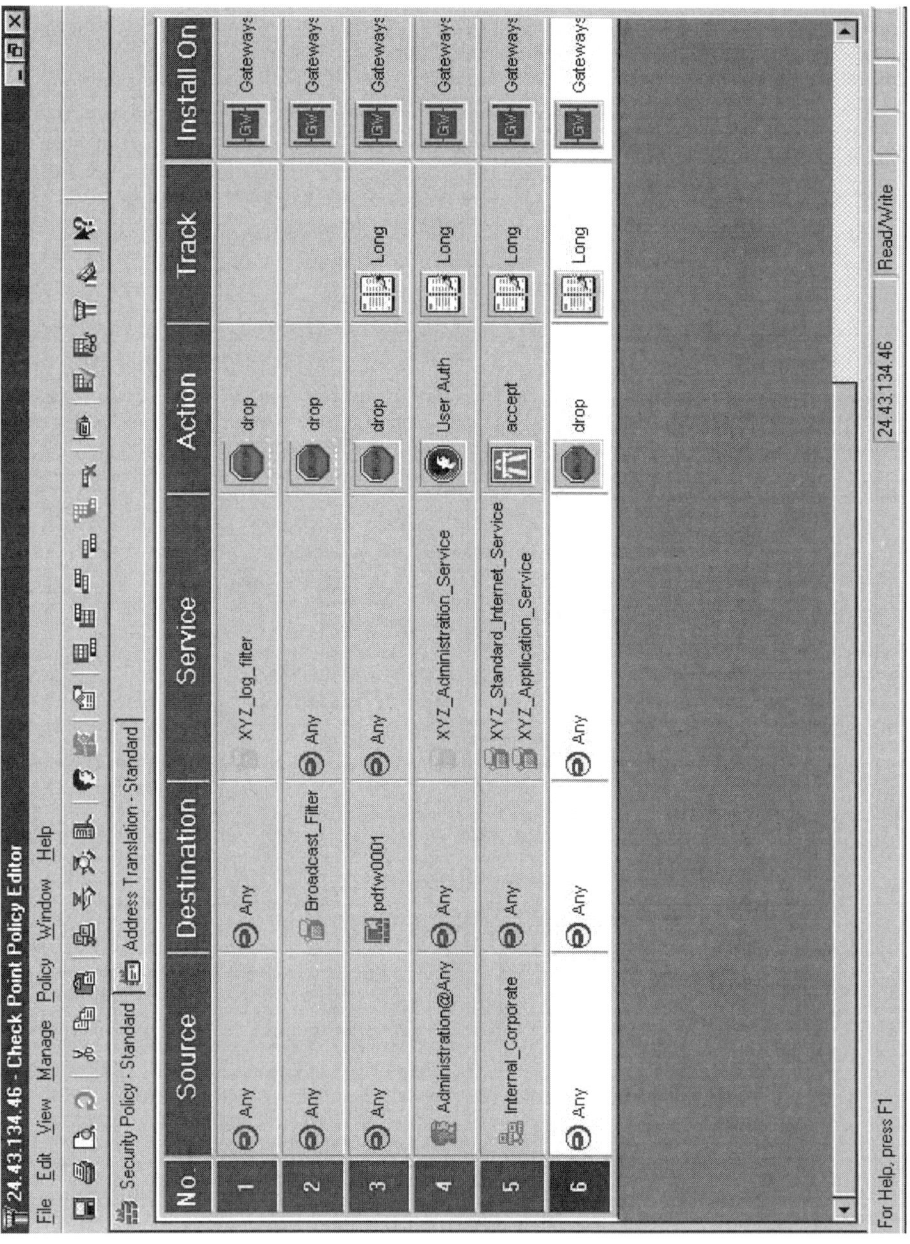

No.	Source	Destination	Service	Action	Track	Install On
1	Any	Any	XYZ_log_filter	drop		Gateways
2	Any	Broadcast_Filter	Any	drop		Gateways
3	Any	pdfw0001	Any	drop	Long	Gateways
4	Administration@Any	Any	XYZ_Administration_Service	User Auth	Long	Gateways
5	Internal_Corporate	Any	XYZ_Standard_Internet_Service XYZ_Application_Service	accept	Long	Gateways
6	Any	Any	Any	drop	Long	Gateways

Exhibit 38. Rule Base without VPN

- The fourth rule is used to restrict access to Telnet and FTP to administrators only. The User Authentication option is used for non-Windows clients. Windows clients can use the Session Authentication client and the action can be set to Session Authentication. If one has a mixed environment, one requires two rules.
  Source = Any
  Destination = Any
  Service = XYZ_Administration_Services
  Action = Drop
  Track = Long
  Install On = Gateways
  Time = Any
  Comment = Admin access to Telnet and FTP
- The fifth rule is used to define allowable services for internal users. These include standard Internet services and also any services that were discovered during an application inventory process.
  Source = Internal_Corporate
  Destination = Any
  Service = XYZ_Standard_Internet_Service
  XYZ_Application_Service
  Action = Accept
  Track = Long
  Install on = Gateways
  Time = Any
  Comment = Authorized services
- Rule six is known as the clean-up rule. It uses drop any service communication that does not fall into any of the other prior rules. It also logs the action to see what people are trying to do to one's firewall.
  Source = Any
  Destination = Any
  Service = Any
  Action = Drop
  Track = Long
  Install on = Gateways
  Time = Any
  Comment = Drop and log unauthorized communications

16. The Network Address Translation (NAT) rules are automatically inserted into the rule base (Exhibit 39). These are set when the interfaces were defined for NAT. The NAT rules basically work out as follows:
    - Any communication within the internal corporate network remains unchanged by the firewall.
    - Any communications that will pass through the firewall to the outside world will be masked by the external IP address of the firewall.

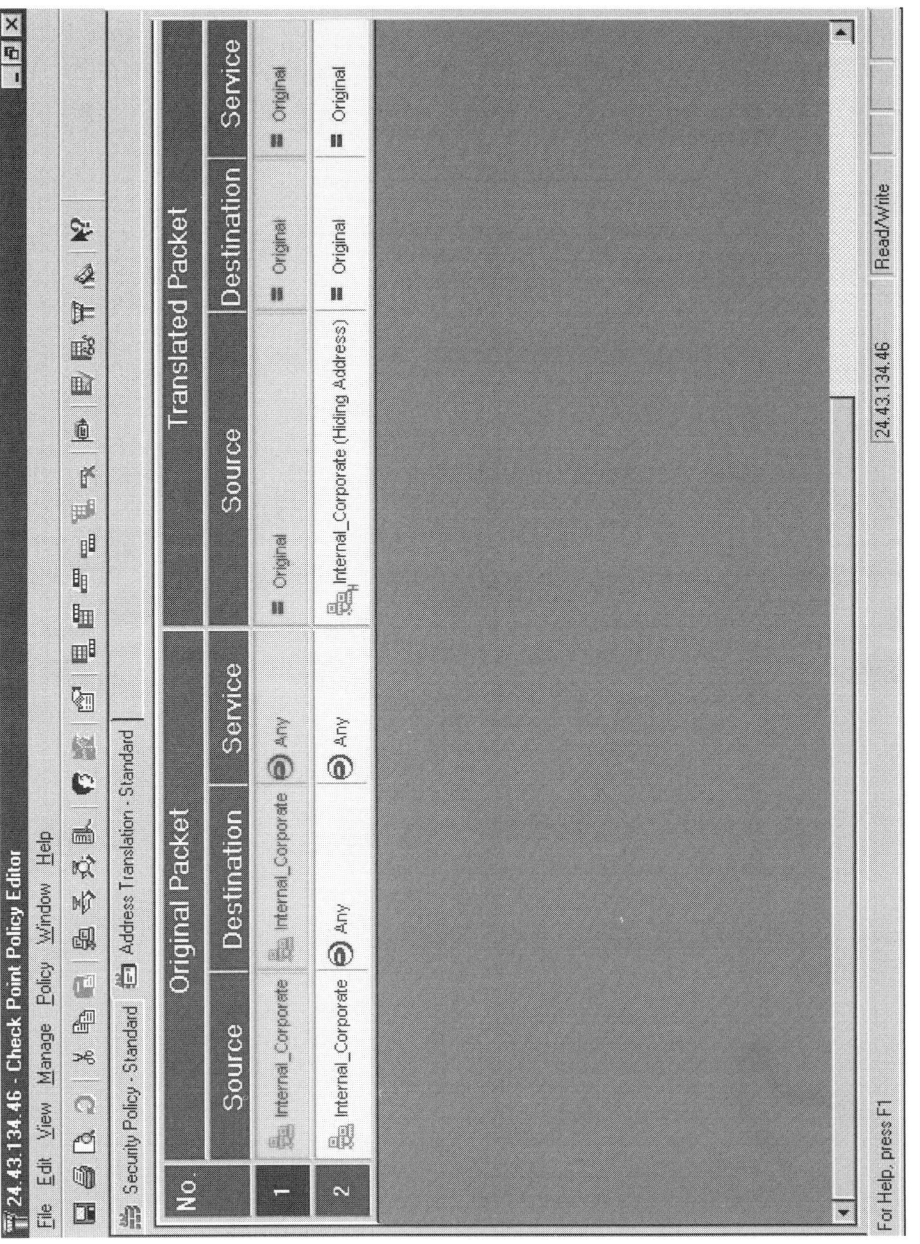

Exhibit 39. NAT Rule Base without VPN

- NAT is necessary only if one is using RFC 1918 addresses for the internal network. Otherwise, NAT is not required. It is highly recommended that one use RFC 1918 class addresses for internal networks because they offer an additional layer of security since they are nonroutable addresses over the Internet.

17. Now that one has a basic rule base, one can load it and test the firewall's functionality. The basic rule base shown here is fine for a dual-homed host, but will not suffice for a multi-homed host scenario. One can begin the rule base installation by selecting Policy from the menu and selecting Install, or by selecting the Install Policy icon from the icon bar.
    - The first message that comes up informs one that address translation is being used. Click the checkbox to prevent further viewing of this dialog in the future. Select OK to continue.
    - The next message that appears informs one that the rule base will contain settings that were defined in the Properties setup (e.g., ICMP and DNS resolution). Click the checkbox to prevent further viewing of this dialog in the future. Select OK to continue.
    - The following window displays where the rule base will be loaded or where the rule base will be applied. In this case, there is only the one firewall, pdfw0001. Select OK to continue.
    - The final message dialog will display a compilation message for the rule base to make sure it is valid and then the installation message. When all is fine and complete, select the Close button to return to the rule base window of the policy editor.
18. Begin testing the rule base.

Configuration for a Multi-Homed Host or DMZ Configuration

For systems that will encapsulate a DMZ, there are a number of changes to the basic rule base that need to take place.

1. First, one needs to create a DMZ network object. This can be done in the same manner as used to create the internal_corporate network object in the previous list, step 5. Set the Name to DMZ and the color of the object to orange.
2. Create an SMTP server definition for the DMZ. This is done as shown before in the previous list, steps 1 and 2. Set the IP address for the object to 10.10.10.zzz and enter a descriptive comment for the object; for example, "Corporate SMTP mail server on DMZ." The only difference with step 2 when defining the NAT rule will be the static IP address that will be used. The address to be used (Exhibit 40) will be from the available pool of static IP addresses that the ISP has assigned.

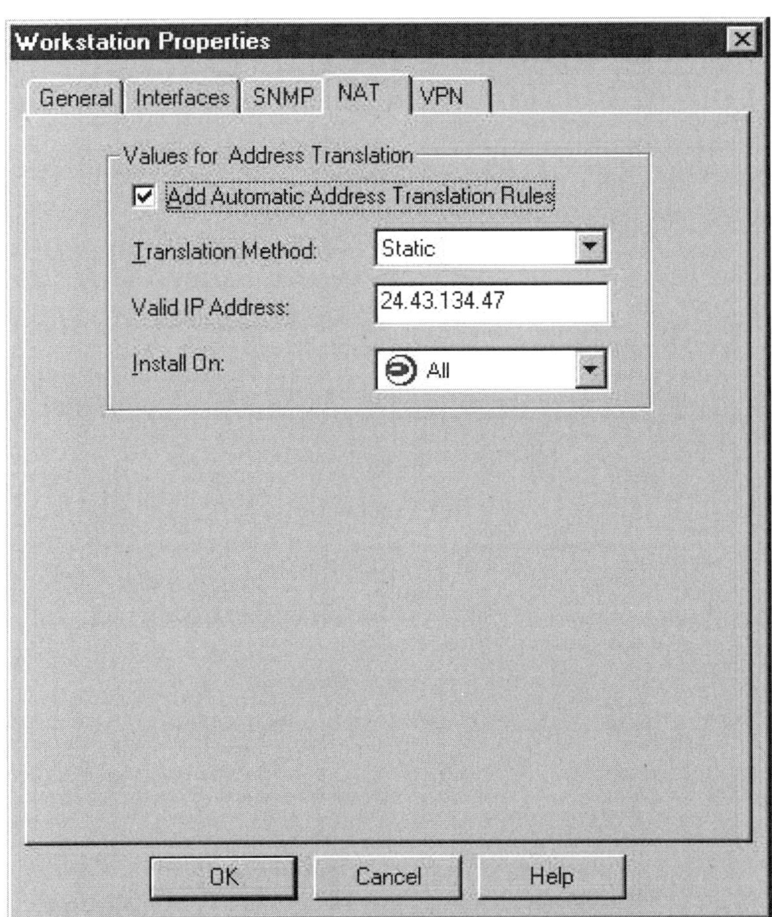

Exhibit 40. DMZ SMTP Server Definition Screen

3. Create an HTTP server definition for the DMZ. This is done as shown before in the previous list, steps 1 and 2. Set the IP address for the object to 10.10.10.zzz and enter a descriptive comment for the object; for example, "Corporate HTTP web server on DMZ." The only difference with step 2 when defining the NAT rule will be the static IP address that will be used. The address to be used (Exhibit 41) will be from the available pool of static IP addresses that the ISP assigned.
4. Next, one needs to create a modified DMZ group object (Exhibit 42) that will be used for anti-spoofing.

As with previous setup instructions, one needs to define the DMZ network objects and then modify the rule base to reflect the DMZ.

The next step to explore is the creation of a point-to-point VPN. We will also define a rule to allow SecuRemote users to gain access to the corporate network by way of the SecuRemote client. Note that to use the SecuRemote product, it will be necessary to contact the vendor from whom the product was purchased and request a SecuRemote license key. Keys are available from 50 to 250 users for the gateway product line.

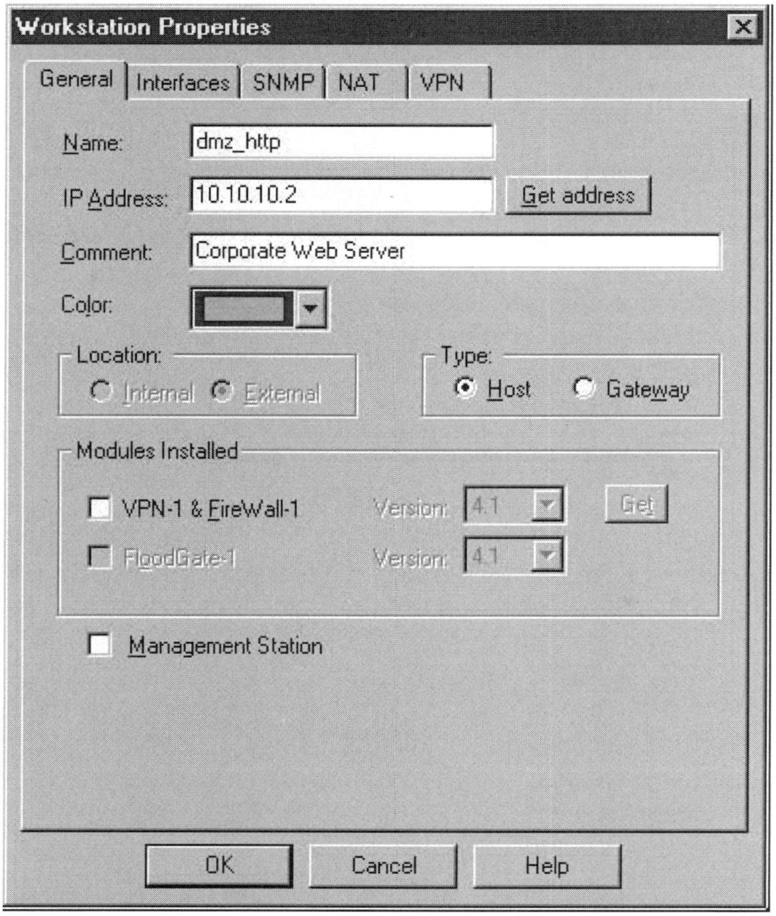

Exhibit 41. DMZ HTTP Server Definition Screen

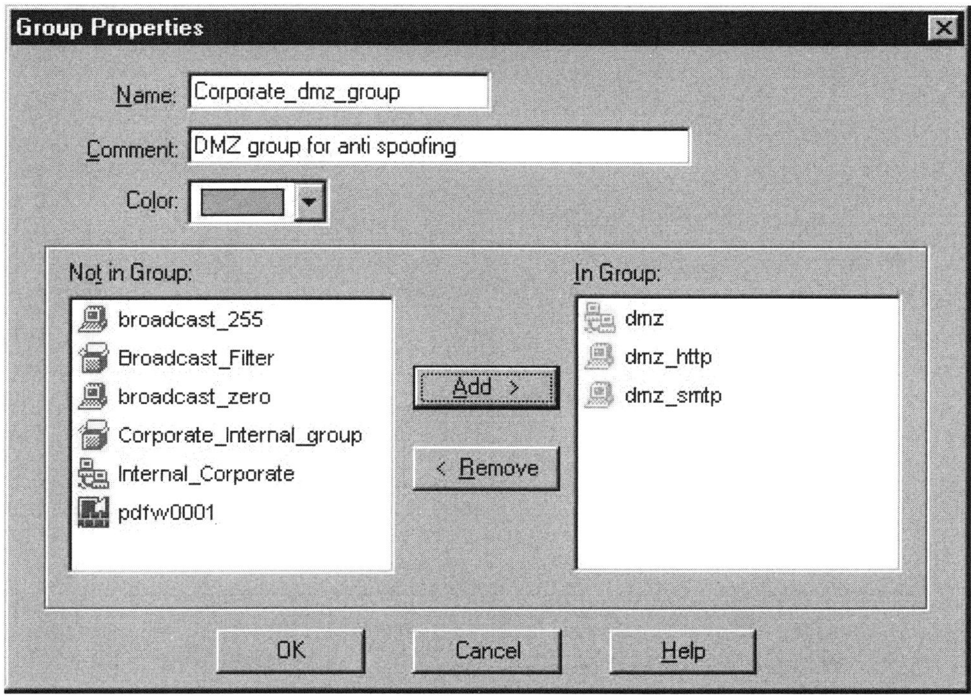

Exhibit 42. Modified DMZ Group for Anti-Spoofing

Defining the VPN

When setting up a VPN for a corporate environment, one has to determine how many sites will comprise the VPN. When determining the number of users per site and the number of subsidiaries and their internal users, the cost of an enterprise license is not that expensive. Check Point licenses its gateway products by the number of IP addresses to be protected behind the firewall. All IP addresses are considered even if they will never use the gateway. An organization's next concern in determining the purchase of an enterprise license will be growth rate. If there are currently two offices, how long will it take before another office will be opened or even if another one is necessary. A small organization with only two offices would not benefit from an enterprise license and may be better off mixing gateway licenses between sites to keep costs to a minimum. One must also consider the management costs. An enterprise license provides the mechanism to manage the entire VPN centrally. A gateway mix requires some rule base entries and accomplishes the same feat. The example will demonstrate a site-to-site VPN between two gateway products. The important difference between a gateway-to-gateway VPN and an enterprise VPN is that the gateways require one to define the other side of the VPN as an external gateway. This is also the way some organizations wish to treat their subsidiary offices. For example, an American organization may have a Canadian subsidiary. However, each office has its own network and operational requirements that differ from each other. The only connection required between the sites is for secure inter-office communications via the VPN over cheap Internet connections:

1. Create the Network object for the external partner network. This will be the internal network of the alternate site. The important items to remember include:
   - Name the object Business_Partner_Network
   - The IP subnet cannot be the same as the internal IP subnet at the local site.
   - The location is external in this case. In addition, there is no need to define NAT for the object.
2. Create the external network object for the external firewall (Exhibits 43, 44, 45). Make sure that the location is set to external. Select the VPN tab, and under the Domain section, select Other; then highlight and accept the Business_Partner_Network object created above. Make sure IKE is the selected encryption scheme. Select Edit to edit the IKE configuration settings. Make sure that both support the same key exchange properties and check the following boxes:
   - Supports Aggressive Mode
   - Support for key exchange for subnets
   - MD5
   - SHA1
   - Pre-Shared Secret

Note 1

During the testing phase, if keys are exchanged properly but an encrypted channel cannot be established, deselect Supports Aggressive Mode and Support for key exchange for subnets. Refer to the Virtual Private Networks manual of the Check Point package, Chapter 14, page 257 — Troubleshooting.

Note 2

The external firewall object IP address here will be the external IP address of the business partners firewall. The Other domain will be the defined Partner external network. The encryption setup must be identical. Any deviation will result in a number of errors.

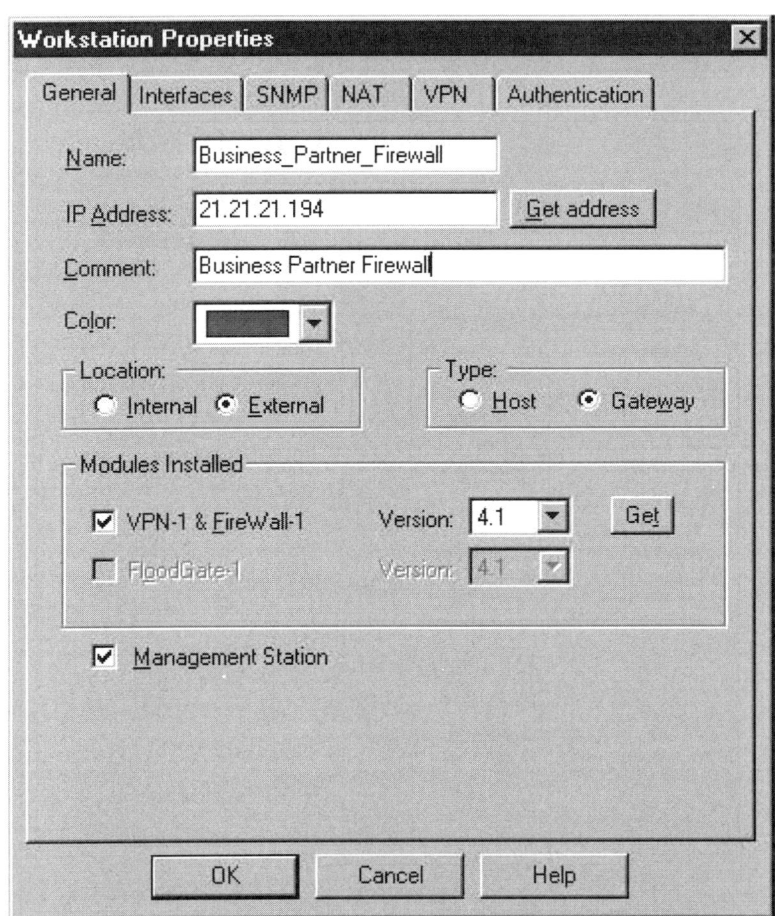

Exhibit 43. Business Partner Firewall Screen 1

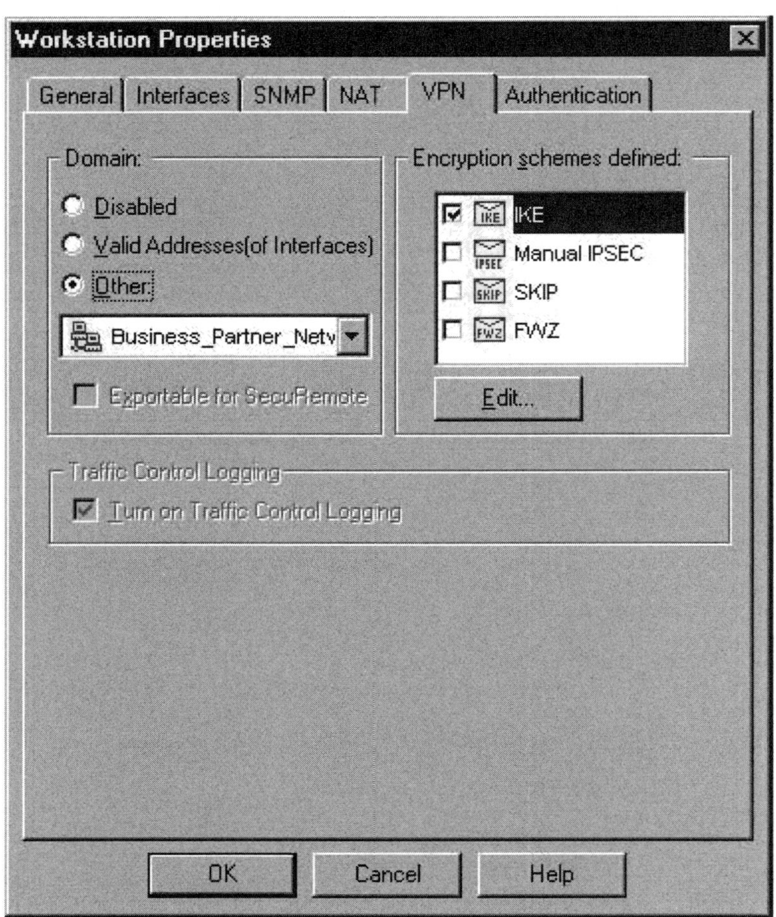

Exhibit 44. Business Partner Firewall Screen 2

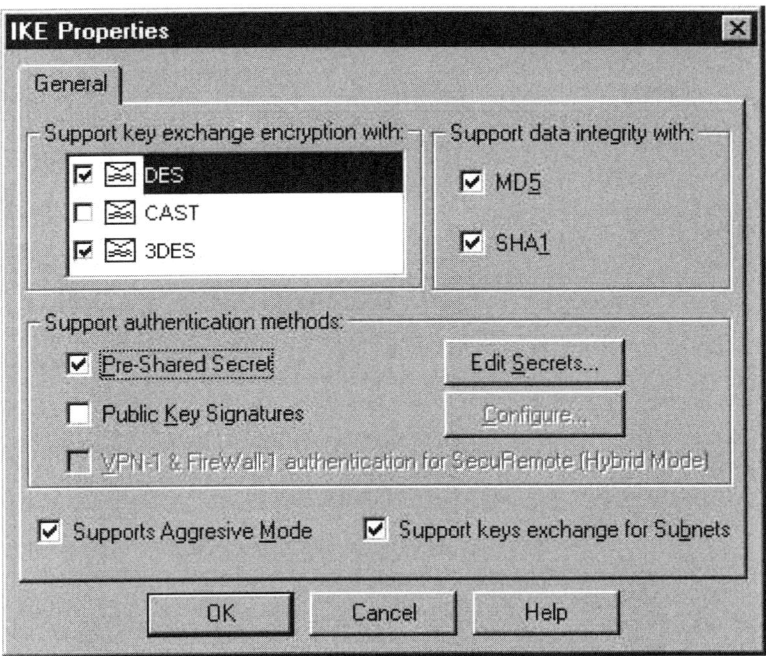

Exhibit 45. Business Partner Firewall Screen 3

3. For each firewall object, one will have to set the secret password that will be used between the firewalls. Select the Edit Secrets button. From the Shared Secret dialog box, select the Edit button. Enter the secret key and select the Set button. Both secret keys must be identical.
4. Next define the security domain for each partner of the VPN. The security domain for the internal domain should include the internal network and the internal firewall. This is known as the internal security domain. Call the object Internal_Security_Domain. The external security domain should include the external network and the external firewall. Call the object Business_Partner_Domain. Open the Firewall object and select the VPN tab to modify the Domain selection. In the Domain section, select the radio button corresponding to the option Other. Highlight and select the object Internal_Security_Domain. This now needs to be completed on the partner firewall also. The only difference is that the roles are reversed.
5. Define the VPN rules for the VPN Partners (see Exhibit 46). There are two rules that comprise the VPN when there are only two hosts involved: one rule to "encrypt to" and one rule to "decrypt from." The VPN rules must be placed at the top of the rule base before any Stealth rule. If they are placed after the Stealth rule, traffic will be dropped. In the example, the rule base also shows a rule defined for SecuRemote client access. Remote User Client setup is defined in the next section. Refer to Chapters 11 and 12 of the Virtual Private Networks manual for additional information on SecuRemote client setup. Set the following rules for each site:
   - Rule 1:
     Source = Internal_Security_Domain
     Destination = Business_Partner_Domain
     Service = Any
     Action = Encrypt
     Track = Long
     Comment = Channel to partner
   - Rule 2:
     Source = Business_Partner_Domain
     Destination = Internal_Security_Domain
     Service = Any
     Action = Encrypt
     Track = Long
     Comment = Channel from partner
   - For each rule, the Encrypt action must be edited and both must be identical. The encryption properties must be set to IKE. Select the Edit button to set additonal IKE properties:
     Transform should be set to Encryption + Data Integrity (ESP)
     Encryption algorithm = 3DES
     Data integrity = MD5
     Allowed peer gateway = Any
     Use Perfect Forward Secrecy

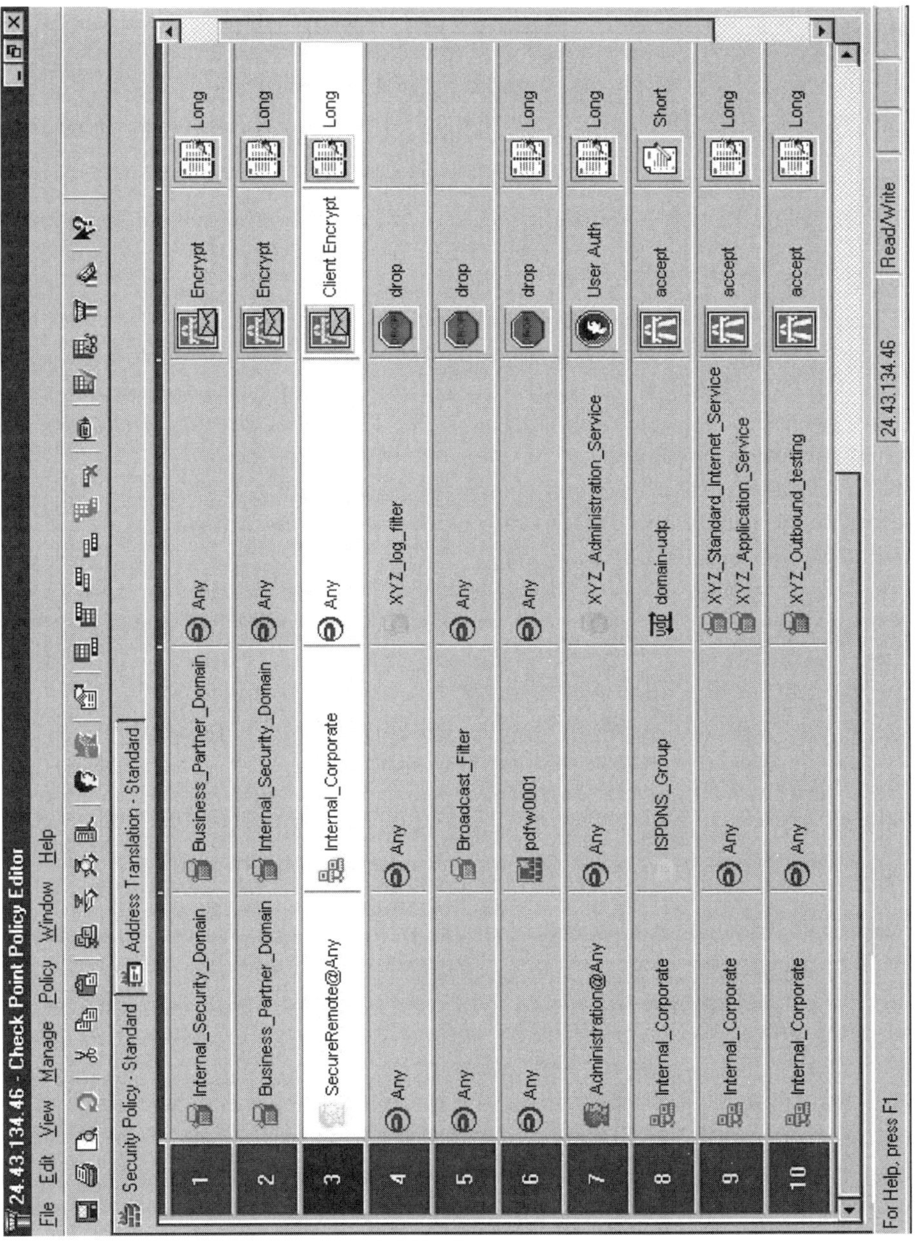

Exhibit 46. Business Partner Firewall Screen Rule Base 9

6. Test the VPN by trying to access a system on the partner network; for example, open a Telnet session to the Partner network (Exhibits 47 and 48).

SecuRemote

Setting up access for SecuRemote requires the setup of remote users in the user database and a rule to allow remote users to access the protected network resources.

1. The installation of the SecuRemote SP4 Client software will be launched from the CD-ROM that was previously created. The first screen is the License screen. Select the OK button to continue. Select the Next button to continue with the installation.
2. When prompted for the default path Installation, keep the default and select the OK button. If one is upgrading client software, select the radio button corresponding to Upgrade. One will see the installation statistics being displayed.
3. Select Install Desktop Security Support and select the Next button.
4. Select Yes to view the *readme* file; otherwise, select No.
5. Select Yes to restart the machine.
6. On system reboot, run the SecuRemote Client.
7. From the Sites menu option, select Create Site or click on the New Site icon. Enter a name for the new site and enter the IP address of the site.
8. The SecuRemote Client will attempt to make a connection.
9. When the connection is successful, one will be prompted to save the site information by selecting the OK button.
10. The SecuRemote Logon screen will appear whenever one tries to access a protected resource on the remote network. All traffic between the client and the firewall is encrypted to ensure data integrity.

Once testing has verified that the operational characteristics of the firewall match one's requirements, it is possible to begin further tweaking and securing of the system. These options are left to the user to decide if they are necessary at this point. If one runs a port scanner against the firewall (Exhibit 49), one can see that it is not listening to very much. The few ports that are open are secured firewall ports. The usual insecure ports of the native Windows NT environment are now secure. The service descriptions for ports 258, 264, and 265 are incorrect because the services file that maps ports to services needs to be manually modified for the machine performing the port scan. Refer to Exhibit 69 for the actual service descriptions.

11Aug2001	20:55:54	dae...	pdfw0001	log	key install		pdfw0001	Business_Partner...		
11Aug2001	20:55:54	dae...	pdfw0001	log	key install		pdfw0001	Business_Partner...	ip	0
11Aug2001	20:56:00	dae...	pdfw0001	log	key install		pdfw0001	Business_Partner...	ip	0
11Aug2001	20:56:00	dae...	pdfw0001	log	encrypt	telnet	pdfw0001	192.168.3.58	tcp	2

Exhibit 47. Internal Firewall Telnet Encryption

2076	11Aug2001	21:01:43	dae...	firewall	log	key install		firewall_external	firewall	
2077	11Aug2001	21:01:43	dae...	firewall	log	key install		firewall_external	firewall	ip
2078	11Aug2001	21:01:50	dae...	firewall	log	key install		firewall_external	firewall	ip
2079	11Aug2001	21:01:50	dae...	firewall	log	decrypt	telnet	firewall_external	csx1	tcp

Exhibit 48. External Firewall Telnet Decryption

Exhibit 49. NMAP Port Scan of a Fully Configured NT 4.0 Check Point FireWall-1 System[3]

```
# Nmap (V. nmap) scan initiated 2.53 as: nmap -v -sS -O -P0 -p1-
65535 -o pdfw0001.txt 24.43.134.46
Interesting ports on PDFW0001 (24.43.134.46):
(The 65530 ports scanned but not shown below are in state: filtered)
Port      State     Service
139/tcp   closed    netbios-ssn
258/tcp   open      yak-chat
264/tcp   open      bgmp
265/tcp   open      unknown
500/tcp   closed    isakmp

TCP Sequence Prediction: Class=random positive increments
                         Difficulty=18246 (Worthy challenge)

Sequence numbers: A224BCDB A2254360 A225E41E A2272920 A227B49A A2288FD6
Remote operating system guess: Microsoft NT 4.0 Server SP5 + 2047
Hotfixes

# Nmap run completed at Thu Aug 09 23:15:28 2001 -- 1 IP address (1
host up) scanned in 5721 seconds
```

Windows 2000 Server Setup, Installation, and Configuration for Check Point FireWall-1/VPN-1

To set up Check Point FireWall-1 on a Windows 2000 server, one will need to download the Windows 2000 SP2 software package from the Check Point Web site (www.checkpoint.com/download). A valid user id and password are required to access this site. To gain access to the site, one must purchase a software subscription for the product.

Windows 2000 has an installation process similar to Windows NT. They both require three phases for installation, setup, and configuration. The first phase is the text mode driver phase (see Exhibit 50). The second phase is the GUI installation and configuration phase; the third phase is the initial configuration phase.

The Windows 2000 Check Point SP2 installation process is:

Exhibit 50. Windows 2000 Server Installation Notes: Phase 1

1. Place the diskette titled Windows 2000 Advanced Server Boot Disk 1 into the floppy drive of the machine (Drive A:).
2. Power up the system.
3. The following message will be displayed as the system boots from the floppy diskette.
   ```
   Setup is inspecting your computers hardware configuration...
   ```
4. Then the screen will go blue and a status bar will appear on the bottom of the screen. The following messages will be displayed on the status bar prior to the final display of screen two.
   ```
   Press F6 if you need to install a third party SCSI or RAID
   Driver...
   Setup is loading files (Machine Identification Data)...
   Setup is loading files (Windows 2000 Executive)...

   Windows 2000 Setup
   ==================
   Please insert the disk labeled Windows 2000 Advanced Server
   Setup Disk #2 into Drive A:
   * Press ENTER When ready.
   ENTER=Continue F3=Quit
   ```
5. Place the diskette titled Windows 2000 Advanced Server Setup Disk 2 into the floppy drive and press the Enter key to continue the installation process. After pressing the Enter key, the status line at the bottom of the screen will display a series of messages as follows:
   ```
   Please wait...
   Setup is loading files (Driver Files)...

   Windows 2000 Setup
   ==================
   Please insert the disk labeled Windows 2000 Advanced Server
   Setup Disk #3 into Drive A:
   * Press ENTER When ready.
   ENTER=Continue F3=Quit
   ```

6. Place the diskette titled Windows 2000 Advanced Server Setup Disk 3 into the floppy drive and press the Enter key to continue the installation process. After pressing the Enter key, the status line at the bottom of the screen will display a series of messages as follows:

```
Please wait...
Setup is loading files (Driver Files)...
```

7. Place the Diskette titled Windows 2000 Advanced Server Setup Disk 4 into the floppy drive and press the Enter key to continue the installation process. After pressing the Enter key, the status line at the bottom of the screen will display a series of messages as follows:

```
Please wait...
Setup is loading files (Driver files)...

Setup is Starting Windows 2000
Processing Information File...

Windows 2000 Setup
==================
Please insert the disk labeled Windows 2000 Advanced Server
Setup Disk #4 into Drive A:
* Press ENTER When ready.
ENTER=Continue F3=Quit
```

8. Press the ENTER key to continue.

```
Windows 2000 Setup
==================
Welcome to Setup.
This portion of the setup program prepares Microsoft Windows
2000(TM) to run on your computer.
To set up Windows 2000 now, press Enter
To repair a Windows 2000 installation, press R.
To quit Setup without installing Windows 2000, press F3.
 ENTER=Continue R=Repair F3=Quit
```

9. Press the Enter key to continue.

```
Windows 2000 Setup
==================
Insert the CD labeled: Windows 2000 Advanced Server CD-ROM into
your CD-ROM drive.
* Press ENTER When ready.
F3=Quit ENTER=Continue
```

10. Once you place the Windows 2000 Server CD-ROM into the CD-ROM drive, the following screen will be displayed.

```
Windows 2000 Server Setup
=========================
Setup has determined that your computer's startup hard disk is
new or has been erased, or that your computer is running an
operating system that is incompatable with Windows 2000.
If the hard disk is new or has been erased, or if you want to
discard its current contents, you can choose to continue Setup.
```

```
If your computer system is running an operating system that is
incompatable with Windows 2000, Continuing Setup may damage or
destroy the existing operating system.
To continue Setup, press C.
CAUTION: Any data currently on your computer's hard disk will
be lost.
To quit Setup, press F3.
C=Continue Setup F3=Quit
```

11. Press C to continue with the installation of Windows 2000 Server.

```
Windows 2000 Licensing Agreement
================================
********************************************
END-USER LICENSE AGREEMENT SERVER LICENSE FOR
MICROSOFT WINDOWS 2000 SERVER PRODUCTS
********************************************

IMPORTANT READ CAREFULLY: This Microsoft End-User License Agree-
ment ("EULA") is a legal agreement between you ...
                .
                .
                .
...lowing rights to the Server Software and Client Software
F8=I agree    ESC=I do not agree    PAGE DOWN=Next Page
```

12. The License Agreement screen is then displayed. Press function key F8 to continue with the installation and accept the terms of the license agreement.
13. The next screen will allow one to select and create a partition on a selected hard disk within the computer.

```
Windows 2000 Server Setup
=========================
The following list shows the existing partitions and unpartitioned
space on this computer.
Use the UP and DOWN arrow keys to select an item in the list.
To setup Windows 2000 on the selected item, press Enter.
To create a partition in the unpartitioned space, press C.
To delete the selected partition, press D.
 xxxx MB Disk 0 at Id 1 on bus 0 on aic78xx
      Unpartitioned space xxxx MB
 ENTER=Install    C=Create Partition    F3=Quit
```

14. Select the partition that you want to install the operating system on and press C to continue.

```
Windows NT Server Setup
=======================
You asked setup to create a new partition on XXXX MB Disk 0 at
Id 0 on Bus 0 on aic78xx.
To create a new partition, enter a size below and press Enter.
To go back to the previous screen without creating the partition,
press ESC.
 The minimum size for the new partition is 8 megabytes (MB).
 The maximum size for the new partition is XXXX megabytes (MB).
```

```
Create partition of size (in MB): XXXX
ENTER=Create ESC=Cancel
```

15. Specify the size of the partition you wish to create and press Enter to create the partition.

```
Windows 2000 Server Setup
=========================
The following list shows the existing partitions and unparti-
tioned space on this computer.
Use the UP and DOWN arrow keys to select an item in the list.
To setup Windows 2000 on the selected item, press Enter.
To create a partition in the unpartitioned space, press C.
To delete the selected partition, press D.
xxxx MB Disk 0 at Id 1 on bus 0 on aic78xx
     C: New Unformatted) xxxx MB
ENTER=Install    D=Delete Partition    F3=Quit
```

16. Press the Enter key to install.

```
Windows 2000 Server Setup
=========================
The partition you selected is not formatted. Setup will now
format the partition.
Use the UP and DOWN arrow keys to select the file system you
want and then press Enter.
If you want to select a different partition for Windows 2000,
press ESC.
Format the partition using the FAT file system
Format the partition using the NTFS file system
ENTER=Continue ESC=Cancel
```

17. Format the partition using the NTFS file system.

```
Windows NT Server Setup
=======================
Please wait while Setup formats the partition
 C: New (Unformatted) XXXX MB
 on XXXX MB Disk 0 at Id 1 on bus 0 on aic78xx.
```

18. Wait while the disk is formatted. The system will automatically reboot and the GUI installation process will begin.

Exhibit 51. Windows 2000 Server Installation Notes: Phase 2

1. Once the system reboots and comes back up, one will be greeted with the GUI Windows 2000 Setup screen. Wait while the interface comes up.
2. Set the regional settings for the system; otherwise, accept the defaults and select the Next button.
3. When prompted, enter the name and organization for the new system. For example, an abbreviation can be used for the name of the organization in the Name field and the full organization name can be placed in the Organization field.
4. Enter the registration number for the software to activate it. Without a proper registration key, the software will not allow one to continue with the installation. The registration code can be found on the back of the CD jewel case.
5. Select either per seat or per server licensing mode. If one selects per server mode, one must have purchased the required license.
6. Enter the computer name that will be used to identify the system on the network (i.e., we will follow the same guidelines as with the Windows NT 4.0 installation process, PDFW0001).
7. When the default installation components for Windows 2000 Server screen comes up, one should select each component area and deselect all their attributes. We do not want to install any of these additional items on the firewall. The only selection one may wish to retain is for the standard screen savers. Once done, press the Next button to continue with the installation.
8. The Windows 2000 installation will prompt for Date and Time settings. Select the correct values for your location. Select Next to continue with the installation process. The system will display a Network Settings progress information screen. Wait while this process completes.
9. Once the Network Settings screen is displayed, select the Custom Settings radio button; typical is the default setting.
10. For each network adapter in the system, disable the File and Printer Sharing option. Then highlight the TCP/IP options and set the networking parameters. As a guide, use the settings established by the ISP for the external adapter and refer to the sample settings used during the Windows NT 4.0 example as a guide for internal and DMZ network settings.
11. When prompted for a workgroup name, select a name that is not currently utilized by any of your production environments. The use of a cryptic name is usually the best choice. Select the Next button to continue with the installation.
12. The next screen will display the final installation process task list. When each of the processes is complete, one must select the Finish button and allow the system to reboot.

Exhibit 52. Windows 2000 Server Installation Notes: Phase 3

1. The first time one logs on to the server, one is greeted by an installation Wizard. Select the radio button "I will configure this server later" and select the Next button. On the next Wizard screen, uncheck the box "show this screen at startup." Open up a command prompt and test the network connectivity. A good test to know that routing is working is to ping an address that lies outside the external NIC interface. Because one is building this system in a lab environment, this will most likely be a router address.
2. Once everything seems to be in working order, place the copy of the Windows 2000 Service Pack 2 CD-ROM that was burned into the CD-ROM drive of the machine and run the Service Pack 2 update. When prompted, reboot the machine.
3. Upon logging on to the system, one can begin to tailor the environment to one's own liking.

Once the Windows 2000 Server is up and patched, one needs to retrieve the Windows 2000 version of the Check Point Service Pack 2 for FireWall-1/VPN-1. This is necessary. The Standard Check Point Service Pack 2 CD-ROM does not contain a build for Windows 2000, nor can one install the NT version from that CD-ROM onto a Windows 2000 system. Doing so will result in the blue screen of death when the system tries to load *fw.sys*. The correct procedures for setting up a Windows 2000 server are as follows:

1. Install Windows 2000 SP2 (downloaded from the Check Point Web site).
2. Install the GUI clients from the Enterprise suite 4.1.2 CD-ROM.
3. Install SP4 for Windows 2000.
4. Install SP4 GUI clients.
5. Apply the SP4 Hot Fix.

The items listed in procedures 1, 3, 4, and 5 are all downloadable from the Check Point Web site if one has a software subscription The following installation procedures assume that you have already downloaded the software from the Check Point Web site and burned a CD-ROM with the service packs.

---

1. Navigate the burned CD-ROM to find the Setup application for the Windows 2000 version of FW-1/VPN-1 SP2. Run the Setup application. The install Wizard will load up and one will be prompted to accept the license agreement. Select Yes to continue. Then select the Next button to continue.
2. At the Selecting Setup Type screen, select the installation type you wish to install. Standalone is for gateway products; Distributed is only for enterprise products. Select Next to continue with the installation. When prompted for the license type, select the radio button that matches the

purchased license type. Then press the Next button to continue with the installation.

3. When prompted for the destination location, leave the defaults as they are. Select the Next button to continue. The installation statistics will come up; wait for the product to finish installing. Once completed, the Check Point configuration application will automatically be launched.
4. The licenses one has will need to be registered on the Check Point Web site before one can proceed with the installation. It is assumed that the product(s) purchased have been licensed. If not, register them at https://usercenter.checkpoint.com/home3/index.jsp. It usually takes a couple of days for a license key to be generated. It is best to perform this function as soon as one takes receipt of the software package. Select the Add button to open the Add License dialog. Select the Fetch from File button to retrieve a license. Then Select the Get Validation Code button to retrieve the validation code. Select OK. Repeat this process for as many product licenses as have been purchased. When complete, select the Next button to continue with the installation process.
5. Next, one is prompted to enter an administrative user for the system. Select the Add button to open up the Add Administrator dialog. Enter the Administrator name and password. Then select the OK button, and then the Next button to continue with the installation process.

Note

This section is used to set up and configure multi-level concurrent access to the firewall management console. It is possible to assign various access levels to administrators and operators. Only one administrator with write privileges is allowed access to the console at any one time. A second administrator with write privileges will be warned that the console is already accessed in write mode and will only be available in read-only mode.

---

6. The next screen will prompt one for the external IP address of the firewall. Enter the desired IP address. Then select the Next button to continue with the installation process.
7. Next, one is required to add any GUI client IP addresses that will be managing the system. Type in the IP address of the machines that will act as GUI interfaces to the management console. When done, select the Next button to continue with the installation process.
8. One is required to enter the device name of the external network interface card of the machine. One can retrieve the device name by issuing a *route print* command. Then enter the value and select the

next button to continue with the installation. Note that the name must be entered exactly as displayed; otherwise, when it comes time to performing a policy load, one will get a warning message regarding the interface. In addition, one will also see similar behavior to that outlined in the Check Point FireWall-1 Installation Process, step 14.

9. When prompted for IP Forwarding, select the radio button to control IP forwarding. Then select the Next button to continue with the installation.
10. The final task is to perform a keyboard run to generate a random cryptographic key for the FW-1/VPN-1 system. When complete, select the Finish key to continue. The next screen will prompt the reboot now or reboot later. It is recommended to reboot now before proceeding further with the installation.

The Check Point Client Software Installation from the 4.1.2 Enterprise CD-ROM is:

1. Place the Check Point CD-ROM into the CD-ROM drive of the firewall machine. If the Auto Run feature is still enabled, the Check Point 2000 screen will be displayed. Exit from this installation screen. See Exhibit 52 for details regarding the error that occurs from this installation interface. Using the explorer, navigate to the \Windows\CPMgmtClnt-41 directory on the CD-ROM and run the setup application. The Setup Wizard dialog box will appear briefly.
2. The Check Point Management Client 4.1 Welcome installation screen will appear. Select the Next button to continue with the installation of the management clients.
3. The Check Point Choose Destination Location screen will appear next. Select the default location path for the management clients.
4. Next, one will be prompted for component selection. By default, all items except the real-time monitor are selected for installation. If desired, one also can deselect System Status.
5. The final screen displays the progress statistics for the installation of the software. Once done, the management clients will be installed on the machine. A final message will appear informing you that you can now run the client software.

If one attempts to install the GUI Clients from the Enterprise 4.1.2 CD-ROM by way of the Auto Run, the Check Point 2000 Installation Interface does not know how to handle the Windows 2000 Operating System and will error out during the process.

The default Check Point 2000 Automatic Installation Interface (Exhibit 53) cannot identify the Windows 2000 Operating System properly. Because of this, attempting to install the client software from the CD-ROM will result in an error that will terminate the installation process.

Before one can install the Service Pack 4 upgrade from Check Point, one must shut down the FireWall-1/VPN-1 service. This can be done manually

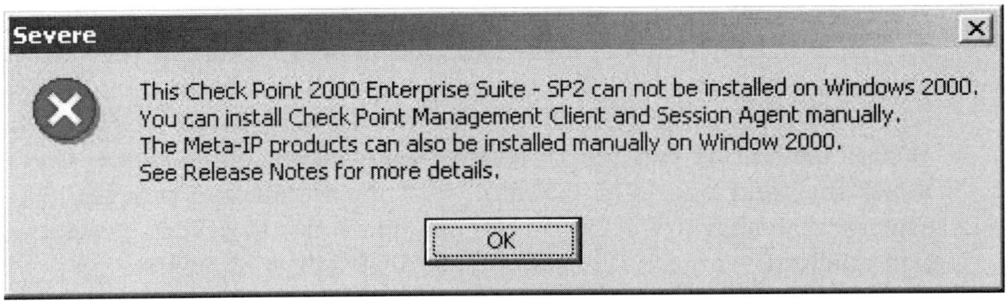

Exhibit 53. CD-ROM GUI Client Installation

from the command prompt by issuing a *c:\winnt\fw1\4.1\bin\fw stop* command or from the Windows 2000 Service Monitor.

To stop the FireWall-1/VPN-1 service:

1. Before the Check Point Service Pack 4 update can be applied for the Server software, the FireWall-1/VPN-1 service must be shut down. The following steps detail the shutdown process:
   - Select the Start button, Programs, Administrative Tools, Services icon.
   - Locate the CheckPoint FireWall-1 service and right-click on the service.
   - Select the Stop button to stop the service. Wait for the service to stop.
   - Verify that the service status is stopped. Then press OK to close the properties window for the FireWall-1 service.
2. One can now continue with the SP4 Server software installation process.

To install Service Pack 4 for Check Point FireWall-1:

1. Disable the FireWall-1 service before applying SP4. This can be done by opening the Windows 2000 service control manager and stopping the FireWall-1 service. Place the Check Point SP4 CD-ROM, created by downloading the patch from the Check Point site, into the CD-ROM drive of the firewall machine. Using the explorer, navigate to the directory on the CD-ROM where the files were burned and run the setup application. The Setup Wizard dialog box will appear briefly, followed by the Welcome screen. Press the Enter key to continue with the installation.
2. The next screen displayed will be the License screen. Select Yes to continue with the installation process and begin installation of the software upgrade. The Statistics installation screen will display the progress of the update.
3. When the software has been installed, one will be prompted to reboot the machine. Select Yes to continue. A message will appear stating that the setup of the software will be completed after the system reboots.

To install Service Pack 4 for the GUI Clients:

1. Place the Check Point SP4 CD-ROM, created when by downloading the patch from Check Point site, into the CD-ROM drive of the firewall machine. Using the explorer, navigate to the directory on the CD-ROM where the files were burned and run the setup application. The Setup Wizard dialog box will appear briefly, followed by the Welcome screen. Select the Next button to continue with the installation process.
2. The License screen will be displayed. Select Yes to accept the license and continue with the installation. The Installation Statistics screen will appear next. Wait until the product is fully installed.
3. The final screen informs one that the process is complete. Press Finish to exit the GUI Clients installation update.

To apply the SP4 Hot Fix:

1. Once the Check Point FireWall-1/VPN-1 4.1 Service Pack 4 installation is complete, one can apply the SP4 Hot Fix. This process does require that the FireWall-1 service be shut down in order for the hot fix to be applied when the service restarts.
2. Copy and place the *crypt.def* and *table.def* files of the SP4 Hot Fix patch into the C:\winnt\fw1\41\lib directory.
   - Rename the existing *crypt.def* and *table.def* files with an extension of *bak* or with an extension that denotes the original patch level (e.g., *sp2*).
   - Copy the new *sp4* file definitions from the burned CD-ROM into the lib directory.
   - For more information, refer to the Check Point SP4 Hot Fix documentation. Once these files have been copied to their destination, one can restart the FireWall-1 service.

To restart FireWall-1/VPN-1 service:

1. After the Check Point Service Pack 4 update has been applied for the server software, the FireWall-1/VPN-1 service must be restarted. The following steps graphically detail the start-up process:
   - Select the Start button, Programs, Administrative Tools, Services icon.
   - Locate the Check Point FireWall-1 service and right-click on the service.
   - Select the Start button to start the service. Wait for the service to start.
   - Verify that the service status is started. Then press OK to close the properties window for the FireWall-1 service.
   - One can now continue to verify that SP4 has been properly applied to the server by issuing an *fw ver –k* command.
   - The output of the command should yield a build number of 41862.

Configuring Check Point FireWall-1/VPN-1 for Windows 2000

The configuration process for Check Point FireWall-1 on Windows 2000 is actually the same as that for Windows NT Server 4.0. The only real differences between the two are the graphical details that differentiate the two platforms. However, the configuration process on Windows 2000 is discussed here for consistency purposes.

Note

Prior to SP4, Local.arp functionality was not supported. A workaround exists; however, it is highly recommended thatSP4 be used to bypass this issue.

This configuration process will assume a multi-homed firewall consisting of three network interface cards: one for the external network, one for the DMZ, and one for the internal network. If one plans to perform an upgrade from Windows NT to Windows 2000, check to make sure that all peripheral devices are supported under Windows 2000 before proceeding with the upgrade. The network interface card that was used as the internal network interface in the Windows NT Server 4.0 installation is not compatible with Windows 2000. Always check to make sure the hardware is compatible before beginning a monumental task such as an upgrade on an existing production machine. It is highly recommended that a new machine be purchased for migration to Windows 2000 and Check Point FireWall-1 SP4 rather than risk unnecessary downtime.

1. Run the Policy Editor 4.1 application from the Start, Programs, Check Point Management Clients menu. Select either the Manage Menu item and then select Network Objects, or select the Manage Network Objects icon from the graphical menu bar. From the Network Objects dialog, one can begin defining objects that make up the computing environment. Select Workstation to begin the creation of a workstation object.
2. The first object to define is the firewall object. Set the following fields in the General tab of the workstation object (Exhibit 54) to the required values.
   - Name = the system name (PDF0001). It should also be defined in the host table under \etc directory. It is added by default by the Check Point installation process, but always check to make sure the entry exists, just in case.
   - IP Address = the external IP address of the firewall

- Comment = place a good descriptive comment in this field
- Select the following radio buttons:
  Location = Internal
  Type = Gateway
  VPN-1 & FireWall-1
  Version 4.1
- Management Station
  Set the color to red

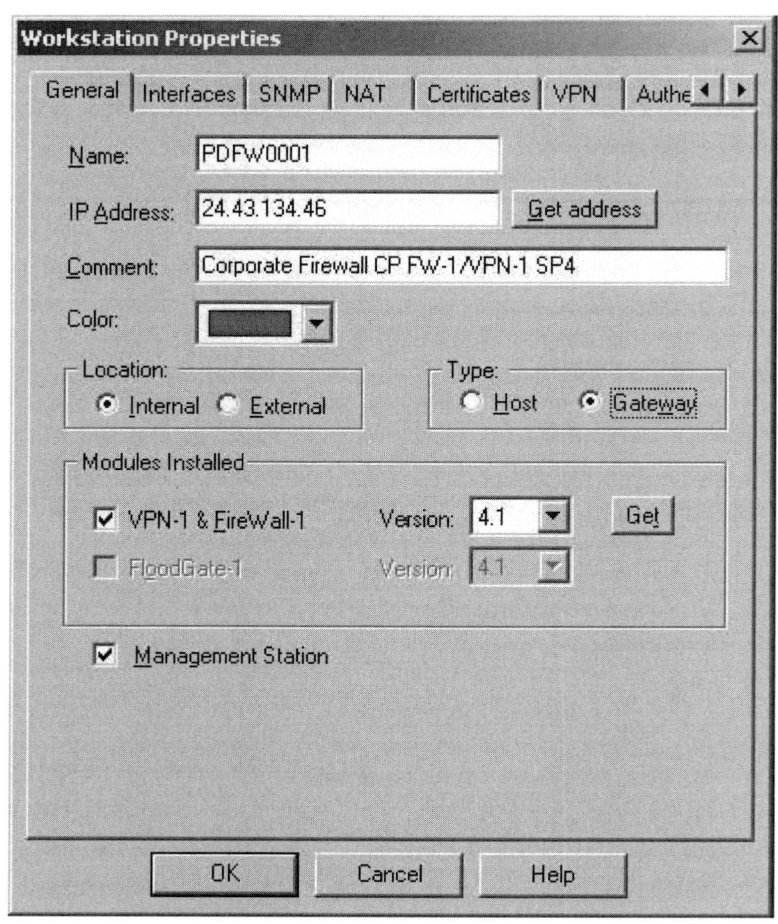

Exhibit 54. Configuration PDFW0001 General Tab

3. Select the Interfaces tab (Exhibit 55) and depress the Get button. If the network interface cards were properly set up, they will be automatically populated. The interface properties will be defined after defining additional network object groups for anti-spoofing security.
4. Select the Authentication tab next and deselect all checkboxes that do not apply. In this example, only VPN-1 & FireWall-1 Password has been selected. Press the OK button to save the object.

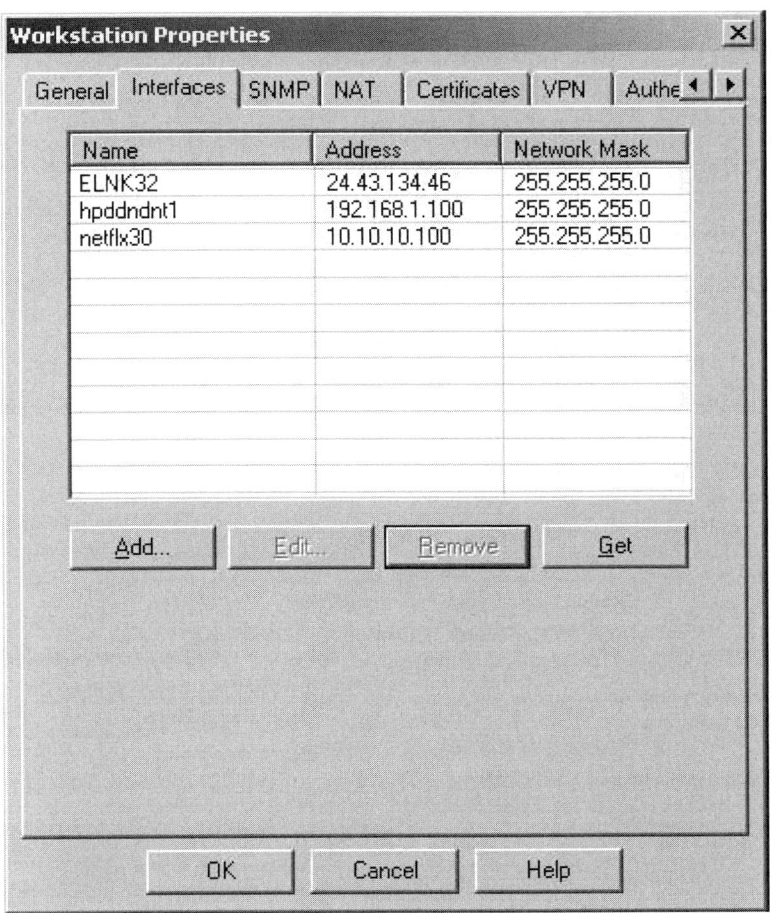

Exhibit 55. Configuration PDFW0001 Interfaces Tab

5. Create the Internal Network Object using the Network Objects Add function and select New Network.
   - Set the field values as follows:
     Name = Corporate_Network
     IP Address = subnet for the network
     Net Mask = network mask for above network
     Comment = suitable description
     Color = green
   - Select the radio buttons as follows:
     Location = Internal
     Broadcast = Allowed
   - Then select the NAT tab for the object to set up the Network Address Translation of the RFC 1918 address. NAT is required if the internal network addresses are nonroutable Internet addresses. Set the following fields for NAT on the Internal Network Object as follows:
     Check the Add Automatic Address Translation Rules checkbox.
     Translation Mode = hide
     Hiding IP Address = external IP address of firewall
     Install On = All
   - This is identical to the steps carried out in the instructions for the Windows NT 4.0 installation.
6. Create the DMZ Network Object using the Network Objects Add function and select New Network.
   - Set the field values accordingly as follows:
     Name = Corporate_DMZ
     IP Address = subnet for network
     Net Mask = network mask for above network
     Comment = suitable description
     Color = orange
   - Select the radio buttons as follows:
     Location = Internal
     Broadcast = Allowed
   - Do not set any Network Address Translation (NAT) for this object.
     Hiding IP address = external IP address of firewall
     Install On = All
7. Create group objects that will be used for anti-spoofing on the interfaces. These groups can be created now but should be updated when the network Definitions change for the internal and DMZ networks. Create the Group Objects using the Network Objects Add function and select New Group. Set the field values accordingly as follows:
   - Internal Group Object:
     Name = Internal_Corporate_Network
     Comment = a suitable description
     Color = green
   - DMZ Group Object:
     Name = DMZ_Corporate_Network
     Comment = a suitable description

Color = orange

8. Once the Anti-Spoofing group definitions have been defined and saved, select the Network Objects icon from the menu bar and highlight the pdfw0001 firewall object and click Edit to edit the object. Click on the Interfaces tab and highlight each interface one at a time and edit the Interface Properties Security tab. For both the internal network and the DMZ network, select the Specific radio button in the Valid Addresses section. Select the appropriate group for each interface. Internal_Corporate_Network for the Internal Interface (Exhibit 56) and DMZ_Corporate_Network for the DMZ interface (Exhibit 57). For the external interface, select the radio button Others in the Valid Addresses section (Exhibit 58). It is recommended that the logging options for each be set to Log.
9. Defining the Properties Setup screen for the firewall. The default Security Policy tab of the Properties Setup needs to be changed for testing of the rule base to proceed. It also requires some default timeouts to be reduced to keep the firewall state tables small by flushing out terminated connection sessions. Select the following settings for the Security Policy tab:

   Set TCP Session Timeout = 300

   Select Log in the Track section of the "IP Option Drop" of the Log and Alert Tab

   Select the SYNDefender tab and set the following entry:

   Select the radio button = Passive SYN Gateway

   Select OK to accept the modifications for the time being
10. The next step is to create a broadcast filter and filter group. These objects will be used to filter out broadcast traffic from the log file. Create two new Network Objects using the Manage Network Objects icon from the menu bar and select the New button to create new workstation objects for the following broadcast filters:

    0.0.0.0 and 255.255.255.255

    - Once these objects are defined, create a broadcast filter group consisting of these two objects. It will be used during the rule base definition later in this exercise. Create the filter group by clicking on the New button of Network Objects and selecting Group.

Note

Refer to the instructions for Check Point Security Objects and Rules Base Configuration, step 10. The process is identical. Refer to Exhibit 31.

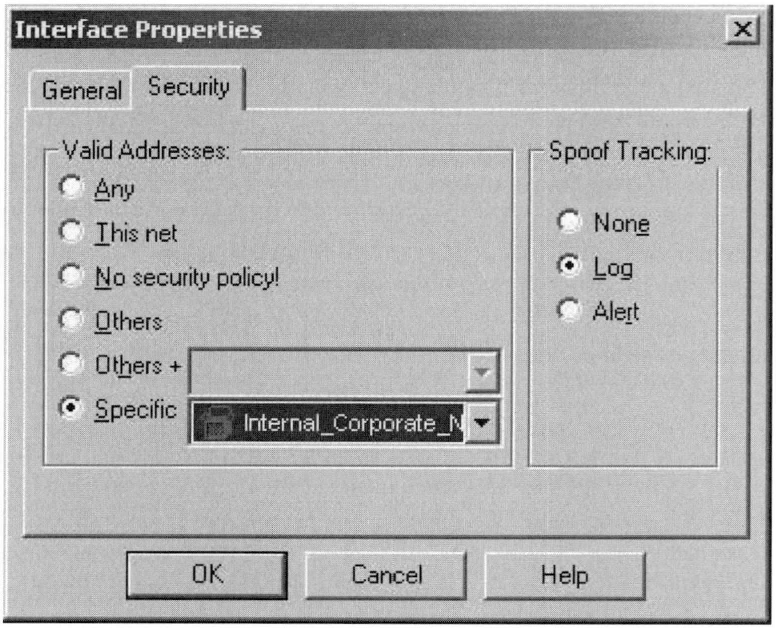

Exhibit 56. PDFW0001 Interfaces Anti-Spoofing Setup for Internal NIC

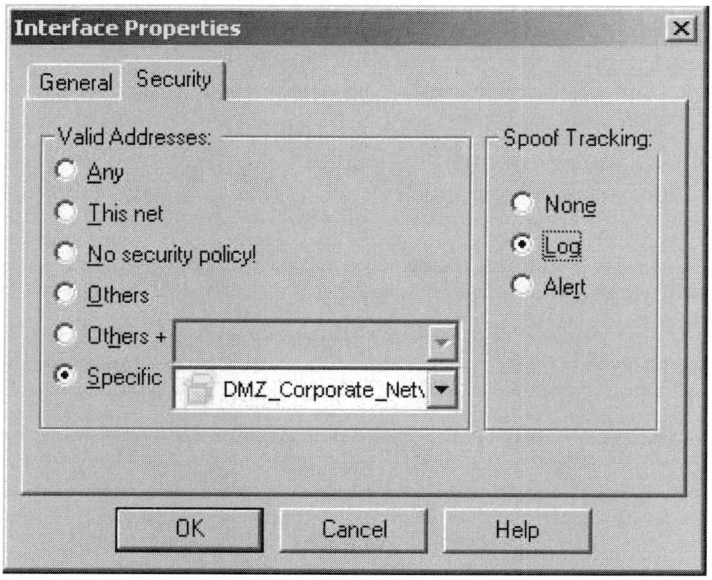

Exhibit 57 PDFW0001 Interfaces Anti-Spoofing Setup for DMZ NIC

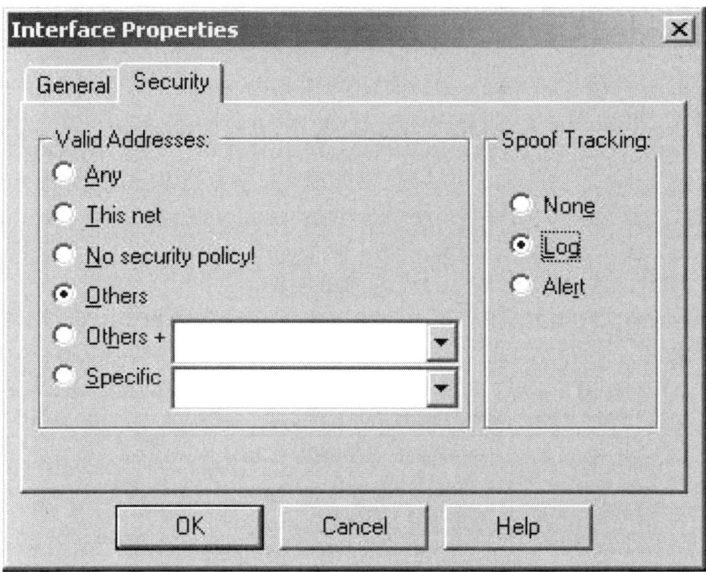

Exhibit 58. PDFW0001 Interfaces Anti-Spoofing Setup for External NIC

11. Creating a service group for Internet applications or administration is done by selecting the Manage Services icon on the menu bar, or by selecting the Manage Menu option and selecting Services. From the Services dialog box, select the New button and select Group. This will allow one to create a group services object that can encapsulate a set of required Internet services. This makes the setup of the rule base easier and simpler to maintain. We define a service group for the following activities with the following services assigned to each:
    - *Standard Internet services.* These are the basic Internet surfing services: HTTP, HTTPS, FTP, and NNTP.
    - *Authenticated services.* These services are restricted for administrative use only: Telnet and FTP.
    - *Application services.* Application services are those that have been identified in an application inventory process. These can range from commercial applications to custom in-house developed applications (e.g., SMTP, POP-3, IMAP, Lotus, or MS-Exchange v5.5
    - *Filter services.* These are services that we wish to filter and remove from the firewall logs. This typically consists of NetBIOS related traffic (i.e., the NBT Service group).
    - *Diagnostics services.* These are services that are used to enable ICMP diagnostic services such as Ping and Traceroute to work through the firewall without having to modify the Properties Setup to enable ICMP. Enabling and disabling these sets of services is a conscious decision on the security administrator's behalf (i.e., echo request and Traceroute for outbound testing and echo reply, time exceeded, and dest-unreach for inbound testing).

Note

For additional details on setting up service groups, refer to the instructions for Check Point Security Objects and Rules Base Configuration, step 11 Exhibits 37–37.

---

12. Creating user groups for system administration and remote access is accomplished from the Manage menu item and selecting the User option, or simply click on the Manger User icon on the menu bar. It will be necessary to create an administrative group for use with restrictive services such as Telnet and FTP. If one will require users to have remote access to the internal network, a SecuRemote users group should be created.
13. Creation of users for each of the above user groups can be accomplished using the same menu option, Manage User interface. However, initially one needs to create a new template for the user class. Using the Manager User icon, select the New button and then select the Template option.

Set the name for the template, comment, color, and expiry date for users created with this template under the General tab. Under the Groups tab, select the group the users will belong to. Under the Authentication tab, select VPN-1 & FireWall-1 Password. Under the Location tab, select Any for both source and destination. Under the Time tab, select the appropriate settings. Under the Encryption tab, select IKE for the encryption method. Edit the IKE properties and select Password in the Authentication tab and under the Encryption tab, select the Encryption and Data Integrity radio button, SHA1 for data integrity and 3DES for the encryption algorithm. Select the Encryption tab to define encryption settings.

Note

Please refer to the following for more information on user management: Getting Started Guide, page 217 — Creating Users; Administrators Guide, Chapter 5, page 153 — Managing Users.

---

14. Creating the remote user is done by selecting the Manage menu option and clicking on Manage Users, or one can click on the Manage Users icon. Click on the New button and select RemoteUser. This is the template that was previously created. From the General tab, enter the user name and provide a more descriptive comment for the user if desired. Then select the Authentication tab and enter an eight-character password for the user. Then select the Encryption tab and select the Edit button to enter the encryption password. Note that both the Authentication and Encryption passwords must match or access will be denied to remote users. One will then need to install the user database by selecting the Load option. The user database is automatically installed when one loads the rule base for the firewall.
15. To set up the firewall to accept hybrid secure remote authentication, it will be necessary to shut down FireWall-1 services to proceed with the setup of an internal management Certificate Authority (CA). Follow the instructions to shut down the FireWall-1 service. Create the CA and then certify the CA using the *fw create internalca create* and *fw create internalca certify* commands (Exhibit 59). Restart the FireWall-1 service once the above have been successfully completed. See the previous list for instructions on restarting the FireWall-1 services. A more detailed document can be obtained from the Check Point Web site, titled "Hybrid Mode IKE for SecuRemote Authentication."
16. Restart the Policy Editor client and select the Manage option on the menu and then select Servers. The Servers dialog will display the Internal Management CA that was created in step 15. Select the Edit

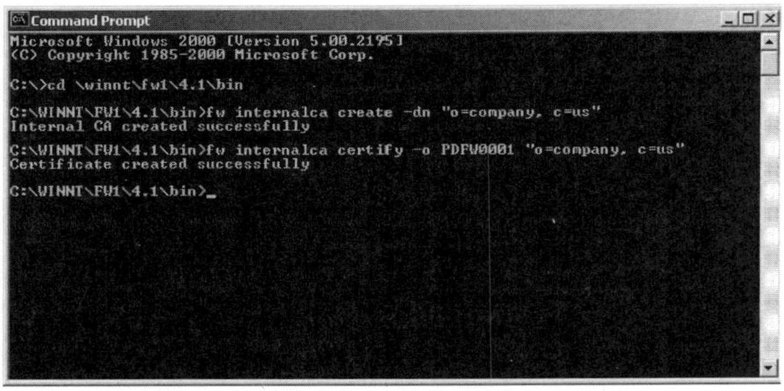

```
Command Prompt
Microsoft Windows 2000 [Version 5.00.2195]
(C) Copyright 1985-2000 Microsoft Corp.

C:\>cd \winnt\fw1\4.1\bin

C:\WINNT\FW1\4.1\bin>fw internalca create -dn "o=company, c=us"
Internal CA created successfully

C:\WINNT\FW1\4.1\bin>fw internalca certify -o PDFW0001 "o=company, c=us"
Certificate created successfully

C:\WINNT\FW1\4.1\bin>_
```

Exhibit 59. Create Internal CA for Hybrid Mode Support

button to view the object. The General tab only allows one to modify the comment. Enter a comment to identify the CA. Click on the VPN-1 CM tab; then click on the View button in the Certificate section. One can view the contents of the CA created in step 15. One can also save the CA for distribution to other administrators and firewalls in the corporate domain.

17. To allow Hybrid SecuRemote connections to the firewall, it will be necessary to modify the Firewall Object PDFW0001 to reflect the required changes. Edit the VPN tab of the PDFW0001 workstation object and in the Domain section, check the "Exportable for SecuRemote" box. Next, edit the encryption scheme IKE. Select the Edit button of the "Encrypted Schemes Defined" section. In the Support Authentication Methods section, check the VPN-1/FireWall-1 authentication for SecuRemote (Hybrid Mode).
18. Create additional objects to complete the configuration of the networking environment. One needs to define additional objects such as the Corporate Web, Mail server, DNS Server (Exhibit 60) and the DMZ Server Group (Exhibit 61) and with the allowable services (Exhibit 62). First, one must define the HTTP Server within the DMZ. Provide a name for the server and its IP address on the DMZ. Next, create Network Address Translation for the HTTP server as a static address supplied by the ISP. Create the SMTP Server in a similar fashion by setting the internal DMZ information and then create NAT to an external IP address. Next, create a Workstation for the Corporate DNS Server. Finally, create the Service group for the allowable services on the DMZ and create a DMZ Server group to encapsulate all the DMZ servers in the DMZ.
19. Create objects for the Branch Office in order to create a secure VPN channel between the corporate office and the branch office. First create a firewall object for the Branch Office. Set the IP address, location to External, and Gateway radio button. Then save the object. Next, create the Branch Office Network object. Enter the Subnet address for the internal network at the branch office and set the location to External. Do not set NAT for the object. Create the Branch Office security domain

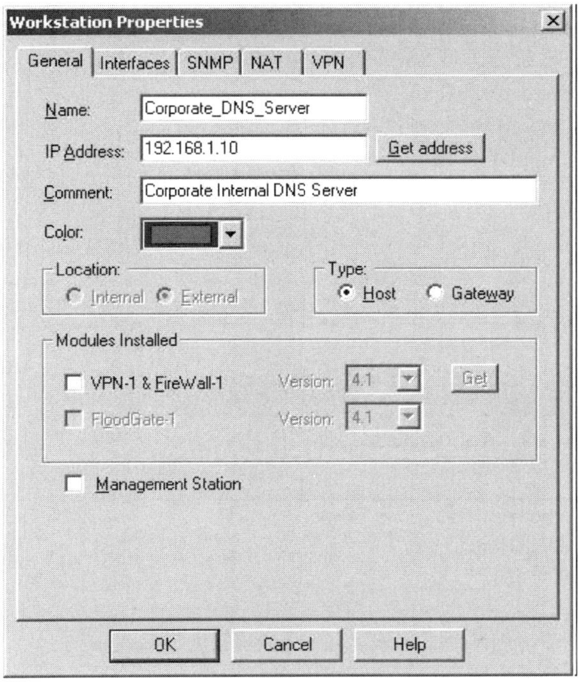

Exhibit 60. Corporate DNS Server

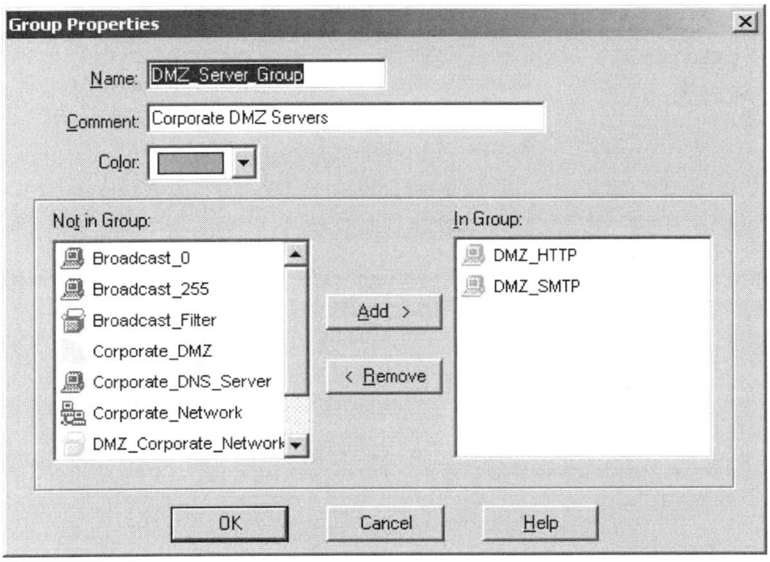

Exhibit 61. Corporate DMZ Server Group

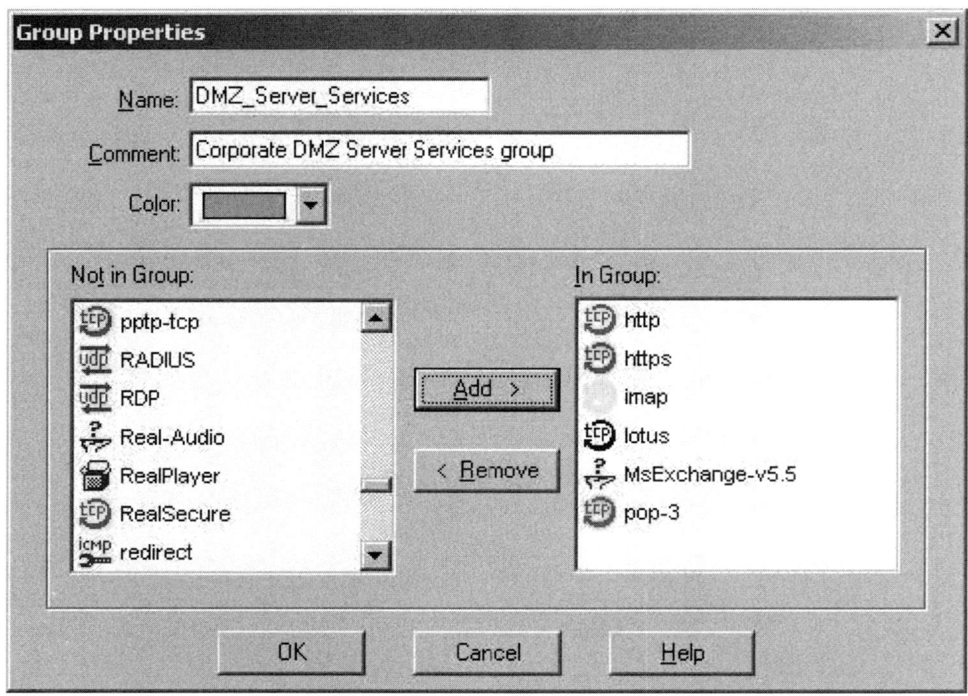

Exhibit 62. Corporate DMZ Server Services Group

and add the Branch Firewall object and the Branch Network to the group. Create the Corporate Security Domain and add the Corporate Firewall and the Corporate Internal Network to the group. Modify the Branch Office Firewall Object and select the VPN tab. In the Domain section, select the radio button for the other option and in the drop-down dialog box, select the Branch_Office_Network object. Then select the Edit button in the Encryption Schemes section. De-select the Cast option, and select the Pre-Shared Secrets checkbox. Then select the Edit Secrets button to open the Shared Secrets dialog. Select the edit button and enter a secret password. Then select the Set button to accept the password. Then select the OK button. Next, one must modify the Corporate Firewall Object to accept VPN connections. Select the VPN tab of the PDFW0001 firewall object. De-select the Cast option. Check the Pre-Shared Secrets to enable the option and then click on the Edit Secrets button. Select Edit from the Shared Secrets dialog and verify that the secret key is identical to that entered for the Branch Office Firewall. Select Set and then select OK to retain settings.

Note

Refer to the instructions on the Check Point VPN Setup Process for additional information.

---

20. Creating the initial rule base for the firewall is accomplished by using either the icon menu bar or the Edit Menu item and selecting Add Rule (Exhibit 63). Based on the objects that we have created we can set up a rule base to reflect the assembled objects (Exhibit 64) and test the functionality of the firewall. Once we confirm that the firewall is operational, we can revisit the rule base to add VPN functionality to the branch office.
    - Rule 1: This rule will be used to allow secure remote users to access the internal corporate network (see Exhibit 65).
      Source = SecuRemoteUsers@Corporate
      Destination = Corporate_Network
      Service = Any
      Action = Client Encrypt
      Track = Long
      Install On = Gateways
      Time = Any
      Comment = Allow authenticated users access to the internal network
    - Rule 2 and Rule 3: These rules comprise the Corporate to Branch VPN network. For each rule on both sides of the VPN, the encryption properties must match (see Exhibits 66 and 67).

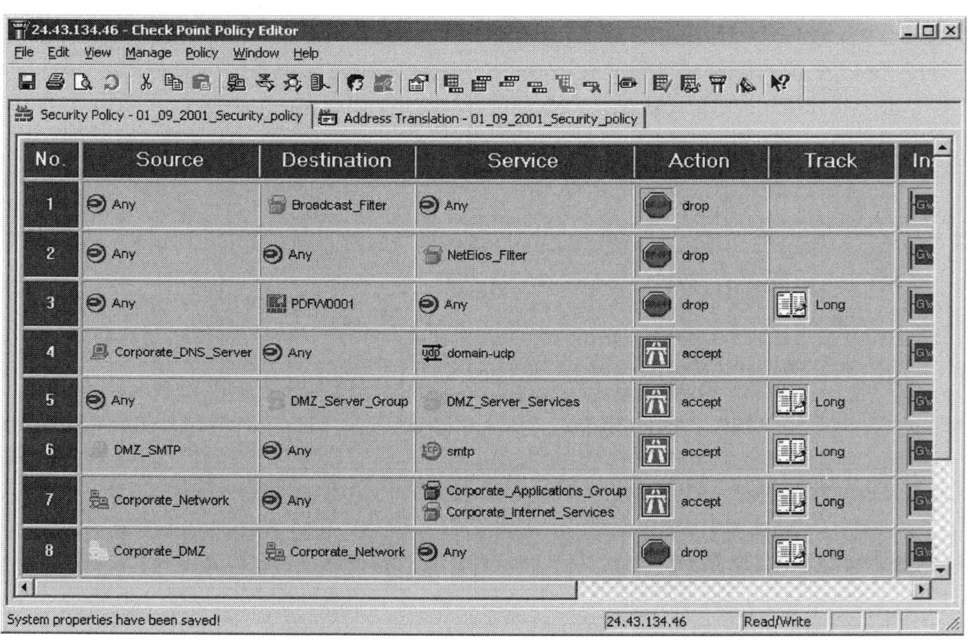

Exhibit 63. Initial Rule Base, Part I

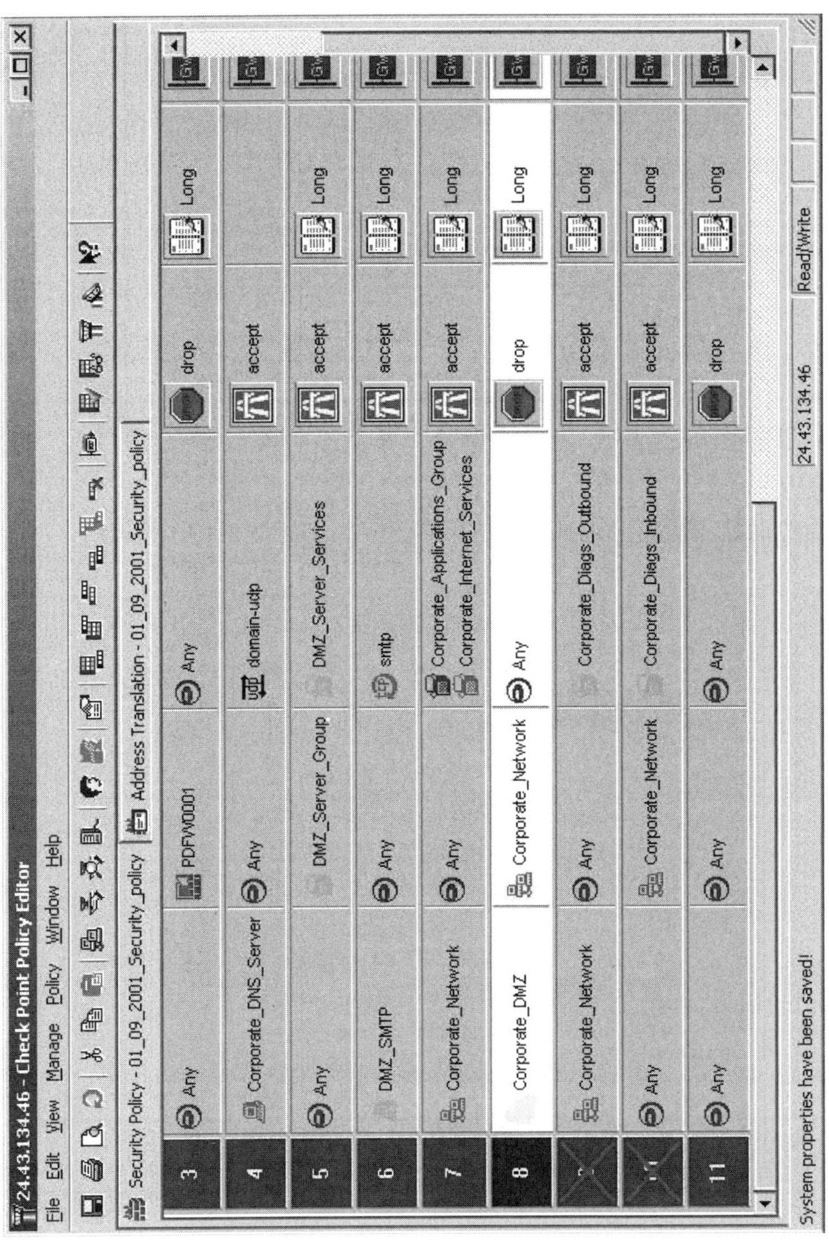

Exhibit 64. Initial Rule Base, Part II

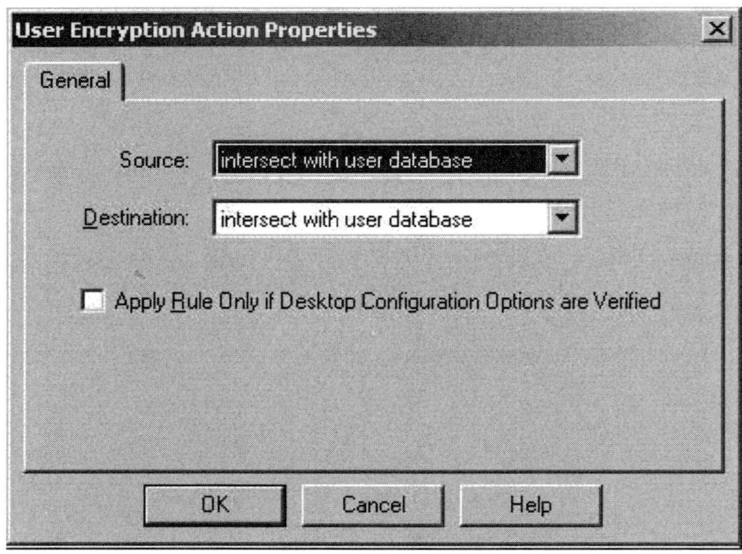

Exhibit 65. Properties for Rule 1: Action Client Encrypt

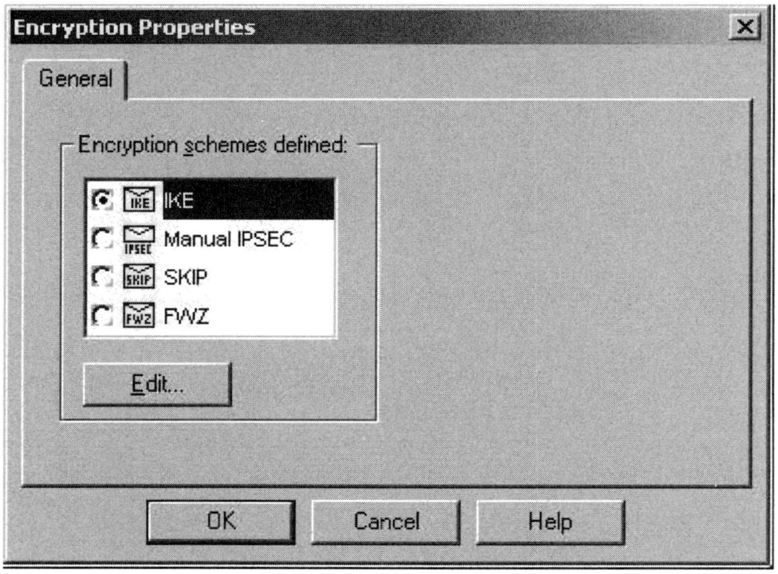

Encryption Properties
General
Encryption schemes defined:
IKE
Manual IPSEC
SKIP
FWZ
Edit...
OK
Cancel
Help

Exhibit 66. VPN Encryption Properties for Rules 2 and 3

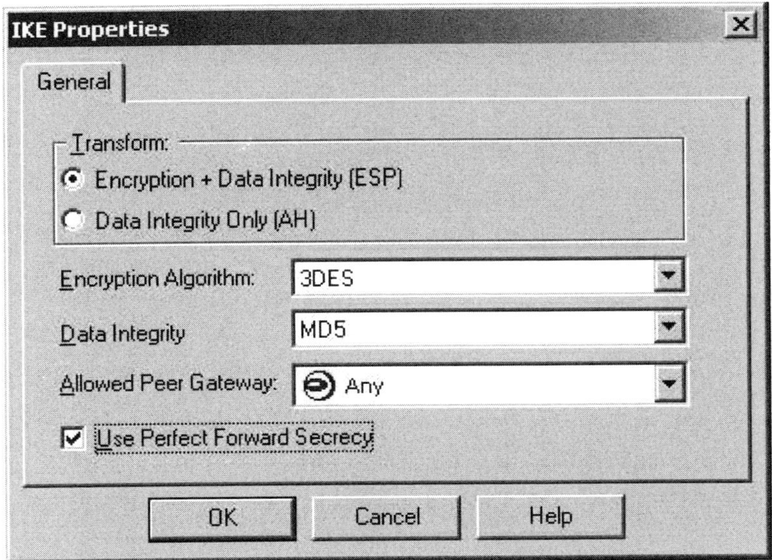

Exhibit 67. Rules 2 and 3: Edit VPN Encryption Properties for Rules 2 and 3

- Rule 2:
  Source = Corporate_Securty_Domain
  Destination = Branch_Office_security_domain
  Service = Any
  Action = Encrypt
  Track = Long
  Install On = Gateways
  Time = Any
  Comment = Encrypt traffic from corporate to branch
- Rule 3:
  Source = Branch_Office_security_domain
  Destination = Corporate_Securty_Domain
  Service = Any
  Action = Encrypt
  Track = Long
  Install On = Gateways
  Time = Any
  Comment = Encrypt traffic from branch to corporate
- Rule 4: This rule will be used to filter broadcast traffic.
  Source = Any
  Destination = Broadcast_Filter
  Service = Any
  Action = drop
  Track = leave blank
  Install On = Gateways
  Time = Any
  Comment = Drop and do not log broadcast traffic
- Rule 5: This rule will set up a log filter for NetBIOS traffic. Set the following options for Rule 1:
  Source = Any
  Destination = Any
  Service = XYZ_Log_filter
  Action = drop
  Track = leave blank
  Install On = Gateways
  Time = Any
  Comment = Drop and do not log NetBIOS traffic
- Rule 6: This rule is used to block all communications to the firewall. This is sometimes called the Stealth rule. We use this rule to hide the firewall from the majority of intruders.
  Source = Any
  Destination = PDFW0001
  Service = Any
  Action = drop
  Track = Long
  Install On = Gateways
  Time = Any

Comment = Drop all to the firewall and log it. Listen on FW-1 services only.

- Rule 7: This rule is used to restrict all domain name service queries to the Internal DNS Server.
  Source = Corporate_DNS_Server
  Destination = Any
  Service = domain_udp
  Action = accept
  Track = Long
  Install On = Gateways
  Time = Any
  Comment = Allow DNS service from corporate DNS server only
- Rule 8: This rule allows administrators equipped with the FireWall-1 Authentication agent to access restricted services such as FTP and Telnet.
  Source = Administrator@any
  Destination = Any
  Service = Corporate_Admin_Services
  Action = Session Auth
  Track = Long
  Install On = Gateways
  Time = Any
  Comment = Allow access to restricted services via authentication client
- Rule 9: This rule allows administrators on alternate platforms to access restricted services such as FTP and Telnet. UNIX and MAC users cannot run the Authentication Agent because it is a Windows-only product.
  Source = Administrators@any
  Destination = Any
  Service = Corporate_Admin_Services
  Action = User Auth
  Track = Long
  Install On = Gateways
  Time = Any
  Comment = Allow access to restricted services via user id and password defined in the firewall's user database
- Rule 10: This rule allows servers on the corporate DMZ to communicate using authorized services to the outside world and internal network.
  Source = Any
  Destination = DMZ_Server_Group
  Service = DMZ_Server_Services
  Action = accept
  Track = Long
  Install On = Gateways
  Time = Any

Comment = Allow authorized communication to the DMZ

- Rule 11: This rule allows SMTP traffic to escape the DMZ.
  Source = DMZ_SMTP
  Destination = Any
  Service = SMTP
  Action = accept
  Track = Long
  Install On = Gateways
  Time = Any
  Comment = Allow SMTP out of the dmz
- Rule 12: This rule is used to define allowable services for internal users. These include standard Internet services and also any services that were discovered during an application inventory process.
  Source = Corporate_Network
  Destination = Any
  Service = Corporate_Applications_Group
  = Corporate_Internet_Services
  Action = accept
  Track = Long
  Install On = Gateways
  Time = Any
  Comment = Authorized services
- Rule 13: This rule prevents intruders from infiltrating the corporate DMZ and using it to gain access to the internal network.
  Source = Corporate_DMZ
  Destination = Corporate_Network
  Service = Any
  Action = drop
  Track = Long
  Install On = Gateways
  Time = Any
  Comment = Prevent intrusion via DMZ
- Rules 14 and 15: These rules are used for diagnostics testing. They are only used for testing and problem resolution purposes and restrict the types of ICMP traffic that can pass through the firewall when invoked. This replaces the "Accept ICMP" option in the Properties Setup Security Policy tab. These rules are disabled until required.
  Source = Corporate_Network
  Destination = Any
  Service = Corporate_Diags_Outbound
  Action = accept
  Track = Long
  Install On = Gateways
  Time = Any
  Comment = Diagnostics outbound
  Source = Any

Destination = Corporate_Network
Service = Corporate_Diags_Inbound
Action = accept
Track = Long
Install On = Gateways
Time = Any
Comment = Diagnostics inbound

- Rule 16: This rule is known as the clean-up rule. It is used to drop any service communication that does not fall into any of the other prior rules. It also logs the action to see what people are trying to do to the firewall.
  Source = Any
  Destination = any
  Service = Any
  Action = drop
  Track = Long
  Install on = Gateways
  Time = Any
  Comment = Drop and log unauthorized communications

21. The Network Address Translation (NAT) rules are automatically inserted into the rule base. These were set when the interfaces were defined for NAT. The NAT rules basically work as follows (Exhibit 68):
    - Translate any traffic from the Internal HTTP server DMZ address to use the external assigned static address.
    - Translate any traffic from the Internal SMTP server DMZ address to use the external assigned static address.
    - Any communication within the internal corporate network remains unchanged by the firewall.
    - Any communications that will pass through the firewall to the outside world will be masked by the external IP address of the firewall.
    - NAT is necessary only if oneis using RFC 1918 addresses for the internal network. Otherwise, one does not require NAT. It is highly recommended that one use RFC 1918 class addresses for internal networks because they offer an additional layer of security since they are nonroutable addresses over the internet.
22. Now that one has a basic rule base, one can load it and test the firewall's functionality. The basic rule base shown here is fine for a dual-homed host but will not suffice for a multi-homed host scenario. One can begin the rule base installation by selecting Policy from the menu and selecting Install, or by selecting the Install Policy icon from the icon bar. The first message that comes up informs one that address translation is being used. Click the checkbox to prevent further viewing of this dialog in the future, and select OK to continue. The next message that appears informs one that the rule base will contain settings that were defined in the Properties setup (i.e., ICMP and DNS resolution). Click the checkbox to prevent further viewing of this dialog in the future, and select OK to continue. The following window displays

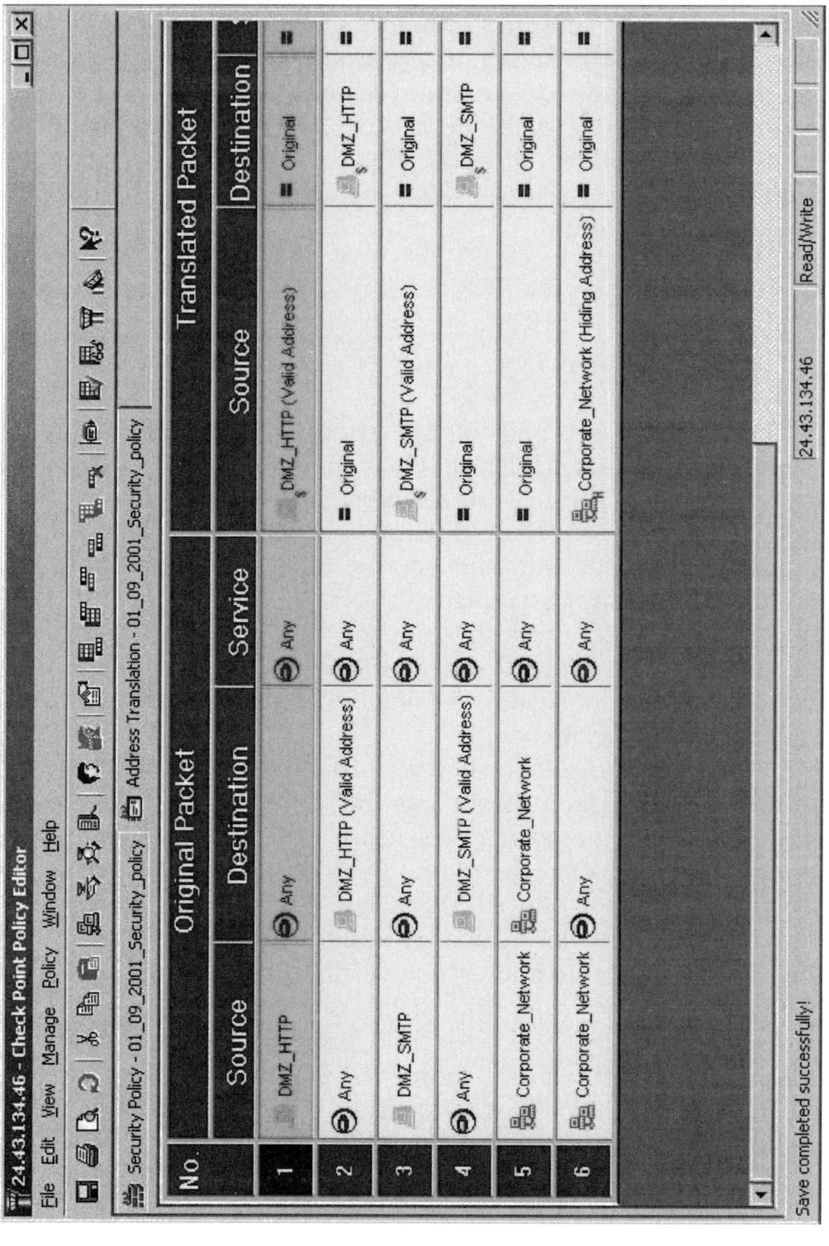

Exhibit 68. Initial Rule Base Address Translation

where the rule base will be loaded or where the rule base will be applied. In this case, there is only the one firewall, pdfw0001. Select OK to continue. The final message dialog will display a compilation message for the rule base to make sure it is valid and then the installation message. When all is fine and complete, select the Close button to return to the rule base window of the Policy Editor.

23. Begin testing the rule base.

As with the Windows NT 4.0 Server configuration, it is left for you to decide if the system requires further security tweaking. After running an NMAP port scan of the system (Exhibit 69), it was found that a Windows 2000 Server is even more quiet than its predecessor.

Exhibit 69. NMAP Port Scan of Fully Configured Windows 2000 Check Point FireWall-1 System[3]

```
# Nmap (V. nmap) scan initiated 2.53 as: nmap -v -sS -O -P0 -p1-
65535 -o PDFW0001w2kcp2.txt 24.43.134.46
Interesting ports on PDFW0001 (24.43.134.46):
(The 65531 ports scanned but not shown below are in state: filtered)
Port      State     Service
258/tcp   open      yak-chat
264/tcp   open      bgmp
265/tcp   open      unknown
500/tcp   closed    isakmp

TCP Sequence Prediction: Class=random positive increments
                           Difficulty=44615 (Worthy challenge)

Sequence numbers: D5A2DDCE D5A398F5 D5A4A7F1 D5A590F5 D5A6218E D5A751B6
Remote operating system guess: Windows 2000 RC1 through final release

# Nmap run completed at Sun Sep 02 00:58:57 2001 -- 1 IP address (1
host up) scanned in 4864 seconds
```

Although in both cases it is still recommended that any TCP/IP tweaking and securing be carried out. These are the most common attack methods that can bring down a server. Keep a watchful eye on the server logs.

It is recommended that both operating system platforms undergo TCP/IP tuning to secure the protocol stack to try and prevent Denial of Service (DOS) attacks from taking down the firewall

Denial of Service attacks are one of the most common forms of attack against a server. These methods are engineered to bring down a server at will. therefore it is necessary to keep a watchful eye on the server's firewall logs to see what individuals are doing to your firewall.

Distributed Denial of Service (DDOS) attacks are even more difficult to discover because attack patterns are random in nature and a multitude of systems are used to coordinate the attack.

To enhance the capabilities of the firewall even further, one should investigate and pursue the implementation of automatically sending alerts to an administrative group on the mail server.

Additional references can be gathered from the Check Point Web site. Exhibit 70 lists a number of excellent sources of publicly available material from the vendor.

Exhibit 70. Check Point Resources

Article
SecuRemote Version 3.0 Quick Reference Guide
How to Hide the Source Address of a Client on the Internet Behind the Firewall's Internal Address
FireWall-1 Version 4.0 SecuRemote Split/Encrypted DNS Quick Reference Guide, Revision 1.4
Configuring Single SignOn
Hybrid Mode IKE for SecuRemote Authentication
Firewall-1 Version 4.0, How to Configure Authenticated & Encrypted SecuRemote Topology Downloads from a FireWall Module
User Authentication with Primary Domain Controller (PDC) in NT

Check Point FireWall-1/VPN-1 Operating Notes

Check Point FireWall-1/VPN-1 has a number of varying operating points of which one should be aware. The first important aspect of the FireWall-1/VPN-1 environment is that of the services that it uses to function. Like any other product, FireWall-1/VPN-1 uses and listens on ports. The services one chooses to operate with will determine what ports will be active on the system. If one performs a *netstat* operation on the server, one will see these ports in use; however, they may not be labeled properly. To get the ports reflecting their true service function, one must edit the services file in the C:\winnt\system32\drivers\etc directory. Refer to Exhibit 71 for a listing of these services.

The definitions for all objects and services defined on the firewall reside within the conf directory (c:\winnt\fw-1\4.1\conf). For recovery or upgrade purposes, this directory must be backed up; see Exhibit 72 for a list of critical files to be backed up. It is recommended that this directory be backed up prior to making any changes to the rule base and after changes are applied to the rule base. This will provide before-and-after configurations of the firewall.

In addition, it is also recommended that rule base changes be saved incrementally by appending the date of the change to the policy being modified (e.g., XYZ_Policy_26_08_2001).

Exhibit 71. FireWall-1/VPN-1 Services

Port	*Class*	*Service*
256	TCP	Encryption/Key Exchange
257	TCP	Remote Policy Management
258	TCP	GUI Policy Editor Communications
259	TCP	Client Authentication
259	UDP	Encryption Services
260	UDP	SNMP Deamon
261	UDP	SNMP Deamon
264	TCP	SecuRemote and Secure Client Hand Shakes
265	TCP	Key Exchange
500	UDP	ISAKMP Key Exchange
900	TCP	HTTP Secure Server Client Authentication

Exhibit 72. Critical Configuration Files

```
objects.C
*.W
rulebases.fws
fwauth.NDB
fwmusers
gui-clients
external.if
fwauth.keys
serverkeys.*
masters
fwauthd.conf
product.conf
fw.license
smtp.conf
fwopsec.conf
```

Finally, one needs to modify the memory pool parameters for the firewall. The defaults are typically fine for small environments that do not impose any stress on the firewall. One modifies this parameter to prevent the loss of data to event logs and to make sure that the firewall can adequately service the environment, both now and in the future.

A memory pool size of between 8 and 16 MB should suffice for most organizations. To adjust the memory pool (Exhibit 73), one will need to use the Registry Editor and insert a new key value called Memory in the Check Point FireWall-1 product key.

Further tuning parameters are possible; however, they should only be applied when necessary. When in doubt, contact Check Point Technical

Support for additional help. If this is going to be your first firewall implementation, at least purchase a minimal support contract. It will save countless hours when something that should work does not work. Your administrators will be grateful.

Exhibit 73. Memory Pool Adjustments

HKEY_LOCAL_MACHINE\SYSTEM\CurrentControlSet\Services\FW1\Parameters

Add a new parameter called "Memory" and set its data type to REG_DWORD

When prompted for the value, enter a number in bytes to set the new memory pool size. For the new parameter to take effect you will need to reboot the machine.

Notes

1. The Security Rollup is a response to the IT community's need for proper security maintenance of the Windows NT operating environment since Microsoft opted to cancel the release of Service Pack 7.
2. Even a completely secured and well-configured firewall can still be susceptible to a Denial of Service attack (DoS). Hardening is not an effective defense against DoS attacks, but it can prevent the system from becoming vulnerable from an attacker using such methods. Should the firewall software components crash and/or fail, vulnerable operating system services will be exposed to further attack. Removing these services will prevent further penetration by an attacker.
3. The machine that performs the nmap scan will need to have the services file corrected to map proper service names to the port numbers.

Chapter 9

Enhancing the Security Infrastructure

Although one knows how and what is required to set up perimeter security and the management tactics for regulating an environment, there are a number of limitations that need to be addressed but are outside the scope of this book. These additional topics include:

- Virus protection and scanning
- Fault tolerance and load balancing
- Reporting and management
- Encryption acceleration
- Public key infrastructure
- Authentication
- Intrusion detection
- Backup and recovery

Each of these topics on its own is a lengthy discussion; but nonetheless, each must be addressed to fulfill the requirements of a well-founded security front. Once the initial constructs of an organization's perimeter security have been put in place, time should be set aside to investigate options to integrate the above items into the corporate security model. These items are discussed in no particular order because each organization will have varied requirements and priorities.

Virus Protection

Today's business environment is highly susceptible to damage caused by computer viruses and worms. The tight integration of application software and operating system software has allowed the proliferation of extremely dangerous virus code to attack a multitude of machines in continuous waves of assault. Although anti-virus software has been around for quite some time, the ability to detect new virus signatures that are not mutant strains of older viruses is difficult. Unfortunately, a virus can have a drastic effect on a business's operations. Not only is a virus damaging to the computing environment, it also takes a toll on Systems staff because they must make sure the virus is scrubbed clean from the environment. Knowing when infection occurred is critical. Backups may be infected and the need to minimize the impact on reintroducing a potentially dangerous virus back into the computing environment from a restore operation is paramount.

Transferring viruses by floppy, CD-ROM, or zip drive is another way that viruses tend to pop into the environment over and over again. But today's medium of choice for infection is e-mail. Appendix E provides a sample memo that can be used to educate and inform staff of virus protection. Not only do servers and workstations require virus protection, but firewalls require it also. Because the firewall is the focal point of entrance for all data communication into the corporate environment, it only makes sense to have it provide scanning services for the organization. Although not to contradict the previous discussion regarding the only function a firewall should perform is firewalling, Check Point FireWall-1 does provide the capability to offload virus protection to an alternate server via the Content Vectoring Protocol (CVP). A CVP server is an out-of-process[1] server that provides a specific service to the firewall. In this case, the service being performed is virus scanning. Also known as a Security Server, all SMTP traffic can be routed to a CVP server that performs the actual content inspection. This relieves the firewall from performing the task locally and impacting other firewall services and functions. If SMTP traffic is found to be free of viral infection, the message is forwarded to its destination, the mail server.

In Exhibit 1, inbound SMTP mail traffic is redirected to the CVP SMTP Security Server as defined in the FireWall-1 rule base. Messages are then scanned and, if found to be free of viruses, they are forwarded to the internal mail server as defined in the FireWall-1 rule base.

Fault Tolerance and Load Balancing

Fault tolerance and load balancing tend to go hand in hand, although they are and cover different functional spectrums of operation. Fault tolerance refers to a system's ability to withstand a system failure and remain in operation to deliver services to an organization. Load balancing, on the other hand, refers to a system's ability to evenly distribute tasks and resource usage across a series of machines that constitutes a single system.

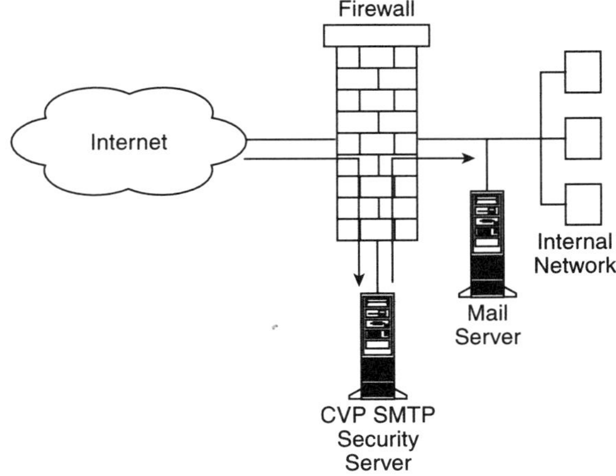

Exhibit 1. SMTP CVP Virus Scanning Model

Fault Tolerance

To maintain high levels of operational service, it is necessary to invest in premium hardware that can support such features as:

- Multiple power supplies with individual power connectors
- Hot pluggable components, such as CPUs, hard disks, and NICs
- Good ventilation and environmental controls

Although some of these features are only available in high-end equipment, similar results can be achieved by setting up duplicate hardware systems and leaving one system configured for hot or cold standby, with hot standby being the ideal solution. This can lower overall hardware costs by utilizing two midrange systems for the cost of a single high-end system. Check Point offers a high-availability product to deliver fault protection. The High Availability add-on feature provides for transparent fail-over for both firewall connections and virtual private network (VPN) connections. Thus, it is possible to achieve higher levels of operating efficiency through the use of a High Availability (HA) module, as opposed to purchasing extremely expensive fault-tolerant computing equipment. The Check Point High Availability Server (see Exhibit 2) achieves its transparent fail-over by sharing the state tables between all servers that operate within the HA cluster.

Load Balancing

Check Point FireWall-1 provides load balancing features that allow a group of servers to service or share a service load across a grouping of servers (see Exhibit 3). The load balancing feature enables the provision of a group of

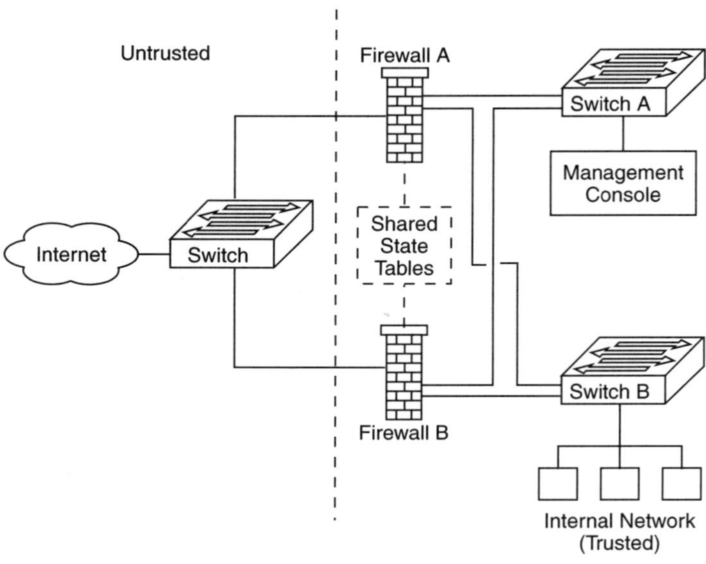

Exhibit 2. Sample High Availability Model

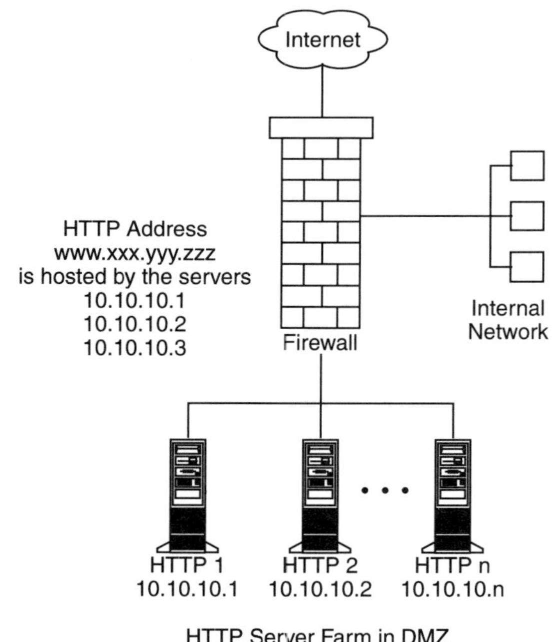

Exhibit 3. Load Balancing Model

servers to appear to operate as a single server; for example, a Web or FTP server farm. Although the site may only have a single IP address, it can be served by two or more systems transparently.

Reporting and Management

System management of the Check Point FireWall-1 product line is very intuitive and easy to work with. The Policy Management console is a completely graphical environment and easy to navigate. Additional add-on products snap into the interface structure and administrators can easily tab between management consoles for a variety of installed products.

Reporting is a separate module that can be used to create management report statistics on the firewall's operational characteristics. Reports can be generated as graphical charts to track specific firewall functions. Default report formats exist and the module also allows for custom reporting. The report module does not delete or modify any of the system log files, but copies the data to its own database to allow one to navigate and generate reports on the firewall operations at one's leisure.

Encryption Acceleration

Encryption acceleration is the ability to offload highly intense computational and CPU-bound encryption services onto an alternate device. This is extremely important when dealing with virtual private networks (VPNs) that service hundreds or even thousands of encryption tunnels.

The ability to offload VPN encryption capabilities to an alternate hardware device is highly desirable, especially with large VPN networks. Using an encryption accelerator relieves the CPU and frees up the entire system to respond to other communications traffic not directly related to VPN traffic.

Public Key Infrastructure

A public key infrastructure (PKI) enables authentication of remote users via the use of certificates from Entrust or Verisign. Root-level certificates are issued to the enrolling organization from either of these public authorities, which allows an organization to create and assign certificates to its own user base. In essence, it allows the organization to create and distribute certificates to the user community to (1) gain access to resources internally or externally and (2) provide a public and private key pair for encryption. These certificates are integrated into the Check Point FireWall-1 architecture to deliver solid authentication and encryption throughout an organization.

Authentication

Authentication is the ability to determine that users wishing to gain access to a site, system, or resource are who they say they are and not imposters. Although similar to the concept of PKI, authentication only encompasses user credentials. Users are still required to identify themselves using user ids and passwords. Strong authentication mechanisms employ one-time cryptographic hardware to generate a one-time password for the user. These passwords share an encryption algorithm that makes it impossible to reuse or even predict a password for the user at anytime. The hardware-generated password and user id combination provides the unique identifiers necessary to identify the user and allow him or her to gain access to the system. RSA, Inc. produces the Secure ID product line that falls into this category of security products in order to provide strong authentication. The Secure ID product line is supported by the Check Point framework as an alternative to traditional user id and password assignment.

Intrusion Detection

Intrusion detection is a fairly young concept in security. Although very promising, it is still not without fault. Intrusion detection system (IDS) engines and algorithms can only monitor and report findings. Most products will send alerts to management consoles even if the source of the alert was caused by an authorized individual; for example, an internal Telnet session by an administrator. IDSs are still in their infancy and it will be a number of years before the technology is ideally perfected. Sorting out the operational characteristics of a network is difficult. Management overhead of an additional reporting system that cries wolf too many times is dangerous and leads to neglect. As IDSs mature, they will become a necessary support vehicles to protect one's network.

Backup and Recovery

As with any system, a sound backup and recovery strategy is not an option — it is mandatory. Loss of a firewall security policy and object hierarchy can be disastrous. Although it is always possible to rebuild and recreate the firewall if required, it is far better to maintain a backup of the firewall's configuration. This is easily accomplished by backing up the content of the /conf directory for FireWall-1. In most cases, this directory will even fit on a floppy diskette. More complex configurations may require multiple floppies or alternate backup media such as a zip drive or tape drive. The proper backup of the /conf directory ensures easy recovery of the corporate security rule base, as well as an easy means for system migration.

Note

1. Not to be confused with the terminology of COM/DCOM, but of a similar nature.

Appendix A

DoD Security Classifications

Security classifications as defined by the U.S. Department of Defense (DoD), also known as the Trusted Computer Standards Evaluation Criteria, are noted below.

Level D1: Minimum Security, Unclassified or Public

This type of system is categorized as untrusted and is extremely vulnerable because there is no authentication for users accessing the system. In addition, there is no capability for access control at the file or directory level. Examples of operating systems that exhibit these traits include MS DOS/PC-DOS and the Microsoft Windows 3.x or 9x product line.

Level C: Medium Security, Confidential or Internal

This security level is composed of two sublevels: C1 and C2. A level C1 system requires user identification to gain access to the system via a user id and password. In addition, file and directory access permissions can be set to tailor access to data files and directories to specific groups or users of the system. These controls are known as discretionary access controls (DACs). System administration of a C1 system falls into the domain of a super-user or system administrator. The super-user or system administrator has complete control over the entire system. This is a vulnerable system should the super-user or system administrator become a disgruntled employee. A C2 type of system introduces auditing of all system security events and also introduces an additional layer of security that allows for granular access control and execution permissions. This additional level of control allows for the segregation of administrative duties without granting full administrative capabilities to a large group of individuals. For example, in Windows NT, one can allow the full backup of all files in the system to a backup operators group. Even if the operator has no access to a file, it will be backed up under the backup operators group. These additional permissions are available as User Rights. Examples of an operating system that exhibits these traits include Microsoft Windows NT 3.51–4.0, Windows 2000, Novell Netware, Sun Solaris, and HP UX.

Level B: High Security, Secret — Top Secret or Need-to-Know Basis

This security level is comprised of three sublevels: B1, B2, and B3. Each level contains all the attributes of level C; in addition, the attributes of each B level is additive of the preceding level's attributes.

A B1 type of system does not allow the creator of a file to modify its permissions. A B2 type of system introduces labeling of all devices within the system to achieve variable levels of security by assigning access permissions to these labels. A level B3 system introduces domain security, in which domains are separate subsystems that have their own security descriptions or definitions, and domains may interact with each other if authorized. However, a domain cannot impose its own privileges on other domains to gain additional access privileges.

Examples of operating systems that exhibit these traits include Trusted Solaris, Trusted IRIX, HP UX LBS, and HP MPE.

Level A: Maximum Security, Top Secret

This type of system contains all the attributes of a level B3 system. It also assumes that the overall design of the system was performed under tight controls and each step in the assembly process was verified. The system must be transported under guard to its destination for installation. Should any component be tampered with, the entire system would be considered untrusted. There are no known systems that exhibit these traits for commercial or industrial use.

Appendix B

Asset Inventory List

Item Number	Location	Department	P.O. Reference	Assigned User	Operating System	Local Installed Applications	Network Access Requirements	Remote Access Requirements	Security Profile Installed

Legend:

Item Number: This is a unique number that can identify the asset. For example, a desktop computer system might be labeled as WK00001-01, its associated monitor labeled as WK00001-02, its printer as WK00001-03, etc.

Location: This is an identifier that informs someone where the asset can be found. For example, Manufacturing Plant A; or, in the case of a building, 12-A for the twelfth floor Section A.

Department: This is the owner of the said asset. For example, Sales.

P.O. Reference: This is the Purchase Order Reference Number of the asset. It is usually required by accounting during an audit.

Assigned User: This is the user who uses the asset.

Operating System: This denotes what operating system the asset is running. Note that if it is a terminal, mark it as a terminal.

Local Installed Applications: These are all the local installed applications found on the machine. For audit verification purposes, this should match the department's software installation profile.

Network Access Requirements: These are a list of network resources that the asset and user profile have access to over the corporate network. For audit verification purposes, this should match the departments' network access profile.

Remote Access Requirements: This denotes if the machine is an access point for remote access purposes. For audit verification purposes, this machine requires additional controls to ensure it is operating within acceptable parameters.

Security Profile Installed: This refers to the installation of a Security Access profile. For example, Production users will use mandatory profiles to ensure proper data and applications access on the local area network (LAN). For audit verification purposes, the profile should be listed here so it can be cross-referenced for accuracy.

Appendix C

Windows NT 4.0 SP6a Post-Security Rollup Patch List

Core OS

- (Q243835) — Improve TCP Initial Sequence Number Randomness
- (Q243649) — Malformed Spooler Request Vulnerability
- (Q246045) — Malformed Resource Enumeration Argument Vulnerability
- (Q248183) — Syskey Keystream Reuse Vulnerability
- (Q248185) — Malformed Security Identifier Request Vulnerability
- (Q247869) — Spoofed LPC Port Request Vulnerability
- (Q249108) — RDISK Registry Enumeration File Vulnerability
- (Q249973) — Malformed RTF Control Word Vulnerability
- (Q248399) — Recycle Bin Creation Vulnerability
- (Q250625) — Registry Permissions Vulnerability
- (Q257870) — Malformed TCP/IP Print Request Vulnerability
- (Q259496) — OffloadModExpo Registry Permissions Vulnerability
- (Q259622) — Malformed Environment Variable Vulnerability
- (Q259728) — IP Fragment Reassembly Vulnerability
- (Q262694) — ResetBrowser Frame and Host Announcement Frame Vulnerabilities
- (Q264684) — Remote Registry Access Authentication Vulnerability
- (Q269239) — NetBIOS Name Server Protocol Spoofing Vulnerability
- (Q269049) — Relative Shell Path Vulnerability
- (Q266433) — Multiple LPC and LPC Ports Vulnerabilities
- (Q274835) — Netmon Protocol Parsing Vulnerability
- (Q275567) — Incomplete TCP/IP Packet Vulnerability

- (Q276575) — Phone Book Service Buffer Overflow Vulnerability
- (Q265714) — Registry Permissions Vulnerability
- (Q279336) — Weak Permissions on Winsock Mutex Can Allow Service Failure
- (Q280119) — Malformed NTLMSSP Request Can Enable Code to Run with System Privileges
- (Q283001) — Malformed PPTP Packet Stream Can Cause Kernel Exhaustion
- (Q293818) — Erroneous VeriSign-Issued Digital Certificates Pose Spoofing Hazard

Internet Information Server 4.0

- (Q188348) — IIS Malformed FTP List Request Vulnerability
- (Q234905) — Malformed HTR Request Vulnerability
- (Q233335) — Double Byte Code Page Vulnerability
- (Q238349) — Unauthorized Access to IIS Servers through ODBC Data Access with RDS
- (Q241805) — Domain Resolution and FTP Download Vulnerabilities
- (Q244613) — Windows Multi-threaded SSL ISAPI Filter Vulnerability
- (Q238606) — Virtual Directory Naming Vulnerability
- (Q246401) — Escape Character Parsing Vulnerability
- (Q252693) — Chunked Encoding Post Vulnerability
- (Q249599) — Virtualized UNC Share Vulnerability
- (Q254142) — Myriad Escaped Characters Vulnerability
- (Q260205) — Malformed Extension Data in URL Vulnerability
- (Q260838) — Undelimited .HTR Request and File Fragment Reading via .HTR Vulnerabilities
- (Q267559) — Absent Directory Browser Argument Vulnerability
- (Q269862) — File Permission Canonicalization Vulnerability
- (Q260347) — IIS Cross-Site Scripting Vulnerabilities
- (Q271652) — Invalid URL Vulnerability
- (Q269862) — Web Server Folder Traversal Vulnerability
- (Q274149) — Session ID Cookie Marking Vulnerability
- (Q277873) — Web Server File Request Parsing Vulnerability
- (Q285985) — Malformed .HTR Request Allows Reading of File Fragments
- (Q295534) — Superfluous Decoding Operation Could Allow Command Execution via IIS

Index Server

- (Q252463) — Malformed Hit-Highlighting Argument Vulnerability
- (Q294472) and (Q296185) — Index Server Search Function Contains Unchecked Buffer
- (Q300972) — Unchecked Buffer in Index Server ISAPI Extension Could Enable Web Server Compromise

Front Page Server Extensions

- (Q280322) — Malformed Web Form Submission Vulnerability

The following patches are not included in the Post SP6a Security Rollup kit.

Core OS

- (Q296441) — WebDAV Service Provider Can Allow Scripts to Levy Requests as User

Front Page Server Extensions

- (Q300477) — FrontPage Server Extension Sub-component Contains Unchecked Buffer

Java Virtual Machine

- (Q277014) — New Variant of VM File Reading Vulnerability

Procedural instructions to prevent unauthorized actions on a server include:

Core OS

- (Q169556) — Disabling Creation of Local Groups on a Domain by Non-Administrative Users
- (Q155197) — Windows NT 4.0 Does Not Delete Unattended Installation File
- (Q242294) — RASMAN Security Descriptor Vulnerability

Internet Information Server

- (Q184375) — Unauthorized ODBC Data Access with RDS and IIS
- (Q232449) — File Viewers Vulnerability
- (Q184375) — Unauthorized Access to IIS Servers through ODBC Data Access with RDS

Front Page Server Extensions

- (Q259799) — Link View Server-Side Component Vulnerability
- (Q260267) — Server-Side Image Map Components Vulnerability

Windows 2000 SP2 Post Patch List

This list is always growing and thus would be obsolete during the next Service Pack. Check the Microsoft Web site for Post Windows 2000 Service Pack 2 updates. Review the security patches for the core operating system and apply them. One should continually check the release of security patches and also enroll in the Microsoft Security Bulletin program (http://www.microsoft.com/security).

Appendix D

Letter Issued to Customers of the Egghead E-Commerce Site and Press Release

Dear Customer,

Egghead.com has discovered that a hacker has accessed our computer systems, potentially including our customer databases. While there is no indication that any customer information has been compromised, as a precautionary measure, we have taken immediate steps to protect you by contacting the credit card companies with whom we work. They are in the process of alerting card issuers and banks so that they can take the necessary steps to ensure the security of cardholders who may be affected.

We wish to underscore that we have taken these steps as precautions. We have no information at this time to suggest that any credit card information has been compromised. We are investigating this possibility, and we are doing everything we can to proactively protect you. If you would like further information, you may wish to contact the issuer of your credit card to determine what steps they are taking. We regret any inconvenience this may cause you.

We issued a press release on this matter earlier today. It is appended below this message. If you have additional questions, please call our customer service team at 1-800-EGGHEAD (344-4323).

Respectfully,

Jeff Sheahan, President & CEO Egghead.com, Inc.

Press Release:

Contact: Joanne Hartzell, Egghead.com, Inc. (650) 470-2713; John Stodder, Shoreen Maghame Edelman Worldwide, (323) 857-9100

Egghead.com Investigates Breach of Company Computer Systems Company Undertakes Immediate Precautionary Measures, Menlo Park, Calif., December 22, 2000

Egghead.com®, Inc. (Nasdaq: EGGS) released the following statement today: "Egghead.com has discovered that a hacker has accessed our computer systems, potentially including customer databases. As a precautionary measure, we have taken immediate steps to protect our customers by contacting the credit card companies we work with. They are in the process of alerting card issuers and banks so that they can take the necessary steps to ensure the security of cardholders who may be affected.

"Simultaneously, we have retained the world's leading computer security experts to conduct a thorough investigation of our security procedures and an analysis of this breach. We are also working with law enforcement authorities, who are in the process of conducting a criminal investigation.

"For many months, we have been in the process of strengthening our security systems in an effort to combat the increasing, industry-wide problem of malicious hacking. We are committed to providing the highest security standards in the industry, a process that has been ongoing and has involved a considerable investment on the part of our company. Those principles will continue to guide us going forward."

About Egghead.com: Egghead.com is a leading Internet direct marketer of technology and related products. With an emphasis on Small- to Medium-sized Business (SMB) customers, Egghead.com offers a wide range of products from computer hardware and software, consumer electronics and office products, to sporting goods and vacation packages. Its Clearance, After Work, and Auction formats offer bargains on excess and closeout goods and services. Egghead.com combines broad selection, low prices, and excellent service to provide an outstanding online shopping experience for businesses and consumers. Egghead.com is located on the Internet at http://www.egghead.com.

This press release contains forward-looking statements that involve risks and uncertainties, including but not limited to statements relating to steps taken to protect our customers. These forward-looking statements are based on information available to the company at the time of this release and we assume no obligation to update any such forward-looking statements. The statements in this release are not guarantees of future performance. Actual results could differ materially from current expectations as a result of numerous factors. For example, our ability to protect our customers from potential misuse of private information is limited, and the impact of compromised computed security on our business is unpredictable. Other risks and uncertainties associated with the business are detailed in our most recent Forms 10-K and 10-Q which are on file with the SEC and available through www.sec.gov.

Shoreen Maghame Edelman Worldwide (323) 857-9100 ext. 231, e-mail: shoreen.maghame@edelman.com.

Due to our desire to ensure every person who may be affected has been notified, you may be receiving this message even if previously expressing a desire not to receive e-mail from Egghead.com. If this is the case, please be assured you will not be receiving promotional e-mails from Egghead.com in the future.

To be removed from our mailing list, please go to:

http://promo2.eggheadlist.com/blist.asp?e=Username@organization.com.

Appendix E

Virus Memo

To: All Staff

From: Systems Operations

Date: month dd, yyyy

Re: Computer Virus Information

What Is a Virus?

A virus is a computer program that has been designed as a joke or to cause sabotage. It replicates itself by attaching to other programs on your personal computer or on the network and performs undesired processes or destroys information.

How Do You Know if Your PC Has a Virus?

The Systems department has a virus scanning package that will detect numerous variations and combinations of viruses.

The Systems department is actively pursuing the implementation of a network virus scanning product that will provide automatic virus detection on a daily basis. However, until this procedure is in place, we will continue to perform manual virus scanning services on incoming diskettes.

What Are the Symptoms of a Virus?[1]

- Disappearing files
- Unable to access files
- Unusual slowdown of software operations
- Strange messages
- Weird things appearing on your screen
- Hard disk errors
- Excessive hard disk activity (the hard disk operates more than should be usual or at strange times)
- Write-protect errors on the floppy drive when no activity is directed there

What Do You Do When You Suspect a Virus?

Call the Help Desk immediately! (Ext. 9999)

Do Not:

- Use the PC
- Sign on to the network
- Loan out any of your diskettes until the machine is determined to be virus-free

When Should You Scan for a Virus?

You should perform a virus scan during any of the following activities:

- Distributing diskettes to other sites, customers, etc.
- Downloading information from public bulletin boards
- Using diskettes from a home PC
- Using demonstration diskettes
- Using software from sources other than major distributors

How to Safeguard Your PC from Viruses

- Backup critical data files regularly. (Contact systems for assistance if necessary.)
- Reformat recycled diskettes prior to use.
- Use only company-approved software — do not use unauthorized copies of software.
- Have Systems scan all diskettes going out to clients or other sites.

- Write-protect all software and data diskettes that will be used on more than one PC.[2]
- Software obtained from Public Domain bulletin boards, the Internet, or schools *should not* be installed on any of XYZ Widget Manufacturing Limited's computers. If you require files from these services, have the files scanned by the Systems department, and never download when attached to the network.
- When work is brought in from home PCs, only pass data on to your work PC; that is, only copy Word Perfect or Excel/123 spreadsheets. This will minimize infections
- If using a home PC for business purposes, exercise the same precautions and scanning procedures applied at the office.
- Should you receive a diskette containing unknown data or files, do not process it until you know who sent it to you and why.
- Demo software received from other business sources may have been in other offices/PCs and should be scanned prior to use.
- When in doubt, have the Systems department scan the diskette in question.

Systems Operations would like to stress the fact that these virus programs are extremely dangerous in a networked environment and can cause serious damage to both data and programs that can lead to critical system downtime.

Notes

1. Many of these symptoms can be hardware-related problems; however, if you do experience them, please contact the Help Desk.
2. Write-protecting a diskette is done by physically altering the disk to prevent the writing of data to the disk. To accomplish this task for a 3.5-inch diskette, hold the disk in your hand with the round center facing you. Slide the tab at the bottom right-hand corner down to the open position. To re-enable writing to the diskette, slide the tab up to the closed position.

Appendix F

Sample Systems Operations Procedures Manual

Systems Department

Systems Operations

Version x.x: Date

The XYZ Company

Document Overview

This document provides an immediate reference to Systems Operations procedures for the XYZ computing environment. It is a guide for what to do in an emergency situation and on a day-to-day basis, as well as some details of who is responsible for what in terms of response time and other issues.

Author, Systems Department

1. What to do in an emergency

1.1 System Down

In the event that no one is able to log onto the network or a server(s) is(are) not functioning normally, follow these steps:

- Write down any error messages exactly as they appear.
- Examine the system error logs on all servers for any possible clues
  - Refer to Section xxx for System 1
  - Refer to Section xxx for System 2
  - Refer to Section xxx for System 3

- Check that all the cables attached to the server and or hubs are securely fastened.
- Examine the hub for any malfunctions or loose connections.
- If possible, shut down the server and restart the network. Notify network users via voicemail explaining the network situation.
- (Refer to "Start/Shut Down Network" in the Daily Network Maintenance section of this document.)
- If the server does not start or you are still not able to log on to the network, contact the Network Administrator. In the event of a major failure, contact the Network Administrator, Manager of Systems, and the V.P. of Systems. The problem will be assimilated and acted upon. In the event that the Systems team is unavailable within a short period of time, contact the external support provider for the system(s) requiring attention.
  - Network Administrator — Name, ext. 999 — Home phone number
  - Manager Systems — Name, ext. 999 — Home phone number
  - V.P. of Systems — Name, ext. 999 — Home phone number
  - External support contact 1 — Name, phone number — Support number, and contact number
  - External support contact 2 — Name, phone number — Support number, and contact number
- Fill out a Post-Mortem and attach additional information if necessary. (Refer to Appendix 3 for a sample Post-Mortem Report. They can be found online at ....)
- Once the problem has been corrected and you are able to log on to the network or server again, notify all network users via voicemail and inform them that they can begin to log on to the network.

1.2 Workstation Down

1.3 Printer Down

1.3.1 Local Printer Down

1.3.2 Network Printer Down

1.4 Tape Backup Down

1.5 Power Down

1.6 General Troubleshooting Methodology

1.7 Communications Down

2. Daily Network Maintenance

2.1 Start/Down Network

2.1.1 Starting the System 1

2.1.2 Stopping the System 1

2.1.3 Starting the System 2

2.1.4 Stopping the System 2

2.1.5 Starting the System 3

2.1.6 Stopping the System 3

2.2 Adding Users/Groups

2.2.1 Maintaining Network Users, Group, and Profile Account Information

2.2.1.1 Adding Users

2.2.1.2. Adding Groups

2.2.1.3. Adding Profiles

2.2.1.4. Adding Users to the Mail System

2.2.1.5. Adding Users to the Production System(s)

2.2.1.6. Adding User/Group Level Security

2.2.1.7. Deleting Users

2.2.1.8. Deleting Groups

2.2.1.9. Deleting/Modifying Profiles

2.2.1.10. Deleting Users from the Mail System

2.2.1.11. Deleting Users from Production System(s)

2.2.1.12. Deleting User/Group Level Security

2.3 Managing Tape Backups and Tape Restores

2.3.1 XYZ Backup Methodology

2.3.2 How to Schedule a Backup on System 1

2.3.3 How to Schedule a Backup on System 2

2.3.4 How to Schedule a Backup on System 3

2.3.5 How to Schedule a Restore on System 1

2.3.6 How to Schedule a Restore on System 2

2.3.7 How to Schedule a Restore on System 3

2.4 Adding Network Resource Assignments

2.4.1 Setting up Shares

2.4.1.1 Assigning Shares

2.4.1.2 Securing Shares

2.4.1.3 Removing Shares

2.4.1.4 Modifying Profiles to Add or Remove Shares

2.4.2 Setting up Network Printers

2.4.2.1 Assigning Network Printers

2.4.2.2 Assigning Network Printer Security

2.4.2.3 Removing Network Printers

2.4.2.4 Modifying Profiles to Add or Remove Printer Shares

2.5 Remote Access Systems

2.5.1 Adding Users to Remote Access Systems

2.5.2 Removing Users from Remote Access Systems

2.6 Maintenance of Updates, Patches, and Service Packs

2.6.1 Installing/Removing System 1 Updates or Patches

2.6.2 Installing/Removing System 2 Updates or Patches

2.6.3 Installing/Removing System 3 Updates or Patches

2.6.4 Standard Procedures for Installing/Removing Microsoft Service Packs/ Patches

2.7 Managing Network Hubs and the Cable Plant

2.8 Managing the Firewall

2.9 Managing the Router and Gateway

2.10 Managing the Mail Server Environment

2.11 Managing the Corporate Intranet and Internet

2.11.1 Managing the XYZ Web Site(s)

2.11.2 Managing the XYZ Internal Web Site

2.11.3 Managing the XYZ External Web Site

2.12 Daily Checklist Maintenance for System 1

2.13 Daily Checklist Maintenance for System 2

2.14 Daily Checklist Maintenance for System 3

2.15 Daily Checklist Maintenance for the Network

2.16 Weekly Checklist Maintenance for the Network

2.17 Daylight Savings Checklist Maintenance for the Network

2.18 Year-End Checklist Maintenance for the Network

3. Commercial Applications Maintenance

3.1 Standard Office Applications Installation

3.2 Standard Desktop OS Installation

3.3 Additional Applications Installation

3.4 Maintenance Standard Office Applications

3.5 Maintenance of Desktop Environment

3.6 Maintenance of Additional Applications Environment

4. In-House Developed Applications

4.1 Production System 1

4.1.1 Subsytem A

4.1.2 Subsystem B

4.1.3 Subsystem C

4.2 Production System 2

4.3 Production System 3

5. Desktop Maintenance

5.1 Maintenance of Hardware Equipment

5.2 Maintenance of Printer Equipment

5.3 Maintenance of Other Equipment

6. Appendices

Appendix 1. Client Contacts

Position	Name	Phone Number

Appendix 2. Vendor Contacts

[Vendor Name]		
Position	Name	Phone Number
[Vendor Name]		
Position	Name	Phone Number
[Vendor Name]		
Position	Name	Phone Number
[Vendor Name]		
Position	Name	Phone Number
[Vendor Name]		
Position	Name	Phone Number

Appendix 3. Post-Mortem Report for Interruption of Service

Systems Department

Recorded Date:

The XYZ Company

Document Overview

This document details specific events leading up to or occurring after a disruption to service in the XYZ computing environment. The Post-Mortem serves as a resource to outline chronological events leading up to or during the service disruption. The background section serves as an orientation of the time frame of the interruption: where, what, and possibly how it occurred.

[Author], Systems Department

1. Overview

1.1 Background to Event

Describe the events and situation leading up to the problem issue.

1.2 Resources

Describe the resources and users affected by this issue.

2. Chronological Description of Problem & Resolution

2.1 Description

Date/Time	*Event*

3. Business Impact

3.1 Systems Affected

The following table lists the applications or batch processing affected by the interruption of service.

List	*Items*	*Status*
Applications		
Batch processing		

3.2 Consequences

The following table describes the consequences of the interruption to service.

List	*Consequences*
Applications	

3.3 Cost Analysis

The attached spreadsheet at the end of this document presents a breakdown of the financial cost of the interruption of service.

4. Recommendations

4.1 Recommendations

There were ... separate problems concerning the [date as day, month, year] interruption to service. List items in full detail here for each problem.

Appendix G

Systems Polices and Guidelines

Systems Polices and Guidelines

Version 1.0

Updated and Distributed [Date]

1. Hardware

1.1 Purchasing and Acquisition

Purchasing of workstations and servers is done by the [Manager of Systems, Director of Systems, or V.P. of Systems]. To requisition PC workstation or server equipment, a written request should be submitted with Project Approval. Such a request should clearly state the benefits to XYZ Company in specific and quantifiable terms. All requests are subject to approval by the President of XYZ Company.

Requests for smaller amounts (up to $x,xxx)of equipment will be reviewed by the Director of Technology, while larger requests (over $x,xxx) will be referred to the President.

1.2 Standard Configurations

To ensure compatibility throughout XYZ Company, only equipment that conforms to one of our "standard configurations" will be purchased. These configurations are currently recorded in Appendix 1, Standard Workstation Configuration.

1.3 Moving Equipment

Physically moving and "trading" equipment should only be done by the Information Systems (IS) department. They have the equipment and expertise to safely move and re-install PCs. In addition, IS keeps track of PC equipment for asset and management purposes. If equipment is moved without authorization, these records will not be accurate.

1.4 Equipment at Employee's Homes

From time to time, we have situations where PC hardware or software will be temporarily moved to an employee's home. In these situations, the IS department must be notified so that asset information can be kept current. In addition, a memo describing the borrowed equipment must be placed in the employee's personnel file. Upon return of the borrowed equipment, the memo will be removed from the employee's file. These systems will also require upgrading from time to time. As such, it will be necessary for employees to bring these machines into the office for maintenance.

1.5 Equipment for New Employees

To ensure that a new employee has a desktop computer and printer, the IS department will require a minimum leadtime for the following situations:

Installation Type	*Required Notice*
New computer	5 working days
Reconfigure existing computer	2 working days

1.6 Employees Leaving the Company

From time to time, employees will leave the company. To prepare for system reconfiguration, the IS department will require notice prior to the employee's departure. In situations where there is an amicable resignation, five (5) days' notice will be required; otherwise, immediate notification will be required.

2. Software

2.1 Standard Software

Based on requirements, any of XYZ Company's standard software packages can be made available to company PC users. The current list of approved software can be viewed in Appendix 2, Standard Supported Software.

2.2 Trial-Basis Software

As new innovations in software occur, the IS group will continue to review new products. Products that are under review will be installed on a trial basis on test machines until their suitability has been determined by the IS group and the user community.

2.3 Non-Standard Software

PC users are not permitted — under any circumstances — to load non-standard software on XYZ Company's machines without the involvement/approval of management. This policy is in place as protection against computer viruses and "bombs" that can cause severe damage. Users wishing to try out software from other sources should contact IS so that standard anti-virus procedures can be run against the diskettes, CDs, or files. This also allows the IS group to evaluate and isolate any installation problems that may be encountered when a new application is loaded onto the PC.

2.4 Local Workstation Environment

With few exceptions, XYZ Company's standard directory file structure should be maintained on local machines. When a machine is first installed, the hard disk will contain standard directories for data.

Standard Directory Configuration for XYZ Company's PCs is:

System Directories	*Backup Directories*
C:\	C:\
C:\WINDOWS	C:\
C:\WINNT	C:\
C:\Program Files	C:\

Users who are familiar with the NT/Windows environment may add directories, but should not remove any of the standard directories. Should any changes occur to the standard directories, this will affect the reliability of the workstation's backup. Changes to the local system's registry files are not permitted without intervention of the IS group. Changes to system and application configurations are discouraged.

2.5 Licensing Policies

All software that is used at XYZ Company must be properly licensed and registered. If the normal purchasing procedures — through the IS group — are followed, this will be taken care of. XYZ Company takes its legal obligation to protect the interests of software developers very seriously. ***We do not*** *permit the use of software that was illegally copied, nor do we permit the illegal copying of software owned by XYZ Company.*

The Systems group recognizes that there will be instances when employees will be performing work at home on their own machines. Arrangements can be made to install standard software on an employee's personal machine. This is available for certain applications software that meets concurrent licensing agreements, or an additional license can be purchased. Once the requirements of use have been filled or the employee leaves the company, the software must be removed from the machine.

3. Backup and Security

3.1 Backups of Local PCs

Backups of key data on local PCs is the responsibility of the Systems group. *Note:* Only data stored within the standard directory structure defined within Section 2.3 will be backed up if the PC is powered on and accessible for the backup server. Backups of key data not contained within the standard directory structure will be the responsibility of the local PC user. Directories or data outside the specified standard needs to be communicated to Systems to be set up and included with the backup streams.

Day and Time of Week		*Type of Operation*
Monday	10:00 pm	Full backup
Tuesday	10:00 pm	Full backup
Wednesday	10:00 pm	Full backup
Thursday	10:00 pm	Full backup
Friday	10:00 pm	Full backup
Saturday		No backup

3.2 Backups of Network Disks

The IS department will back up the network servers onto DAT tape each day. Backups are performed as follows:

Day and Time of Week		*System 1*	*System 2*	*System 3*
Monday		No backup	No backup	No backup
Tuesday	2:00 am	Full backup	Full backup	No backup
Wednesday	2:00 am	Full backup	Full backup	No backup
Thursday	2:00 am	Full backup	Full backup	Full backup
Friday	2:00 am	Full backup	Full backup	No backup
Saturday	2:00 am	Full backup	Full backup	No backup

The tapes are cycled on a monthly basis and month-end tapes are stored for permanent retention. Tapes are sent off-site each day.

3.3 Password Rotation

The Windows NT network will force users to modify their passwords every 30 days. This is an important part of our security position. Users who have forgotten their passwords and locked themselves out of the network should contact IS for assistance. The requirements for passwords are as follows:

- Passwords are to be eight alphanumeric characters.
- Passwords must always be unique from previously used passwords.

Network users are reminded that access to the account is limited to three attempts. Access to the account is disabled after the third invalid attempt. To reestablish the account, contact the IS group.

3.4 Confidentiality of Passwords

Your network access password should be kept strictly confidential. If you have made it known to anyone — internally or externally — press the Ctrl+Alt+Del keys together and select Change Password from the Windows NT Logon Security dialog box. To change any other system passwords, contact the IS group.

3.5 Confidentially of Dial-In Numbers

Users dialing in to the network from external locations should treat XYZ Company's dial-in telephone number(s) as strictly confidential. Under no circumstances should it be divulged to anyone. At this time, dial-in privileges are reserved for individuals with specific business requirements.

3.6 Use of Admin Privileges

Network Administrator privileges are granted to those people who are specifically trained to make adjustments to the network and whose job requires it. These privileges can only be accessed through specific log-in IDs. No users, including IS staff, will have administrator privileges through their normal personal log-in IDs. Only the members of the Systems Operations staff will be entitled to access Administrator privileges on XYZ Company's network systems. In no manner will administrative privileges be granted outside the control of XYZ Company to third-party vendors, support providers, or affiliated companies unless a service level agreement/contract is in place or such privilege is beneficial to XYZ Company. Performing such action would be a serious breach of XYZ Company's security controls and expose the company to unnecessary risks.

XYZ Company's Network Administrator and System Administrator passwords are subject to the following:

- Passwords are to be 14 alphanumeric characters.
- Passwords are to be cycled every quarter.
- Passwords can never be reused and must be completely random in nature.

3.7 Virus Prevention

It is the responsibility of all XYZ Company employees to prevent the exposure of viruses to the corporate network by adhering to the following:

- Scan all diskettes received from *ANY* source (even vendor shrink-wrapped software) for viruses prior to their installation on a XYZ Company machine using the approved, current version of virus detection software. You will be able to determine if the anti-virus software is running by viewing a small icon on the task bar that resembles a shield.
- If a virus is suspected or detected, shut down the machine immediately and contact the IT group to investigate.

3.8 Systems Event Logging

Network events are audited for error, fault detection, and access violations. Any events that fall into these categories are documented and tracked in the Systems Operations Log Book. This book is stored in the computer room and maintained on a daily basis. Significant events are assessed by the Manager of Systems and a course of action is set to deal with the event. In the event of error or fault detection, staff members are trained to assess the situation and perform corrective maintenance. During error or fault detection events, senior management and staff will be notified immediately of the nature of the event and provide an estimate of its correction. After such events, a Post-Mortem will be issued outlining the situation and recommended procedures to limit future exposure. Any events that reflect an access violation will be immediately investigated and reported to senior management as to the cause and source of the violation. Access violations are defined as follows:

- *True violation:* an attempt to bypass XYZ Company's internal access control systems either through hacking or deliberately accessing areas of the system that one is not authorized to be accessing.
- *Apparent violation:* an attempt to access an area of the system that one is supposedly authorized to access but cannot.

3.9 Bulletin Board/Internet Downloading

Generally, the downloading of files from PC "bulletin boards" or the Internet at the office is discouraged. The downloading of files should only be done when there is a clear benefit to XYZ Company. If you must download files, use discretion; make sure the bulletin board or Internet site is reputable. Under no circumstances are applications software or shareware programs to be downloaded; refer to Section 2.3, Non-Standard Software.

3.10 Removal of Electronic Media

As a general rule, staff members are not allowed to remove diskettes containing corporate data from the office without managerial approval. This includes all network data files and subsets thereof. It does not include word processing documents for work at home. In all cases where XYZ Company information is taken from the office, it is the staff member's responsibility to ensure that the confidentially of this data is preserved.

3.11 Computer Room Physical Access Control

In general, only authorized Systems Operations staff and Human Resources will be granted physical access to the computer room and all its facilities.

3.12 Resource Access

Access to network resources is granted to network groups that are composed of the departments users. The users in these groups gain access through the group's Access Control Lists, which are linked to the resources that the group is authorized for. It may be necessary for an individual user to have his or her account tailored to their job function. This is required in instances where the user is in transition from one department to another, or the individual lacks sufficient privileges at the group level, as opposed to other members of the group, to perform a specific job function.

4. Electronic Communication Policy

4.1 Introduction

E-mail is information sent and received electronically between terminals linked to internal networks, telephone lines, or public communications networks such as the Internet. It includes point-to-point transmission of data or information via computer.

4.2 Access and Disclosure

XYZ Company reserves the right to access and disclose the contents of a user's electronic and telephonic communications at anytime, but intends to do so only when it has a business reason. Determining when such a business reason exists shall be within XYZ Company's sole and absolute discretion. Business reasons to access and disclose these communications may include, but are not limited to, the need to solve technical problems, the investigation of a theft or other crime, the prevention of unauthorized disclosure of confidential or proprietary information, suspicion of personal abuse of XYZ Company communications systems, and the review of communications upon the departure or death of a user. XYZ Company may use information regarding the number, sender, recipient, and address of communication for any business reason.

4.3 Password Security

The security and protection of individual passwords is a prime responsibility of the individual owner of the password. If something is authored out of a password-protected system, the presumption will be that the owner of the password authored it.

4.4 Confidential Information and Privileged Communications

Staff should proceed with caution in sending or forwarding confidential information on the communications systems because incorrect or inadvertent distribution can occur more easily than with some other means of communicating information.

4.5 Copyrighted Information

Use of XYZ Company's communications systems to copy or transmit documents, software, information, or other materials protected by the copyright laws, without copyright authorization, is prohibited.

4.6 Internet E-Mail

Employees may, without permission, send appropriate e-mail over the Internet in the normal course of business. However, because employee Internet e-mail addresses indicate an affiliation with XYZ Company, messages posted to listserv lists (or any other publicly available bulletin boards or forums) that in any manner refer to XYZ Company or any of its affiliated clients must be approved by Management. Messages that state an official XYZ Company position on any matter may only be posted by Executive Management.

4.7 Other Prohibited Use

- Engaging in any communication that is unlawful or in violation of XYZ Company's policy, including (but not limited to) communication that is defamatory, obscene, or prohibited by XYZ Company.

- The unauthorized use of passwords to gain access to another person's information or communications
- Using communications systems for electronic "snooping," i.e., to satisfy idle curiosity about the affairs of others, with no business reason for obtaining access to the files or communications of others (this prohibition applies to all staff, including XYZ Company's Systems personal and supervisors)
- Sending, forwarding, redistributing, or replying to "chain letters"
- Knowingly introducing a computer virus into the communications systems
- Using or advocating for issues, causes, or organizations of any kind when such solicitation or advocacy is deemed personal in nature and not recognized as furthering the reputation and interest of XYZ Company
- Unauthorized fundraising of any kind
- Excessive personal use of the communication systems

5. Miscellaneous Guidelines

5.1 Remote Network Access

Users dialing in to the network, particularly during office hours, should keep their sessions as short as possible. This will keep the line open for other users. Remote network access is currently reserved for mobile users, users with special requirements for their job function, and systems administration and maintenance.

5.2 Service Requests

Software and hardware service requests should be directed to the IS department (to the attention of xxx). These requests should be sent in writing using the Systems Request Form. A sample Systems Request Form is attached in Appendix 3, along with an explanation of usage.

5.3 Documentation of Programs and Queries

Programs and queries in regular use must be documented according to company standards and should be filed in the Information Systems Library and source code control facilities. In addition, diskettes with the actual program code and supporting requirements should be filed (using plastic sleeve) with the documentation.

A description of Methodology and Standards goes here.

All applications that modify values in any XYZ Company system, or create accounting or financial records or reports, *must be* controlled and secured.

5.4 Training and Education

The IS group will host a variety of internal PC-related courses. These will be targeted at specific training needs and, in most cases, will be open to all employees (pending manager's approval).

In most cases, these courses will be communicated via an "All Staff" memo, a voicemail or e-mail message. In situations where the course will not be generally available, the communication will be with department managers.

In addition, the IS group will be updating a Systems Library with useful resource books that can be signed out.

6. Appendices

Appendix 1. Standard Hardware Configurations

Standard Workstation Configuration

Hardware brand and CPU classification
Monitor brand and size standard
Memory, hard disk drive, network interface standard
CDROM and sound standard

Standard Laptop Configuration

Hardware brand and CPU classification
Display standard for laptops
Memory, hard disk drive, CD-ROM, and network interface standard

Standard Hardware Peripherals

Desktop printer standard
Departmental printer standard
Mouse standard
Modem standard
Additional hardware requirements standard list

Client Operating Systems and OS extenders

Standard laptop OS
Standard desktop OS

Network Operating Systems

Standard network OS

Appendix 2. Standard Supported Software

Standard Software Packages		
Title	Function	Manufacturer
Accounting Software Packages		
Title	Function	Manufacturer
Systems Development/Operations		
Title	Function	Manufacturer
Communications Software		
Title	Function	Manufacturer
Other Packages		
Title	Function	Manufacturer
In-House Developed Systems		
Application 1	Function	Department
Application 2		
Application 3		
Application 4		
Software Packages Being Phased Out		
Title	Function	Replacement
Software Packages Being Phased In		
Title	Function	Replacing
Software Package Being Evaluated		
Title	Function	
Unsupported Software Packages		
Title	Function	Manufacturer
Software Requested for Review		
Title	Function	Manufacturer

Appendix 3. Systems Request Form

Change Request Reference Number #______

Date Received		Date Required		Actual Installation Date
Target System(s)				
Systems Documentation	End-User Documentation	Operations Documentation	Emergency Patch	Other
(Y/N)	(Y/N)	(Y/N)	(Y/N)	
Risk	Change Code	1 – Communications 2 – Network 3 – Hardware 4 – Security	5 – Commercial Software 6 – In-house Software 7 – OS/Patch Software 8 – Other	
(L/M/H)				
Change Request from				
Change Approved by				
Change Implemented by				
Documentation Filed by				
Change Reason				
Users Affected by Change				
Business Impact of Change				
Change Description				
Test Results of Change				
Acceptance Sign-off				
Scheduled Installation Date			Notification of Change Sent	(Y/N)
Operations Back-out Procedures				
Manager Operations Completion Sign-off				
Operator Sign-off				

Appendix 4. Systems Logs and Post-Mortem Report

Operations Log Date: dd/mmm/yyyy

System/Device	Function Code: 1 Normal Ops 2 Impaired Ops 3 Critical Impairment	Description of Issue	Users Notified (Y/N)	Estimated Service Downtime	Documented (Y/N)	Operator Initials

Post-mortem Report

Systems Department

Recorded Date:

The XYZ Company

Document Overview

This document details specific events leading up to or after a disruption to service in the XYZ computing environment. The Post-Mortem serves as a resource to outline chronological events leading up to or during the service disruption. The background section serves as an orientation of the time frame of the interruption, where, what, and possibly how it occurred.

[Author], Systems

1. Overview

1.1 Background to Event

Describe the events and situation leading up to the problem issue.

1.2 Resources

Describe the resources and users affected by this issue.

2. Chronological Description of Problem and Resolution

2.1 Description

Date/Time	Event

3. Business Impact

3.1 Systems Affected

The following table lists the applications or batch processing affected by the interruption to service.

List	Items	Status
Applications		
Batch processing		

3.2 Consequences

The following table describes the consequences of the interruption to service.

List	Consequences
Applications	

3.3 Cost Analysis

The attached spreadsheet at the end of this document presents a breakdown of the financial cost of the interruption to service.

4. Recommendations

4.1 Recommendations

There were ... separate problems concerning the [date as day, month, year] interruption to service.
List items in full detail here for each separate problem.

Estimated Cost of <Named> Problem: <Date>

<table>
<tr><td colspan="7">Repair Support</td></tr>
<tr><td colspan="4"></td><td>% of Day</td><td>Hours</td><td>Cost</td></tr>
<tr><td colspan="4">Staff member</td><td></td><td></td><td></td></tr>
<tr><td colspan="4">Staff member</td><td></td><td></td><td></td></tr>
<tr><td colspan="4">Staff member</td><td></td><td></td><td></td></tr>
<tr><td colspan="4">Staff member</td><td></td><td></td><td></td></tr>
<tr><td colspan="6" align="right">Total Cost of Repair:</td><td></td></tr>
<tr><td colspan="7">Lost Productivity</td></tr>
<tr><td></td><td>Number of Staff Affected</td><td>% of Time</td><td>System Downtime</td><td>Lost Hours</td><td>Rates</td><td>Cost</td></tr>
<tr><td>Senior management</td><td></td><td></td><td></td><td></td><td></td><td></td></tr>
<tr><td>Tax department</td><td></td><td></td><td></td><td></td><td></td><td></td></tr>
<tr><td>Accounting</td><td></td><td></td><td></td><td></td><td></td><td></td></tr>
<tr><td>Other</td><td></td><td></td><td></td><td></td><td></td><td></td></tr>
<tr><td colspan="6" align="right">Total Cost of Productivity:</td><td></td></tr>
<tr><td colspan="7">Totals</td></tr>
<tr><td colspan="6" align="right">Support:</td><td></td></tr>
<tr><td colspan="6" align="right">Productivity:</td><td></td></tr>
<tr><td colspan="6" align="right">Total:</td><td></td></tr>
</table>

Appendix H

Computer Security and Usage Policy

XYZ Company

Computer Security and Use Policy

Sample Policy

DRAFT – Dated dd/mm/yyyy

1. Authority

This document was approved by [Senior Management Group or Systems Steering Committee] of the XYZ Company.

2. Introduction

Users of XYZ Company computer system resources have a responsibility not to abuse the computer system and to respect the rights of others. The computer systems are critical to the proper functioning of the company. It is the responsibility of every member of the company to ensure that the systems they use are protected from destruction, unauthourized access, unauthourized modification, and loss. This document will serve as a guideline to address these issues.

3. Policy Purpose

The purpose of this Computer Security and Usage Policy is to ensure an information infrastructure that promotes the basic missions of XYZ Company. Computers and networks are powerful enabling technologies for accessing and distributing the information and knowledge developed within XYZ Company and elsewhere. As such, they are strategic technologies for the current and future needs of the company. Because these technologies give individuals the ability to access and copy information from remote sources, users must be mindful of the rights of others to their privacy, intellectual property, and other rights. This Usage Policy codifies what is considered appropriate usage of computer systems with respect to the rights of others. With the privileges to use the information resources of the company come specific responsibilities outlined in this policy.

4. Policy Scope and Applicability

This policy is applicable to all XYZ Company employees and to others granted use of XYZ Company computer systems. This policy refers to all XYZ Company computer systems, whether individually controlled or shared, stand-alone or networked. It applies to all computer and computer communication facilities owned, leased, operated, or contracted by XYZ Company. This includes word processing equipment, personal computers, workstations, minicomputers, and associated peripherals and software, regardless of whether used for business, administration, research, or other purposes.

XYZ Company does not exist in isolation from other communities and jurisdictions and their laws. Under some circumstances, as a result of investigations, subpoena, or lawsuits, XYZ Company may be required by law to provide records (electronic or otherwise) or other information related to those records or relating to use of information resources.

5. Computer Security Officer

The XYZ Company Computer Security Officer or the person designated by [Senior Management or Systems Steering Committie] shall be the primary contact for the interpretation, enforcement, and monitoring of this policy and the resolution of problems concerning it. Any issues concerning law shall be referred to the General Counsel for advice.

The Computer Security Officer shall be responsible for interpretation of this policy, resolution of problems and conflicts with local policies, and special situations.

Where violations of this policy come to his attention, the Computer Security Officer is authorized to work with the appropriate administrative units to obtain compliance with this policy.

Only the XYZ Company Computer Security Officer or designate can authorize the inspection of private data or monitoring of messages (including electronic mail) when there is reasonable cause to suspect improper use of computer or network resources.

In cases where the inspection of personal data is required, a "Right to Access" report form must be completed and signed by the Human Resources manager in conjunction with a senior-level director of the company.

6. Management Responsibility

Each manager is responsible for the security of information resources in all offices under their jurisdiction and for implementing information security requirements on an office-wide basis.

7. System Administrator Responsibilities

While XYZ Company is the legal "owner" or "operator" of all computers and networks purchased or leased with company funds, oversight of any particular system is delegated to the "System Administrator." The System Administrator has additional responsibilities to the company as a whole for the system(s) under his oversight, regardless of the policies of his department or group.

The System Administrator should use reasonable efforts to:

- Take precautions against theft of or damage to the system components
- Faithfully execute all hardware and software licensing agreements applicable to the system
- Treat information about, and information stored by, the system's users in an appropriate manner and to take precautions to protect the security of a system or network and the information contained therein
- Promulgate information about specific policies and procedures that govern access to and use of the system, and services provided to the users or explicitly not provided. This information should describe the data backup services, if any, offered to the users. A written document given to users or messages posted on the computer system itself shall be considered adequate notice.
- Cooperate with the System Administrators of other computer systems or networks, whether within or without the company, to find and correct problems caused on another system by the use of the system under his control

Where violations of this policy come to his attention, the System Administrator is authorized to take reasonable actions to implement and enforce the usage and service policies of the system and to provide for security of the system.

A System Administrator may temporarily suspend access privileges if he believes it necessary or appropriate to maintain the integrity of the computer system or network.

7.1 Systems Event Logging

Network events are audited for error, fault detection, and access violations. Any events that fall into these categories are documented and tracked in the Systems Operations Log Book. This book is stored in the computer room and maintained on a daily basis. Significant events are assessed by the [Manager of System, Director of Systems, or V.P. of Systems] and a course of action is set to deal with the event. In the event of error or fault detection, staff members are trained to assess the situation and perform corrective maintenance. During error or fault detection events, senior management and staff will be notified immediately of the nature of the event and provide an estimate of its correction. After such events, a Post-Mortem will be issued, outlining the situation and recommended procedures to limit future exposure. Any events that reflect an access violation will be immediately investigated and reported to senior management as to the cause and source of the violation. Access violations are defined as follows:

- *True violation:* an attempt to bypass XYZ Company internal access control systems either through hacking or deliberately accessing areas of the system that one is not authorized to be accessing.
- *Apparent violation:* an attempt to access an area of the system that one is supposedly authorized to access but cannot.

7.2 Computer Room Physical Access Control

In general, only authorized Systems Operations staff and Human Resources will be granted physical access to the computer room and all its facilities.

8. Review and Revision of Policy and Procedures

The policies and procedures outlined in this document are subject to revision as systems, and the methods used to compromise them, change. Any staff member seeking to clarify or request revisions to the policies or procedures outlined in this document should contact the Computer Security Officer.

9. Electronic Communications Policy

E-mail is information sent and received electronically between terminals linked to internal networks, telephone lines, or public communications networks such as the Internet. It includes point-to-point transmission of data or information via computer.

9.1 Access and Disclosure

XYZ Company reserves the right to access and disclose the contents of a user's electronic and telephonic communications at anytime, but intends to do so only when it has a business reason. Determining when such a business reason exists shall be within XYZ Company's sole and absolute discretion. Business reasons to access and disclose these communications may include, but are not limited to, the need to solve technical problems, the investigation of a theft or other crime, the prevention of unauthorized disclosure of confidential or proprietary information, suspicion of personal abuse of XYZ Company communications systems, and the review of communications upon the departure or death of a user. XYZ Company may use information regarding the number, sender, recipient, and address of communication for any business reason.

9.2 Password Security

The security and protection of individual passwords is a prime responsibility of the individual owner of the password. If something is authored out of a password-protected system, the presumption will be that the owner of the password authored it.

9.3 Confidential Information and Privileged Communications

Staff should proceed with caution in sending or forwarding confidential information on the communications systems because incorrect or inadvertent distribution can occur more easily than with some other means of communicating information.

9.4 Copyrighted Information

Use of XYZ Company communications systems to copy or transmit documents, software, information, or other materials protected by the copyright laws, without copyright authorization, is prohibited.

9.5 Internet E-Mail

Employees may, without permission, send appropriate e-mail over the Internet in the normal course of business. However, because employee Internet e-mail addresses indicate an affiliation with XYZ Company, messages posted to listserv lists (or any other publicly available bulletin boards or forums) that in any manner refer to XYZ Company or any of its affiliated clients must be approved by Management. Messages that state an official XYZ Company position on any matter may only be posted by Executive Management.

9.6 Approved Uses

XYZ Company computer systems may only be used for the business activities of the company and occasional personal use. The use of a computer is subject to audit at anytime by XYZ Company management.

Personal use of XYZ Company computer equipment may only be approved by management if such use is clearly insignificant, does not interfere or compete with XYZ Company business, and does not involve any incremental cost to XYZ Company. Any questions concerning the personal use of XYZ Company computer resources should be discussed with one's manager.

9.7 Prohibited Uses

- Engaging in any communication that is unlawful or in violation of XYZ Company policy, including (but not limited to) communication that is defamatory, obscene or prohibited by XYZ Company
- The unauthorized use of passwords to gain access to another person's information or communications
- Using communications systems for electronic "snooping," i.e., to satisfy idle curiosity about the affairs of others, with no business reason for obtaining access to the files or communications of others (this prohibition applies to all staff, including XYZ Company Systems personnel and supervisors)
- Sending, forwarding, redistributing, or replying to "chain letters"
- Knowingly introducing a computer virus into the communications systems
- Using or advocating for issues, causes, or organizations of any kind when such solicitation or advocacy is deemed personal in nature and not recognized as furthering the reputation and interest of XYZ Company
- Unauthorized fundraising of any kind
- Excessive personal use of the communication systems

10. Legal Issues

10.1 Software Licensing

A valid license must be held for all licensed software that is installed on XYZ Company computers. Any licensed software installed on the computer systems of XYZ Company must have licenses stored in a secure location and be produced during periodic audit by the Systems department.

10.1.1 Licensing Policies

All software that is used at XYZ Company must be properly licensed and registered. If the normal purchasing procedures are followed, this will be taken care of. XYZ Company takes its legal obligation to protect the interests of software developers very seriously. We do not permit the use of software that was illegally copied, nor do we permit the illegal copying of software owned by XYZ Company.

The Systems group recognizes there will be instances where employees will be performing work at home on their own machines. Arrangements can be made to install standard software on employee's personal machines. This is available for certain application software only that meets concurrent licensing agreements or an additional license can be purchased. Once the requirements of use have been filled or the employee leaves the company, the software must be removed from the machine.

10.2 Trial-Basis Software

As new innovations in software occur, the IS group will continue to review new products. Products that are under review will be installed on a trial basis on test machines until their suitability has been determined.

10.3 Non-Standard Software

PC users are not permitted — under any circumstances — to load non-standard software on XYZ Company machines without the involvement/approval of management. This policy is in place as protection against computer viruses and "bombs" that can cause severe damage. Users wishing to try out software from other sources should contact IS so that standard anti-virus procedures can be run against the diskettes, CDs, or files. This also allows the IS group to evaluate and isolate any installation problems that may be encountered when a new application is loaded onto the PC. This statement is in place to protect both XYZ Company and the user from violating software licensing laws.

11. Personal Computers

11.1 Purchasing and Acquisition

Purchasing of workstations and servers is done by the [Manager of Systems]. To requisition PC workstation or server equipment, a written request (memo or e-mail) should be submitted with Project Approval. Such a request should clearly state the benefits to XYZ Company in specific and quantifiable terms. All requests are subject to approval by the [Systems Steering Committee or departmental V.P.].

Requests for smaller amounts (up to $x,xxx) of equipment will be reviewed by the [Manager of Systems], while larger requests (over $x,xxx) will be referred to the [Systems Steering Committee].

11.2 Standard Configurations

To ensure compatibility throughout XYZ Company, only equipment that conforms to one of our "standard configurations" will be purchased. These configurations are currently recorded in Appendix 3, Standard Hardware Configurations.

11.3 Moving Equipment

Physically moving and "trading" equipment should only be done by the Information Systems department. They have the equipment and expertise to safely move and reinstall PCs. In addition, IS keeps track of PC equipment for asset and management purposes. If equipment is moved without authorization, these records will not be accurate.

11.4 Equipment at Employee's Homes

From time to time we have situations where PC hardware or software will be temporarily moved to an employee's home. In these situations, the IS department must be notified so that asset information can be kept current. In addition, a memo describing the borrowed equipment must be placed in the employee's personnel file. Upon return of the borrowed equipment, the memo will be removed from the employee's file. These systems will also require upgrading from time to time; as such, it will be necessary for employees to bring these machines into the office for maintenance.

11.5 Equipment for New Employees

To ensure that a new employee has a desktop computer and printer, the Operations department will require a minimum leadtime for the following situations:

Installation Type	*Required Notice*
New computer	5 working days
Reconfigure existing computer	2 working days
Cycle down	7 working days

From time to time, new equipment will also be purchased to accommodate new employees. These new acquizations may require both an installation and reconfiguration when equipment is cycled down. In those situations, seven days' leadtime will be required.

11.6 Resource Issue

Not all members of staff have access to the same resources. Each staff member has access to resources that enable her or him to carry out her or his purpose of employment.

11.7 Theft

It is the responsibility of each staff member to help reduce the possibility of theft of XYZ Company equipment and information. The following are some suggestions to help reduce this threat.

- Use power-on, screen-saver, or other such passwords to prevent unauthourized access to your computer system. Power-on passwords must be communicated to your manager to access your system in case of emergency when you are not available.
- Where possible, it is suggested that you lock your office to reduce access to the computer system and information contained within your office. Locking printouts, diskettes, and other information in file cabinets is also recommended.
- When traveling, keep portable computers in your posession. Do not leave them exposed in cars or hotel rooms. Do not leave computer equipment or information with hotel staff or airport baggage.
- Remove confidential information that is unnecessary for your current business needs from your portable computer.
- If you are a portable computer user and have been provided with a Windows NT Emergency Repair Disk or other such recovery disk, do not store this disk with your computer. Store this disk separately from your computer and treat it as a key to a safe.

11.8 Local Workstation Environment

With few exceptions, XYZ Company standard directory file structure should be maintained on local machines. When a machine is first installed, the hard disk will contain standard directories for data.

Standard Directory Configuration for XYZ Company PCs

System Directories	*Backup Directories*
C:\	C:\DVL (data directories for systems development)
C:\WINDOWS	C:\WINDOWS\PROFILES\User
	(all data stored under the "Personal" folder is backed up)
C:\WINNT	C:\WINNT\PROFILES\User
	(all data stored under the "Personal" folder is backed up)
C:\Program Files	Any specific configuration files (e.g., bookmarks)

Users who are familiar with the NT/Windows environment may add directories, but should not remove any of the standard directories. Should any changes occur to the standard directories, this will affect the reliability of the workstation's backup. Changes to the local systems' Registry files are not permitted without the intervention of the IS Operations group. Changes to system and application configurations are discouraged.

11.9 Standard Software and Configuration

Based on requirements, any of the XYZ Company standard software packages can be made available to company PC users. The current list of approved software can be viewed in Appendix 4, Standard Supported Software.

Standard Development Workstation Layout. Please refer to the document on XYZ Company Development Workstation Installation and Configuration. This document can be obtained from the [Manager of Systems Development].

Standard Desktop Workstation Configuration Layout. Please refer to the document on XYZ Company Standard Workstation Installation and Configuration. This document can be obtained from the [Manager of Systems Development].

Standard Server Configuration Layout. Please refer to the document on on XYZ Company Server Installation and Configuration. This document can be obtained from the [Manager of Systems Development].

12. Passwords and Access Controls

A password is the primary method of securing a computer. It identifies you, allows you to access restricted computer services, and associates you with what occurs on a computer system. Your password should be kept secret and not shared with anyone else.

12.1 Password Rotation

The Windows NT network will force users to modify their passwords every 30 days. This is an important part of our security position. Users who have forgotten their passwords and locked themselves out of the network should contact IS for assistance. The requirements for passwords are as follows:

- Passwords are to be eight alphanumeric characters
- Passwords must always be unique from previously used passwords

Network users are reminded that access to the account is limited to three attempts. Access to the account is disabled after the third invalid attempt. To reestablish the account, contact the IS group.

12.2 Confidentiality of Passwords

Your network access password should be kept strictly confidential. If you have made it known to anyone — internally or externally — press the

Ctrl+Alt+Del keys together and select change password from the Windows NT Logon Security dialog box. To change any other system passwords, contact the Network Administrator.

12.3 Handling Passwords

Under no circumstances should a password be written down on paper and stored in an unsecured fashion. If you have a concern with forgetting your password, write it on a piece of paper, seal it in an envelope, and then store it in a locking cabinet or company safe.

12.4 Use of Admin Privileges

Network Administrator privileges are granted to those people who are specifically trained to make adjustments to the network and whose job requires it. These privileges can only be accessed through specific login IDs. No users, including IS staff, will have administrator privileges through their normal personal login IDs. Only the members of the Systems Operations staff will be entitled to access Administrator privileges on XYZ Company network systems. Under no circumstances will administrative privileges be granted outside the control of XYZ Company to third-party vendors, support providers, or affiliated companies, unless a service level agreement/contract is in place or such privilege is beneficial to XYZ Company. Performing such action would be a serious breach of XYZ Company security controls and expose the company to unnecessary risks.

XYZ Company Network Administrator and System Administrator passwords are subject to the following:

- Passwords are to be 14 alphanumeric characters.
- Passwords are to be cycled once each year.
- Passwords can never be reused and must be completely random in nature.

13. Business Continuity

13.1 Manager Access to Equipment

It is the responsibility of the manager to ensure that he or she can access the systems of those whom he or she manages.

13.2 Recoverability of Data

In most cases, the Systems department has provided the manner in which your data is backed up and recovered. In those cases, the Systems department will provide for the recovery of this data in the event of computer malfunction or accidental deletion. XYZ Company computer systems are backed up every weeknight. As a result, information created and lost between backup intervals is unrecoverable.

In some cases, individual users or project groups have taken the responsibility for backing up certain types of data. In these cases, it is the responsibility of the individual creating this data and the manager of the project group to ensure that this information is adequately stored and recoverable. It is required to have recovery procedures documented and stored with the data. It is imperative that the backup media be labeled properly and secured against unauthourized access. In the case of legacy software, it is also necessary that the means to recover the data are stored as well (such means typically contain the hardware and software required to install the program used to create the data).

Requests to backup additional data should be directed to the Systems department, Network Administrator, or Manager of Systems.

13.2.1 Backup of Local PC Data

Backup of data on local PCs is the responsibility of the Systems Operations group. Only data stored within the standard directory structure defined in Section 11.8 will be backed up if the PC is powered on and accessible for the backup server.

Local backup of data is performed after the main server data backup operation has been completed.

Backups of data not contained within the standard directory structure will be the responsibility of the local PC User.

13.2.2 Backup of Data Residing on Network Shares

The IS department will backup the network server(s) onto tape each day. Backups are performed as follows:

Day of Week	*Server*
Monday	9:00 pm
Tuesday	9:00 pm
Wednesday	9:00 pm
Thursday	9:00 pm
Friday	7:00 pm

Local server backups are performed each night to a local system hard disk. This local copy is then transferred to the master backup server for tape backup.

Day of Week	*Server*
Monday	6:30 pm
Tuesday	6:30 pm
Wednesday	6:30 pm
Thursday	6:30 pm
Friday	6:30 pm

The tapes are cycled on a monthly basis and month-end tapes are stored for a period of one year. Month-end tapes are stored off site. [Additional location and responsibility to be added here]. Please refer to the document on XYZ Company Backup and Recoverability strategy for a full explanation of the backup process being exercised at XYZ Company.

14. Confidential Information

Information of a confidential nature shall only be provided to those who need to know it. Storage of confidential information must be done with appropriate access controls. Under no circumstances should confidential information be stored with unrestricted access. If you have concerns regarding this, or are uncertain how to ensure that access controls are in place, contact the Systems department, Network Administrator.

The following suggestions will help you secure the confidential information that you create and manage.

- Do not leave hardcopy, diskettes, or tapes in an unsecured area when they are not in use.
- Hardcopies of confidential information (such as phone lists and company memoranda) should be destroyed (shredded) before being disposed of.
- Avoid using cellular or cordless phones to discuss confidential information.
- Avoid discussing confidential information while using public phones or within the hearing range of others.
- If sending confidential information via fax, verify the destination fax machine's phone number.
- Do not divulge system information or passwords over the telephone to unauthourized individuals. It is extremely rare for anyone outside of XYZ Company to need to know this information for appropriate XYZ Company business. Anyone requesting this type of information should be redirected to the Systems Security Officer.

Any member of XYZ Company staff who obtains confidential information from another organization and wishes to store this data on XYZ Company property or with XYZ Company systems must comply with the appropriate usage and security policies of the organization from which the information was obtained.

14.1 Access and Disclosure of Client Data

XYZ Company works together with its clients and, in doing so, trusts each other's ability to protect its assets. It is thus necessary to make sure that any and all client-related data be treated as confidental and not be left in full view for others to see. Please make sure that all printouts, screen shots, CDs, or diskettes that contain client data are secured. Once specific client data has been used and finished with, it should be either returned or destroyed. Please maintain a conscious effort to protect client data as XYZ Company invites clients on site from time to time.

14.2 Removal of Electronic Media

As a general rule, staff are not allowed to remove diskettes containing corporate data from the office without managerial approval. This includes all network data files and subsets thereof. It does not include word processing documents for work at home. In all cases where XYZ Company information (or entrusted client information) is taken from the office, it is the staff member's responsibility to ensure that the confidentially of this data is preserved.

15. Computer Viruses

Be alert to the potential dangers of accepting programs from public sources such as the Internet. Although anti-virus software has been made available for XYZ Company computers, new viruses are constantly being created. If you have any concern about the safety of a program or file that you wish to download or install, please contact the Systems department.

If you suspect that a virus has infected the computer you use, contact the Systems department, Network Administrator, immediately to help prevent its spread to other computers.

False alarms and hoaxes regarding viruses and other harmful code are extremely prevalent. If you receive an e-mail concerning any security warning, please do not forward it to other employees. Send a copy to the Computer Security Officer only.

16. Networks

When your computer is connected to the XYZ Company network, do not misrepresent yourself (i.e., represent someone else).

Do not connect communications devices such as modems to the computer you use without the assistance of a member of the Systems department. If such a requirement is necessary, the system must be locked down for security reasons. Applications such as PC Anywhere, Carbon Copy, and Co Session must be properly secured to prevent unauthorized access to the network.

Do not attempt to modify your computer or its configuration to share information with others. If you wish to do so, please contact the Systems department, Network Administrator, to aid with this to ensure that the information is secured against unauthourized access.

17. Remote Access and Other External Connections

Connecting XYZ Company systems and networks to non-XYZ Company systems and networks through modems or direct-line attachments can present a very serious risk to XYZ Company. It is possible to expose the entire XYZ Company network systems and data without even knowing that you are doing so. For this reason, it is recommended that you contact a member of the Systems department, Network Administrator, before connecting any devices to your computer.

17.1 Confidentially of Dial-In Numbers

Users dialing in to the network from external locations should treat XYZ Company dial-in telephone number(s) as strictly confidential. Under no circumstances should it be divulged to anyone. At this time, dial-in privileges are reserved for individuals with specific business requirements.

18. The Internet

The Internet is a rapidly growing network that is controlled by many people with different views of what is and is not appropriate. While it is an important resource and in some cases provides for the only way to complete some job-related tasks, the use of the Internet is not without risk.

18.1 Downloading Files

Generally, the downloading of files from PC "bulletin boards" or the Internet at the office is discouraged. The downloading of files should only be done when there is a clear benefit to XYZ Company. If you must download files, use discretion; make sure the bulletin board or Internet site is reputable. Under no circumstances are applications software or shareware programs to be downloaded. Refer to Section 10.3, Non-Standard Software.

18.2 Confidentiality

The Internet is available to people in different organizations and countries. These people may have different views on the appropriate use of computers and information. Not all of these people will have XYZ Company's best interests in mind. For this reason, it is best to presume that any information sent across the Internet has the ability to be read by a number of unknown people.

18.3 Inappropriate Materials

Many Internet Web sites contain and distribute material that is objectionable in the workplace. While it is impossible to list every possible Web site or form of objectionable material, some clear examples include:

- Sexually explicit images and related material
- Advocation of illegal activities
- Advocation of intolerance for others

XYZ Company employees are not to access such Web sites, or distribute or obtain such material through the Internet or any computer system owned by XYZ Company. Compliance with this policy is a condition of employment. Questions regarding the appropriateness of Web sites should be directed to one's manager.

Although XYZ Company does not routinely scan Web sites for inappropriate material, maintain a list of inappropriate Web sites, or block access to sites containing inappropriate material, staff shall not assume that providing access to inappropriate sites implies that XYZ Company condones the access to such sites or the use of its materials.

18.4 Unsolicited E-Mail

XYZ Company employees hold Internet e-mail addresses and on occasion may receive unsolicited e-mail messages to those addresses. Sometimes referred to as spam or junkmail, these messages are dealt with most effectively by ignoring the sender and deleting the message.

In the case that an individual or organization demonstrates that they are to be a continuous source of this type of mail, technical control may be necessary. If this situation is affecting you, please contact the Computer Security Officer.

Your use of the Internet should be guided by this document. Should you require clarification or request that additional guidelines be provided, please contact the Computer Security Officer.

19. Contract Employees and Business Associates

It is imperative that the work done on any XYZ Company computer system by contract employees or business associates be understood by the XYZ Company staff member assigned to manage the project or task.

Non-XYZ Company personnel have access to a great deal of sensitive information in various forms. It is possible to either intentionally or unknowingly compromise a secure computer system.

Software applications (including macros) must have complete source code provided to the XYZ Company project manager/liaison. It is customary that programmers place hidden features (known as Easter eggs, backdoors, mockingbirds, or logic bombs) in their code. A hacker or disgruntled employee may make use of such a feature to compromise XYZ Company systems. It is the responsibility of each project manager/liaison to ensure that any system developed by a person on her or his project team does not contain such code. In addition, it is the responsibility of each project manager/liaison to ensure that such source code must also be stored off-site for data recovery and business continuity purposes.

20. Termination of Employment

It is the responsibility of the Human Resouces department to notify the Computer Security Officer immediately upon the termination of employment of any staff member. The Systems department will ensure that computer system accounts and points of access are secured.

21. Personal Use

Although the use of XYZ Company computers is deemed to be primarily for business purposes, it is understood that, on occasion, the computers may be used for personal purposes as well. It must be understood that the personal use of computer systems must:

- Not interfere with one's job or the jobs of any other staff member
- Not interfere with XYZ Company business
- Comply with the security and usage guidelines contained within this document

In addition to the above, personal use of XYZ Company computer systems shall not include:

- Solicitation of XYZ Company employees
- Provision of information about or lists of XYZ Company employees to others
- Commercial solicitations of one's non-XYZ Company business enterprise

Questions or concerns about the appropriate use of computer equipment assigned to you should be directed to your manager.

22. Conclusion

Users of XYZ Company computer systems have a responsibility not to abuse these and to respect the rights of others. The computer systems are critical to the proper functioning of the company. It is the responsibility of every member of the company to ensure that the computers they use are protected from destruction, unauthourized access, unauthourized modification, and loss. It is expected that all XYZ Company employees will abide by this document. In the event that a circumstance arises in which the application of this document to the circumstance is confusing or inappropriate, this document will be revised to include an appropriate course of action. Such issues should be directed to the Computer Security Officer immediately.

23. Appendices

Appendix 1. Definitions of Terminology

Terminology related to computers and other information systems are used throughout this document. Rudimentary definitions are provided here to assist in the communication of the issues.

Associate: Someone who is contracted or volunteering to assist but is not employed directly by XYZ Company.

Company Data: See *Company Information.*

Company Information: Any information or data, in any medium or form, that is owned and used by a member of the company to conduct its business or the business of any of the subsidiaries.

Company Purposes: Except for minimal personal use, the computer systems purchased by XYZ Company are to be used to perform tasks related to a job function.

Computer System: A complete, or any component of a computer system. This includes but is not limited to personal computers (PCs), laptops/notebooks, workstations, and mini-computers. Supplies such as printer paper, floppy disks, and tapes may also be considered part of the system as a whole.

Computer Virus: A program designed to copy itself into other programs. It may cause the loss or alteration of data on a computer, or in extreme cases, to completely disable a computer. A virus is actived when the program it has infected is executed/run/loaded.

Disaster: A hostile act, or a natural occurrence that severely impedes the operational status of the systems.

Encryption: The conversion of data into a secret code for secure storage or transmission over a public network. The original data is converted into a coded equivalent called ciphertext via an encryption algorithm. The ciphertext is decoded (decrypted) at the receiving end and turned back into plaintext.

Encryption Key: A sequence of numbers, typically from 40 to 128 bits in length, that allows information to be scrambled so that it is unreadable. The scrambled information only becomes readable again when it is decrypted using the encryption key.

Manager: A person to whom other staff members report.

Network Infrastructrue: Includes but is not limited to network cabling and network devices such as hubs, switches, routers, and repeaters.

Physical Asset: Computer and network communications equipment, magnetic media, technical equpment, furniture, etc.

Software Asset: Application software, system software, development tools, and utilities.

Staff: A term used to include anyone who is employed by XYZ Company.

System: See Computer System.

System Administrator: A person who has been designated to manage a computer or network system.

Appendix 2. Selecting a Good Password

The following guidelines are designed to help you select passwords that are not easily compromised by unauthourized persons. Your password should:

- Be at least eight characters in length
- Contain at least one alphabetic and one non-alphabetic character
- Contain no more than three characters identical to your previous password
- Contain no more than two identical consecutive characters
- Not contain your username
- Be changed at least once every six months

Note:

On occasion, you may access computer systems on the Internet or elsewhere that are not under XYZ Company control. Under no circumstances should you use a password for these systems that is identical to a password you use to secure XYZ Company computers.

Appendix 3. Standard Hardware Configurations

Company Workstation Standard

- Brand and CPU class of machine
  - Single or dual processor capable
- Memory standard
- Hard drive standard
- Floppy drive standard
- CD-ROM standard
- Video standard
- Keyboard standard
- Mouse standard
- Network interface standard
- Operating system standard
- Monitor standard

Company Server Standard

- Brand and CPU class of machine
  - Dual or Quad processor capable
- Memory standard
- Tape drive standard
- Hard drive configuration standard (RAID 0, 1, 5)
- Floppy drive standard
- CD-ROM standard
- Video standard
- Keyboard standard
- Mouse standard
- Network interface standard
- Operating system standard
- Monitor standard

Appendix 4. Standard Supported Software

Standard Software Packages		
Title	Function	Manufacturer
Accounting Software Packages		
Title	Function	Manufacturer
Systems Development		
Title	Function	Manufacturer
Systems Operations		
Title	Function	Manufacturer
Communications Software		
Title	Function	Manufacturer
Other Packages		
Title	Function	Manufacturer
In-House Developed Systems		
Title	Function	Manufacturer

Appendix 5. Right to Access Form

Right to Access Confidential Information for: [person's name]

I hereby declare that access to all confidential information be granted to XYZ Company for the purpose of: ____________________________ .

Access to confidential information has been granted to [third party] .

Persons authorizing this access:

__________________ __________________ __________________

President Security Officer General Counsel

Appendix I

References

Commercial and Vendor Web Sites

- www.microsoft.com/security — Microsoft security information bulletins
- www.ntbugtraq.com — vulnerability tracking
- www.l0pht.com, www.atstake.com/research/redirect.html — Penetration tools
- www.securityfocus.com — vulnerability information
- www.securityportal.com — vulnerability information
- www.iss.net–xforce.iss.net — vulnerability information
- www.ntsecurity.com — *Windows 2000 Magazine* security Web site

Tools and Probing

- www.netcraft.com — server analysis
- www.insecure.org — port scanning software
- grc.com — shield up interactive port scanning

Black Hat Sites

- www.phrack.com
- www.2600.com
- www.attrition.org
- cryptome.org — Information
- www.interhack.net
- www.fastlane.net/homepages/thegnome/faqs/index.html
- www.cultdeadcow.com
- www.soci.niu.edu/~cudigest

Check Point Firewall Sites

- www.checkpoint.com
- www.phoneboy.com
- www.dreamwvr.com/bastions/fw1_faq.html
- www.deathstar.ch/security/fw1
- www.secure-1.com

Security Sites

- www.sans.org
- www.gocsi.com
- www.cert.org
- packetstorm.org
- www.first.org
- ciac.llnl.goc
- www.nipc.gov
- sac.saic.com
- www.issa-intl.org
- www.icsa.net

Standards Sites

- csrc.nist.gov
- www.icsa.net
- www.ietf.org

Informational

- grc.com/dos/grcdos.htm

Miscellaneous

- softail.visi.com/security/links.html
- *TCP/IP Illustrated*, Volumns I, II, and III, Gary R. Write and Richard Stevens, ISBN 0-201-63354-X

Magazines

- *Windows 2000 Magazine*
- *Internet Week*
- *E-Week*

Books

- *Building Internet Firewalls*, ISBN: 1-56592-871-7
- *Check Point FireWall-1 Administration Guide*, ISBN: 0-07-134229-X
- *Internet Firewalls and Network Security*, ISBN: 1-56205-437-6
- *Implementing Internet Security*, ISBN: 1-56205-471-6
- *Windows NT 3.5 Resource Kit*
- *Windows NT 4.0 Resource Kit*
- *Windows 2000 Resource Kit*

Index

A

B

C

D

E

F

G

H

I

K

L

M

N

O

S

W

X

Z